THE INCREDIBLE STORY
OF EDWARD LEE HOWARD

"It reads like fiction
But is as real as next month's rent . . ."
New York Daily News

"Extraordinary . . .
a unique and authoritative
—and disturbing—
chronicle about the most secret activity
of the most secret agency"
Seymour Hersh

"A triumph . . .
It offers a rare insight into
the hidden battle between spies and spycatchers
where the naive, as well as the vengeful,
get trapped and maimed in the crossfire."
Nicholas Daniloff, *Chicago Tribune*

"Chilling . . .
the account of one of the worst
intelligence blunders in U.S. history"
Scripps-Howard News Services

"Compelling . . .
A revealing and damning account.
A searing indictment of the CIA."
Washington Post Book World

"A fine book . . .
David Wise knows his way around
the world of intelligence
and he is at his best here."
Larry King, *USA Today*

Other Avon Books by
David Wise

Fiction
THE SAMARKAND DIMENSION

THE SPY WHO GOT AWAY

**THE TRUE STORY OF THE ONLY CIA AGENT
TO DEFECT TO THE SOVIET UNION**

DAVID WISE

AVON BOOKS  NEW YORK

AVON BOOKS
A division of
The Hearst Corporation
105 Madison Avenue
New York, New York 10016

Copyright © 1988 by David Wise
Cover illustration by Alan Ayres
Published by arrangement with Random House, Inc.
Library of Congress Catalog Card Number: 87-43229
ISBN: 0-380-70772-1

First Avon Books Printing: October 1989

AVON TRADEMARK REG. U.S. PAT. OFF. AND IN OTHER COUNTRIES, MARCA
REGISTRADA, HECHO EN U.S.A.

Printed in the U.S.A.

K-R 10 9 8 7 6 5 4 3 2 1

To Jonathan

Contents

It wasn't just the human assets. It was far deeper than that. All the technical assets were rolled up. The damage was tremendous. He closed us down over there.

—U.S. intelligence official, commenting on Edward Lee Howard

Prologue

Budapest, June 1987.

The first warm day of summer, and the sun was setting behind the Buda Hills, casting its last golden rays on the Danube. The call came at dusk to my hotel room. We would meet on the Margit-sziget, an island in the middle of the river.

I waited at the appointed place, and in a few moments he came walking toward me, rather tentatively, a slender, mustached man in a light gray suit. He was the Central Intelligence Agency's first defector, a fugitive from justice accused of espionage, of selling the CIA's most sensitive secrets to the Soviet Union.

He had escaped from the FBI and vanished into the New Mexico desert twenty-one months before. Now he was under the protection of the KGB. He had been granted asylum by the Russians, but he was still a wanted man in every country of the Western world.

I began walking toward him. I knew, as he must have, that the moment was unprecedented. Never before had a defector to Moscow from an intelligence agency been interviewed by a writer from the West. He extended his hand.

"I'm Edward Lee Howard."

1

"Yurchenko's Come Over"

Gus Hathaway was smiling.

The chief of counterintelligence of the Central Intelligence Agency was not a man who smiled very often. His name and face were unknown to the public. But he was very well known indeed in the arcane, closed world of American intelligence, whose most powerful leaders were gathering now in the reception area outside the seventh-floor dining room of the director of the CIA. It was Thursday, August 1, 1985.

Over cocktails before lunch, Hathaway broke the news to his opposite number, Edward J. O'Malley, the counterintelligence chief of the Federal Bureau of Investigation, and Phillip A. Parker, O'Malley's deputy.

"Yurchenko's come over," he said.

The CIA man did not have to explain the bombshell he had just dropped. Vitaly Yurchenko, as the FBI men knew, was the KGB officer in Moscow in charge of all operations inside the United States and Canada. His value as a defector was beyond measure. He could provide information of enormous importance to American intelligence. It was a major coup for the CIA; no wonder Hathaway, a wiry patrician of normally serious demeanor, was smiling.

Hathaway, whose formal title was chief/CI staff—the initials stand for counterintelligence—quickly filled in the details. Yurchenko had defected that morning in Rome, only hours ago; the CIA was moving swiftly to make the necessary arrangements to get him out.

As the electrifying news spread around the room, CIA

3

Director William J. Casey busily greeted his guests, his tall, stooped figure moving among them. The grandees of the secret world of intelligence were there: Casey; Hathaway; John N. McMahon, a handsome, silver-haired Irishman who was the deputy director of the CIA, the agency's number two official; and Clair E. George, a graying, athletic-looking man of medium height and ruddy complexion who had the most secret job of all. George was the CIA's deputy director for operations; as the official in charge of the agency's clandestine arm, he was the nation's top spy.

The director of the FBI, William H. Webster, was present, along with O'Malley, Parker, two section chiefs from the intelligence division, and Jay Aldhizer, the FBI agent who served as liaison with the CIA.

The gathering was a farewell luncheon for O'Malley, who was retiring from the FBI at age fifty after five years as head of Division 5, the FBI's intelligence division. It was O'Malley's job to catch spies, especially Soviet spies. Thus, the luncheon on the seventh floor was, upon closer examination, more than an ordinary conclave of intelligence officers. It was, more precisely, a meeting of the key players in the special arena of *counterintelligence*, whose members formed a separate society within the secret world. Because O'Malley was leaving the FBI, his colleagues across the river in Langley thought it appropriate to honor him. But the news about Yurchenko overshadowed all else. The buzz of conversation in the room was not about the departing FBI man but about the defector.

It was not only a dramatic development; it also came at a time when the U.S. intelligence community needed some good news. A little more than two months earlier a former Navy chief warrant officer, John A. Walker, Jr., the leader of a family spy ring that sold vital naval communications secrets to the Soviet Union for nearly eighteen years, had been arrested. In time Walker, his son, Michael, his brother, Arthur, and a friend, Jerry A. Whitworth, all were convicted of espionage and sent to prison.

The Walker case had already had a devastating impact

on the image of U.S. intelligence. To Congress and the public, it seemed as though American security were a sieve and the intelligence agencies at fault. Only three weeks before, a CIA employee, Sharon Scranage, had been arrested, charged with passing CIA secrets to Ghana. In the next few months other important espionage cases were to surface in such profusion that 1985 became known as the Year of the Spy.

The defection of Vitaly Yurchenko was, therefore, more than a feather in the cap of Gus Hathaway. Quite aside from the information that Yurchenko could provide, the very fact that the CIA had a high-ranking KGB defector might, if it were delicately made known, help offset the unfavorable aura surrounding the U.S. intelligence community.

After drinks Casey's dozen or so guests filed into the CIA director's private dining room and took their places at three little round tables set with gleaming silver and crystal on white tablecloths. Red and white wines were served. Through the picture window, from their vantage point on the top floor of the CIA, the guests could enjoy the bucolic view of the lush, green trees surrounding the isolated headquarters building.

Jay Aldhizer, a six-foot Virginian from Roanoke with a soft southern accent, was pleased. The FBI liaison man with the CIA regarded the lunch as a symbol of the good relations between the agency and the bureau that he had worked so hard to build for five years. Aldhizer was satisfied that relations were admirable at every level. He took pride in that; it was his job as liaison to keep them that way. There had even been two softball games between the FBI and the CIA at a high school field near Langley headquarters. Of course, the two agencies were traditional rivals, but the days of J. Edgar Hoover, when the director of the FBI had actually broken off relations with the CIA, were gone.

During the lunch Casey delivered some remarks praising O'Malley, extolling the cooperation among the various elements of the intelligence community, and dwelling on counterintelligence successes during the FBI official's tenure. Afterward a citation was read, and O'Malley was presented with a medallion of the CIA seal, a fierce eagle atop a shield emblazoned with a starburst design.

At the three round tables the FBI men were bantering with their CIA colleagues, reminding them, once again, of the time the agency had served roast beef to O'Malley on Good Friday and of how O'Malley had struck back, serving corned beef and cabbage to the CIA men when it was his turn to host lunch at the bureau, a pointed reminder to the largely WASP agency that he was a good Irish Catholic.

The bonhomie surrounding Ed O'Malley was genuine, and the praise generous. But the truth was that the intelligence officials were preoccupied. Their thoughts were really about the man who wasn't there but soon would be: Vitaly Sergeyevich Yurchenko.

2

"Robert"

The passenger who had stepped off an Aeroflot flight at Rome's Fiumicino Airport one week earlier, on July 24, had clear blue eyes, thinning red hair, and a drooping handlebar mustache. His big frame and broad shoulders suggested an athlete or at least a man who kept himself trim. He was neatly dressed, almost dapper.

Vitaly Yurchenko was about as far as one could get from the stereotype of a KGB man, the squat, beetle-browed Russian in an ill-fitting suit who scowled at the world and unthinkingly obeyed Moscow Center's orders. Yurchenko, by contrast, had a rather breezy manner, spoke English, and, but for his accent, could easily have passed for an American. He had lived in Washington for five years. In appearance he would not have looked out of place in California, perhaps driving a van along the Pacific Coast Highway on his way to Malibu.

In fact, however, the arriving passenger was deputy chief of the First Department of the First Chief Directorate of the Committee for State Security, or Komitet Gosudarstvennoi Bezopasnosti, the KGB. The directorate is in charge of Soviet clandestine activities abroad.

Yurchenko's department was responsible for all espionage activity and covert operations against North America. In all major cities around the world where the Soviet Union has diplomatic representation, the KGB operates through residents under embassy cover, much as the CIA has station chiefs posing as diplomats. Yurchenko was the man in charge of the five residents in the United States

7

and Canada.[1] At the age of forty-nine, he had risen to a rank just below the very top circle of KGB leaders.

Yurchenko was in Rome on a pretext, he later told his CIA interrogators. He said he had informed his superiors in the KGB that his presence in Rome was required to deal with a high-level agent in that city. But the agent did not exist; in the argot of the intelligence world, he was "notional." The CIA accepted his explanation; the agency's officials were aware that KGB officials of Yurchenko's rank had considerable freedom of movement.

Later there was speculation that Yurchenko had come to Rome on a special assignment: to prevent defections among the twelve members of a delegation of Soviet nuclear scientists who were scheduled to attend an international conference at Erice, Sicily, due to begin on August 20.

American intelligence officials do not believe Yurchenko's arrival was linked to the scientists, although the Russians may have had reason to worry. Four months earlier Vladimir Alexandrov, one of the Soviet Union's most distinguished scientists—and a delegate to the Sicily conference the previous year—had disappeared without a trace in Madrid.[2]

Yurchenko remained in Rome for eight days, apparently

---

[1] In Washington, New York, San Francisco, Ottawa, and Montreal.

[2] Alexandrov, a mathematician and computer expert, had helped develop the theory of nuclear winter, which predicts that a nuclear war would create a new ice age. He had traveled frequently to the West and had even testified to the United States Senate.

Alexandrov was last seen in Madrid's Hotel Habana on March 31. He had been reported uncharacteristically drunk and disorderly. According to one account, he tried to leap from a car returning him from a scientific meeting in Córdoba when he realized it was headed for the Soviet embassy. Soviet officials escorted him back to his hotel, but when they called for him the next day, on April 1, he had vanished. The Soviet government feared he had defected to the CIA.

The Soviet government newspaper *Izvestia* charged on December 23, 1985, that Alexandrov had been "kidnapped" by the CIA. "Alexandrov's address is known—it is the CIA headquarters in Langley," the newspaper said. Officially, at least, U.S. intelligence agencies deny any knowledge of Alexandrov's whereabouts or fate.

staying at the Villa Abamelex, the Soviet ambassador's residence. At 9:00 A.M. on Thursday, August 1, Yurchenko told his colleagues at the Soviet embassy at 5 Via Gaeta, near the Stazione Termini, Rome's main railroad station, that he was going to take a walk and visit the Vatican museums.

When he did not return by nightfall, embassy officials were frantic. Not until the next day did they file a missing persons report with the Italian police. By that time the KGB resident in Rome must have suspected the worst: Vitaly Yurchenko, a high-ranking official of the Soviet intelligence service, a veteran of twenty-five years with the KGB, had defected to the West.[3]

Yurchenko asked for a CIA officer by name when he contacted the CIA's Rome station, in the American embassy on the Via Veneto, on the morning of August 1. The station flashed word to headquarters in northern Virginia. Casey, Clair George, Hathaway and other top CIA officials were alerted, and the machinery for handling priority defectors was put into motion. By the time the Russians went to the Italian police, Yurchenko was long gone, in the hands of the CIA, flying across the Atlantic in a military plane.

The CIA flight landed at Andrews Air Force Base, on the southeastern edge of Washington, early on Friday morning. A team of FBI agents and CIA officers met Yur-

---

[3] Italian authorities did not announce until August 8 that they had been asked by the Soviet embassy to investigate the disappearance of Vitaly Yurchenko, a diplomat with the rank of counselor. Nicolai Esimov, the Soviet chargé d'affaires in Rome, called on Italian Foreign Minister Giulio Andreotti that day with a message from Soviet Foreign Minister Eduard Shevardnadze demanding that Italy "shed full light on the circumstances of the [Yurchenko] disappearance and . . . provide assurances concerning his physical condition and the place where he is presently located." Andreotti promised the Russian that Italian authorities would do everything in their power to comply with the request. A dispatch from Rome published in the *Times* of London on August 9 said that "inquiry had been made throughout Rome hospitals to see whether he had been taken ill or had an accident . . . the search had drawn a complete blank and both the Americans and British said they had nothing to do with the disappearance."

chenko. The FBI provided countersurveillance at the air base; by now the KGB would have a worldwide alert for Yurchenko, and Andrews was a likely place it might watch. It was not that American intelligence thought that the KGB would try to snatch Yurchenko back on U.S. soil and under heavy security—no one expected that—but the Russians might seek to follow him and find out where he was being held.

On the ride from Andrews, Rodney L. Leffler, acting chief of the FBI's Soviet section, rode in the front seat next to the driver; Yurchenko and a CIA officer occupied the back seat. Other security cars swept ahead and trailed behind them.

From the air base Yurchenko was spirited to a CIA safe house in northern Virginia, not far from the agency's headquarters, a house that to the neighbors in the area seemed like any other. The safe house was only a temporary way station; soon afterward Yurchenko was moved to an elegant, two-story safe house in Coventry, a development in the Virginia countryside forty miles southwest of Washington, near Fredericksburg.

Now Yurchenko was in the hands of his main adversaries, the CIA's directorate of operations (DDO).[4] His arrival was a major event inside the directorate. Despite the supposed glamour of espionage, life in the agency's covert side is often routine. The CIA is a large bureaucracy, and the officers in the DDO spend a great deal of their time pushing paper, reading reports, and dealing with humdrum administrative chores. On an average day James Bond would be bored in the DDO.

When, as happens only rarely, the agency gets a high-level Soviet defector, it is a truly exciting development that breaks the clandestine routine. And everyone, including

---

[4]The initials *DDO* actually stand for deputy director for operations, the chief of the directorate, but are often used interchangeably to refer to the directorate itself. Since the early 1970's, in an effort to avoid confusion, some CIA hands have taken to referring to the directorate as the DO. To complicate matters even further, the DDO or DO is also known as the Clandestine Services (CS).

the director of Central Intelligence, wants a piece of the action. William Casey's mind-set had been shaped by his service in World War II, when he served with the Office of Strategic Services in London. There he helped coordinate the work of French resistance forces before the Normandy invasion and supervised airdrops of Allied agents into Nazi Germany. That experience explained his lifelong interest in covert operations, the number of which increased greatly under his aegis at the CIA.

But Casey could not be expected to commute to the safe house near Fredericksburg or personally to supervise Yurchenko's debriefing. The responsibility for handling the defector fell primarily to Burton Lee Gerber, chief of the CIA's Soviet division, and Gus Hathaway, the counterintelligence chief, with both men reporting to Clair George, the DDO. Their staffs debriefed Yurchenko.

All three men, although veteran CIA clandestine officers, were relatively new to their jobs. Clair George had become the DDO a little more than a year earlier, in an unexpected manner. George, who celebrated his fifty-fifth birthday on Saturday, August 3, as the questioning of Yurchenko began in earnest, was born in Pennsylvania and graduated from Pennsylvania State University. He had joined the CIA in 1955 and served in a series of overseas stations, including Hong Kong, Paris, Bamako (the capital of Mali), and New Delhi. In the 1970's he was chief of station (COS) in Beirut and Athens. One former CIA official, not an admirer, called George "ruthless, cunning, ham-handed, contemptuous of his underlings, toadying to his superiors."

Other colleagues had a higher opinion of him; by the early 1980's George was assistant director of the DDO. Then, in 1983, Casey sent him to Capitol Hill as the agency official in charge of congressional relations. The move was a disaster. Many of the members and staff of the Senate Intelligence Committee, in particular, found him arrogant and uninformative. By April 1984 the Senate panel was at loggerheads with the CIA over Casey's failure to brief them fully on the mining of Nicaraguan harbors by the agency.[5] The Senate voted 84–12 to condemn the CIA's action, and in the aftermath Clair George had to go.[6] Casey, in a musical-chairs shift of four top officials, pulled George back and promoted him to deputy director for operations. Having alienated Congress, with help from Casey, George was rewarded by being made the DDO.

Although George, as the DDO, now had overall responsibility for the handling of Yurchenko, the two officials who reported to him had the primary responsibility for the assessment and debriefing of the defector.

As chief of counterintelligence, Gardner Rugg "Gus" Hathaway—no one called him Gardner—now faced, in the Yurchenko case, his first major challenge. Although a veteran officer of the Clandestine Services, Hathaway, at the age of sixty, had occupied the counterintelligence post for only a few months.

Within the agency Hathaway was regarded as FFV (the initials stand for First Families of Virginia).[7] He was a lean, energetic man of average height, who favored Ivy League three-button suits and striped ties. A cowlick of brown hair dipped over the right side of his thin, patrician face, which usually wore an acerbic expression. He re-

---

[5] Senator Barry Goldwater, the committee chairman, exploded in anger, dispatching an unprecedented letter denouncing Casey: "Dear Bill . . . I am pissed off . . . this is no way to run a railroad. . . . It is an act of war. For the life of me, I don't see how we are going to explain it."

[6] The CIA official who ran the covert operation against Nicaragua, Duane R. "Dewey" Clarridge, had assured the committee staff that the mines were the "pop-in" type that make a lot of noise but are harmless. After the story of the mining had broken publicly, staff members studied sea charts and harbor depths to learn enough so that the CIA would have to tell the truth. The agency then admitted to the committee that some of the mines had been placed at a depth of twenty-five feet and contained three hundred pounds of C-4 explosive, enough to blow a ship to smithereens. Had a ship of a friendly Western European nation blown up, or, worse yet, a Soviet tanker, the agency's actions could have had dire consequences. "We're lucky we didn't go to war over it," said one committee source.

[7] Hathaway's colleagues were using the term generically, not literally; the Order of the First Families of Virginia does not list him in its registry of members.

tained a distinctive Virginia accent; he had been born in Danville, deep in the southern part of the state, one of three sons raised by his mother and a stern stepfather, a local realtor. For a time he went to Virginia Episcopal School, in Lynchburg. He had served as a young first lieutenant in the Army during World War II, then earned a bachelor's degree at the University of Virginia in 1950. He was married the following year.

Recruited by the CIA, he went into the operations directorate and after clandestine training was assigned to the Soviet/East European (SE) division, the most elite and prestigious of the geographic divisions of the directorate of operations.[8] By the late 1950's he was running operations against the Poles for SE division out of the Berlin base. In the argot of the agency, he was "on the Polish target." In Berlin Hathaway earned a reputation as something of a wild man, a headstrong young officer who sometimes took more risks than necessary. "In those days Gus had a I-don't-give-a-rat's-ass attitude," one veteran CIA officer recalled.

In the 1960's Hathaway was posted to Rio de Janeiro and Buenos Aires, and by 1973 he was in Montevideo as chief of station. Along the way he divorced and remarried. Although serving in Latin America, he was still targeting Soviet-bloc diplomats and installations. "Gus ran some good ops in Latin America," a CIA colleague said. Later Hathaway did a tour of duty as the chief of station in Moscow. He was the deputy chief of SE division when he was tapped to head counterintelligence.[9]

As chief/CI staff Hathaway had the job of protecting CIA operations from penetration by hostile intelligence services and of finding moles inside the agency. It is an

---

[8]Known as SE today, the Soviet division in the past has had several names, including Soviet Russia (SR) and Soviet Bloc (SB). To avoid confusion, the division will normally be referred to here as SE.

[9]Within the DDO a division is the top level, and below that come branches, then sections. There are also several senior staffs, which historically were not equal to divisions but today are. Thus, as chief of counterintelligence Hathaway was equal in status to a division chief, even though he headed a "staff."

unenviable position that requires the occupant to suspect everyone.

The flip side of his job was to penetrate the opposition, to acquire moles inside the KGB, if at all possible, but at a minimum to find out as much as could be learned about the internal and external operations of Soviet intelligence. The best way to accomplish this task, of course, is to develop "an agent in place," an officer of Soviet intelligence who remains on the job while reporting to the CIA. An agent in place is a rara avis in the intelligence world, however. The next best thing is a defector, a Soviet intelligence agent who, for one reason or another, chooses to change sides and come over to the West.

The two halves of Hathaway's job were inextricably linked because perhaps the most likely way to find a mole inside the CIA is through information provided by a defector. In fact, a CIA officer who betrays his country by providing secrets to the Soviets—and there have been several—must, if he is at all intelligent, live in fear of the possibility that a Soviet defector will one day reveal his identity. No matter how careful a mole inside the CIA may be, no matter how professionally he covers his tracks, he cannot guard against the possibility that there may come a time when a defector will give away the game.

Thus, Gus Hathaway, for many reasons, had a great interest in Vitaly Yurchenko. But the counterintelligence chief also needed to establish in the months ahead whether Yurchenko was what he seemed. Hathaway had to know what he was dealing with.

There are two kinds of defectors, real and false. Real defectors are what they appear to be: intelligence officers who trade their inside knowledge of Soviet secrets for a passport to a new life in the West. A phony defector, on the other hand, is dispatched by the KGB to mislead and confuse the opposition or to learn something about the workings of opposition intelligence services.

In order to establish his "bona fides," the false defector has to reveal genuine information of value. There is a cost, therefore; he must disclose real secrets to peddle the false ones. The more valuable the information he reveals, the more likely he is to be believed as a genuine defector. Then, once accepted by his handlers, he can begin to feed them false information. Perhaps he will even be hired by the CIA, metamorphosing from defector to mole.

But a real defector also reveals true information, and that is the difficulty and the dilemma for his interrogators. The truth about the defector may always remain elusive, as fragile as a flower's wisp on a summer breeze. Counterintelligence has been called a "wilderness of mirrors" because suspicion among human beings, like mirrors reflecting upon each other, reaches to infinity.

As chief of counterintelligence Hathaway was one of the successors to the legendary and controversial James Jesus Angleton, a chain-smoker who cultivated prize orchids, wrote poetry, and prospected for semiprecious gems in underground caves in the Southwest. Angleton was also an expert trout fisherman, and his admirers saw that as symbolic of the way he patiently studied and then reeled in his KGB quarry. But he held one Soviet defector, Yuri Nosenko, locked up in solitary confinement, and frequently drugged, for three and a half years. His conviction that Nosenko was a fake nearly tore the CIA apart. Angleton's detractors claimed that he had long since stepped through the looking glass into a convoluted, subterranean world more analogous to Tolkien than Le Carré. Angleton was fired in 1974 by CIA Director William E. Colby.[10]

If Hathaway was not a seasoned expert in counterintelligence, it was also true that the other CIA official handling the Yurchenko debriefing was relatively new on the job. Burton Lee Gerber, the chief of the Soviet division, had been named to that position a little more than a year earlier.

A tall, thin, soft-spoken man of fifty-two, Gerber had

---

[10]Colby said he found Angleton's "tortuous theories" about a "wily KGB" planting moles and false defectors to undermine the West "impossible to follow." Colby added: "I did not suspect Angleton and his staff of engaging in improper activities. I just could not figure out what they were doing at all." Angleton died on May 11, 1987, of lung cancer, five days after William Casey died of pneumonia following an operation for brain cancer.

wavy gray hair, glasses, and an almost professorial manner. Although a conservative dresser, he would occasionally dare to wear a bright shirt at the division's Christmas party. Married, and a family man, he owned a dog and liked to swim for relaxation. But like Hathaway, he was faceless, unknown outside the intelligence world.

Gerber, born in Illinois, had graduated from Michigan State in 1955 with a bachelor's degree and disappeared into the CIA. He learned Bulgarian and was posted to Sofia under State Department cover in the 1960's. In the early 1980's he served as the chief of station in Moscow.

The goal of every operations officer in the DDO is to head a division, and Gerber's chance came in the summer of 1984 when he was selected as chief/SE division. For Gerber, like Hathaway, Vitaly Yurchenko was the first major-league Soviet defector to come into his net since he had taken over the division.

On Friday, at the safe house in northern Virginia, the debriefing of Yurchenko began. When the Russian arrived, he was met by Gerber, who headed the CIA team. The safe house had a kitchen, dining area, and living room on the ground floor. Rodney Leffler headed the FBI group.

Yurchenko was urged to go upstairs and take a nap; he must be tired after his long flight, his hosts said. But the KGB man was anxious to get started. The CIA officers huddled privately with Yurchenko for a while, off to one side in the living room, making the FBI agents uneasy. But the representatives of both agencies then took their places around the dining-room table.

Yurchenko asked for tea. The CIA didn't have any, so he sat at the table sipping hot water as he spoke. Gerber and the CIA men who would be handling Yurchenko sat at the debriefing table, as did Leffler, representing FBI headquarters. Three agents from the bureau's Washington field office (WFO) were in the room as well.

The first order of business when a defector is interrogated is to learn whether he knows of any penetrations of United States intelligence; other matters can wait. Yurchenko knew of two.

He had actually talked to one; the man, a recent employee of the National Security Agency (NSA), the nation's supersecret code and electronic eavesdropping agency, had telephoned the Soviet embassy in Washington on January 15, 1980. At the time Yurchenko was stationed in Washington as the KGB officer in charge of security for the Soviet colony, or SK, as it is referred to by American intelligence. Yurchenko had taken the call, and he had suggested the caller come to the embassy.

A few moments later the man entered the embassy, but watching FBI agents had no way of knowing who he was. Inside the embassy the ''walk-in,'' as such a volunteer spy is know, revealed sensational information: the NSA had, by using submarines, been able to tap into an underwater communications cable the Soviets used in the Sea of Okhotsk, between the Soviet mainland and the Kamchatka Peninsula. The United States was listening in to Soviet military communications; the highly sensitive project had been code-named Ivy Bells.

The NSA visitor offered to reveal more but demanded payment in ''gold bullion.'' In a scene straight out of a Woody Allen movie, Yurchenko at first thought the man was referring to chicken soup. Soon the confusion was cleared up, but in the meantime, a Soviet electronics technician rushed into the room. He had picked up a burst of radio activity from the FBI's walkie-talkies and radio cars.

The Soviets ordered the American to shave his beard. They had him change into Soviet work clothes and slipped him, surrounded by several Russian workmen, out a side door. The group got into a van and drove away, dropping the American off when they were out of sight of the embassy. The FBI was unable to identify the mysterious visitor.

Yurchenko, questioned now by CIA officers at the safe house, did not remember the name of the man who had come to the embassy five years ago. But he was able to provide the American's physical description—he recalled he had red hair, for example—and his KGB code name: Mr. Long.

Yurchenko also remembered another detail. He knew the man lived in a run-down house in the Washington suburbs; Yurchenko himself had driven to the house to check out the address given by the visitor to the embassy. While he could no longer recall the exact location, he remembered it was near Beltsville, Maryland. Armed with Yurchenko's clues, the FBI would begin a massive hunt for the NSA walk-in.

Yurchenko also told his interrogators of the second penetration. The other man, he said, had worked for the Central Intelligence Agency.

He did not know the CIA man's true name. He knew, however, that his KGB code name was Robert. He had never met the CIA penetration, as he had the NSA man, and could not provide a physical description.

But Yurchenko provided two crucial clues to his identity. He said that the CIA man had met with senior KGB officials in Austria in the fall of 1984, had turned over classified intelligence secrets to the Soviets, and had been paid.

Moreover, he said that "Robert" had been prepared for posting to Moscow by the CIA and then had been taken off that assignment. But "Robert" was familiar with the complex procedures used by the CIA for contacting its agents in the Soviet capital, and he knew their code names and other information that might establish their real identities.

The news horrified Yurchenko's CIA interrogators. If true, it meant there was, or had been, a mole in their inner sanctum, the most secret and sensitive part of the entire agency, the Soviet division. The prospect of a mole anywhere inside the CIA sent chills down the spines of the debriefers. But a mole in SE division was unspeakable, the ultimate catastrophe. It was the agency's worst nightmare come true.

There had already been disturbing intimations that something was wrong in Moscow; the chief of station had cabled Langley headquarters months before, warning of signs that both human and technical operations were being compromised. At least one major operation had been blown, and the CIA's Soviet contact, Adolf G. Tolkachev, a defense researcher, arrested by the KGB. His case officer, Paul M.

"Skip" Stombaugh, Jr., who was under diplomatic cover as a second secretary in the American embassy, had been caught by the Soviets and expelled for espionage. He had been attempting to collect secrets from Tolkachev when he was seized. That had happened in June, only six weeks earlier. If "Robert" had talked to the Soviets, the entire CIA network in Moscow was in mortal danger.

Agents, such as Soviet citizens, whom the CIA recruits are known in agency jargon as assets. If Yurchenko was correct, the news was grave. It meant that the CIA no longer had any assets in Moscow.[11]

Gus Hathaway wasn't smiling anymore. For the counterintelligence chief, and Burt Gerber, the head of SE division, Yurchenko's disclosures were frightening even beyond their grim intelligence implications. Although neither Yurchenko nor almost anyone else knew it, the two CIA men were personally involved in, perhaps some would say in part responsible for, the calamity that Yurchenko had just revealed.

They knew—they had to have known—almost instantly whom Yurchenko was talking about. "Robert" could be only one man. He had been a new officer of the Clandestine Services in SE division. In the spring of 1983 he had been getting ready for assignment to the CIA's Moscow station, his first overseas post, when, at the last moment a polygraph test disclosed petty theft by the man.

Instead of sending the young officer to Moscow, the most sensitive post in the CIA, the agency took the unusual step of firing him. The case was a cause célèbre inside the CIA and especially in SE division. For the division's involvement with the man had not ended with his dismissal.

Afterward the officer had acted bizarrely and caused

---

[11]In the CIA a career spy is called a case officer or, more broadly, an officer of the CIA. Case officers serving overseas in turn recruit agents, usually foreign nationals of the countries where the officers serve. These agents or assets are not career CIA employees. Because most people outside the agency ordinarily refer to CIA case officers as agents, the technical distinction between officers and agents, while certainly important, will not always be observed here.

continuing problems for headquarters. The affair went far beyond Hathaway and Gerber. From top to bottom the agency had made every effort to cover up the potentially explosive case. Months earlier senior officials had decided not to notify the FBI. Specifically it had been decided to conceal the case from the one official in the United States government who had the greatest need to know: Edward O'Malley, the FBI's chief of counterintelligence, the very man who had been honored at William Casey's luncheon twenty-four hours before.

The dismissed CIA officer's bizarre behavior culminated with his confession to the CIA that he was a security risk; in September 1984 the man had volunteered to the agency that he had contemplated selling to the Soviet Union the agency's most sensitive secrets—the details of SE division's operations in Moscow.

Hathaway knew that, and so did Gerber. They had personally handled the man's case over the past years. And they had decided after his astonishing confession that there was still no need to tell the FBI about him. The CIA would contain this on its own.

There was only one man who fit Yurchenko's description.

His name was Edward Lee Howard.

3

Bucaramanga

Bucaramanga lies deep in the Andes in the remote, rural
north of Colombia, close to the border of Venezuela and
almost two hundred miles from Bogotá.

In the spring of 1973 a small group of young, idealistic
Americans worked there, members of the Peace Corps that
had been established more than a decade earlier by President John F. Kennedy. They were part of what Kennedy
had termed "an immense reservoir of dedicated men and
women" who had responded to his call.

In June of that year Mary Cedarleaf, a twenty-three-
year-old graduate of the University of Minnesota, arrived
in Bucaramanga, or "Buke," as the Peace Corps workers
dubbed it, where she was to take up her duties as a teacher
in a rural village on the outskirts of town.

She had grown up in a suburb of St. Paul, and her roots
were in that area. The Cedarleafs lived in Mahtomedi, a
pleasant suburb seven miles northeast of the city. Although a shy girl, she had many friends, joined the Girl
Scouts and the 4-H Club, sang in the school choir, and
took piano lessons until the twelfth grade. She also found
time for sports and the outdoors; she liked to swim, ski,
fish, and ride horses. She played tennis and volleyball, and
one summer in her teens she taught swimming in the icy
waters of nearby White Bear Lake.

Her father, Evar, was a veterinarian who switched ca-
reers and joined with his brothers in the family's successful insurance business in the Twin Cities. He was a solid,
kindly man who had served in the Marines during World

War II. Her mother, Adelaide, an outspoken and deter-mined woman, was an ophthalmologist and an eye surgeon in an era when relatively few women were admitted to the ranks of the medical profession. The Cedarleafs were Re-publicans and good Lutherans.

Mary, the second of their three daughters, had grown up to be an attractive young woman, petite, with curly brown hair and blue eyes. She was so eager to begin her work that she did not wait for her diploma from the Uni-versity of Minnesota. One of her sisters picked it up for her; Mary was already in Colombia with the Peace Corps, fulfilling an ambition she had held since 1962, when she was twelve. The ideas behind the Peace Corps, established only a year earlier by President Kennedy, had fired her imagination. Mary Cedarleaf liked helping others who were less fortunate.

It was in Bucaramanga that she met another Peace Corps volunteer, a dark-haired young man of twenty-two, a year and a half her junior. Ed Howard could hardly have come from a more different background. His mother's family was Hispanic. He had been born in Alamogordo, New Mexico, but lived in half a dozen states and three coun-tries as his father, a career air force sergeant, moved from base to base, working as a missile guidance technician on Sidewinders and Sparrows.

Where Mary Cedarleaf's world was comfortable, upper-middle-class, and Lutheran, Ed Howard's was working-class, Catholic, part Hispanic, and peripatetic. The Howard family, of necessity dictated by his father's career, had never lived in one place long enough to put down roots.

Kenneth Howard retired from the Air Force in 1972, the same year that his son joined the Peace Corps. The senior Howard had been raised in a series of foster homes on poor farms around Marine City, Michigan, during the De-pression. He never knew his father.

Kenneth Howard had joined the Air Force three years after the end of the war and was stationed at Holloman Air Force Base in Alamogordo in 1950, when he met Mary Jaramillo, a handsome woman from Albuquerque who was working as a waitress. They married the same year, and their first child, whom they christened Edward Lee, was born on October 27, 1951. A daughter, Debora, came along five years later.

When Howard was seven months old, his father was transferred to Tachikawa, Japan; mother and baby remained behind in Albuquerque. When Kenneth Howard returned, the family moved to Victorville, California, where he was stationed at George Air Force Base, then to New Mexico for two more years, then to Michigan at the Selfridge Air National Guard Base.

By 1962 the Howards were living at Hahn Air Base in Lautzenhausen, West Germany, forty-five miles west of Frankfurt. Ed Howard was eleven when he moved to Germany, and he quickly picked up the language. He took part in the activities organized for the families of the American servicemen.

"He played Little League and everything," Kenneth Howard recalled. "Ed played catcher. He was kind of on the chubby side. He had lots of friends and was in the Boy Scouts, up to Explorer."

And Ed, or Eddie, as his parents called him, did something else that pleased his mother and father. Both Roman Catholics, they were proud when their son became an altar boy in Germany.

In 1965 the Howards returned to the States, and Kenneth was stationed in Amarillo, in the Texas Panhandle, for a year. Then it was time to pull up stakes and move to Wichita Falls, Texas, for two years at Sheppard Air Force Base. Ed, a teenager by now, also served as an altar boy in Wichita Falls.

But his interest were not confined to religion. Ed Howard like guns. On vacations he visited his grandparents in Reserve, New Mexico, and shot rabbits. "He went down to hunt and fish with them," his father said. "He had my rifle. He was a good shot." Howard was ten when he began hunting rabbits, prairie dogs, and rattlesnakes in the New Mexico desert.

In 1969 the Howards moved to England. Kenneth Howard was assigned to the Bentwaters Royal Air Force Base northeast of London near the Channel. The family lived nearby in Woodbridge. Edward enrolled in the Lakenheath American High School in Brandon, forty miles to the north. He boarded at the school and commuted home on the weekends. Although their son was away much of the time, the Howards tried to go on picnics together when he was home. Ed played football and tennis, did well academically, and graduated from high school in three and a half years.

In the fall of 1969 Edward Howard returned to the States to go to college. The chaplain at Hahn Air Force Base offered to get him a scholarship to Notre Dame to study for the priesthood, but Howard turned it down. He enrolled instead at the University of Texas at Austin. He joined the university's karate club and a student group that supported the United Nations.

The Vietnam War was in full swing. Now eighteen, Howard joined the engineers branch of the Army's Reserve Officers Training Corps, to protect himself from the draft and to enable him to finish college in four years. But Howard drew a high draft number and realized he no longer needed the ROTC; there was little chance he would be called.[1] To break his ROTC contract, he left Austin in the fall of 1970 and enrolled for a semester at the University of Maryland campus in Munich, Germany.

Early in 1971 Howard's family returned to the States, and Kenneth was stationed at England Air Force Base in Alexandria, in central Louisiana. His son was back in college at Austin. In May of the following year Edward Howard was graduated with honors with a bachelor's degree in international business and economics. He was in the top 10 percent of his class. In July Kenneth Howard retired from the Air Force and moved with his wife to Garland, Texas, a suburb of Dallas.

---

[1] In 1969, under a presidential order, Selective Service established a draft of twenty-year-old men based on a lottery keyed to birth dates. Each day of the year was randomly assigned a number from 1 to 365. If a man had a number in the 300's, the chances were very low that he would be called. In fact, the highest number ever reached during the entire Vietnam War was 195. Howard's number was 363.

After graduation Edward Howard joined the Peace Corps. He talked about his motives for doing so in the course of thirty hours of interviews with the author in Budapest over six days. It was late afternoon on a warm day in June. We were sitting in an outdoor café under the trees on the Margit-sziget, or Margaret Island, not far from the spot where we had first met.

"I had talked to a CIA recruiter," Howard said, "just looking for a job, but I was told I was too young. Some Peace Corps recruiter grabbed me between classes, just like the agency, and I applied. They sent a telegram asking, 'Do you accept?' I had applied for graduate school. All of a sudden I had to decide. I consulted friends and a priest. I decided to get out of school." But he said he joined the Peace Corps more for adventure than out of a sense of idealism. "Sure, I wanted to help people, but it was more that I wanted to see the world."

He was sent to Costa Rica for language and other training and then began work in the Dominican Republic. In February 1973 he was reassigned to Colombia.

He was working in Bucaramanga when Mary Cedarleaf arrived. "In June," Howard recalled, "Mary came down from Bogotá. She was dressed all in blue. Blue jeans, blue sweater. I was attracted to her immediately."

Mary Cedarleaf was only visiting on that day, but she was formally assigned to Bucaramanga in August. For three months she and Howard both worked in "Buke." They dated and went dancing.

It wasn't a case of love at first sight, but Mary thought Howard was bright and "fun to be around." They did not see each other often in Colombia, however, because in October Howard was sent off to Cali, a major sugar and manufacturing center in the tropical Cauca River valley, fifty miles from the Pacific.

"I was in the north, and he was in Cali, in the south," Mary recalled. "But in any country Peace Corps workers get to know each other."

Colombia is, and was then, the world's leading source of processed cocaine. Although Cali was not a major growing area, cocaine, marijuana, and other drugs were cheap and plentiful. Howard regularly used a variety of drugs in Colombia, including marijuana and cocaine.

There is no reason to believe that Howard was already working for the Central Intelligence Agency when he served in the Peace Corps. Sargent Shriver, the first head of the corps, realized that it offered tempting cover for the CIA. He went to his brother-in-law President Kennedy and exacted a promise that the intelligence agency would keep hands off. Kennedy issued orders to CIA Director Allen W. Dulles, and the Peace Corps, in its screening process, went to great lengths to make sure that no spooks slipped through the net. CIA employment of any kind remains a permanent barrier to service as a Peace Corps volunteer or staff member.

Howard completed his tour in Colombia on August 31, 1974, and Peace Corps records show that he served satisfactorily. For several months he worked as a Peace Corps recruiter out of Dallas; while recruiting in Puerto Rico that year, he was thrown off two college campuses because the students thought he was there for the CIA. In January 1975 Howard moved to Washington and enrolled as a graduate student at American University.

Mary Cedarleaf finished her service in Colombia in April of that year. Early in 1976, on a trip to Washington to visit her former roommate in Bucaramanga, she met Ed Howard again. They began seeing each other that spring, and Mary made two trips back to Washington to be with him. That summer Howard wangled a Peace Corps assignment in St. Paul and rented a house on White Bear Lake to be near Mary. In August he proposed, and she accepted. On November 26, a few months after Howard had earned his master's in business administration from American University, they were married in a Lutheran church in St. Paul. Both sets of parents were at the wedding.

Kenneth Howard, a heavyset man with thinning sandy hair, did not have his son's educational advantages. He was an intelligent but plainspoken man. His wife, still handsome in middle age, was a straightforward woman without pretensions, who spoke with a noticeable Spanish accent and sometimes worried about her background, her grammar, or the fact that she had not gone to college. The Cedarleafs were as nice as could be to their daughter's new in-laws, but to the Minnesotans at the wedding it was clear that socially and economically Ed Howard had "married up."

Two months earlier Howard had decided on the next step in his career; he had joined the Agency for International Development (AID) as a trainee. The entry-level program could qualify him to become a career Foreign Service officer.

In February the Howards were assigned to Lima, Peru. The young couple looked forward to returning to South America, this time together.

In Peru Howard worked as a project development officer for AID, helping small rural industries and farmers to obtain loans from private banks and public agencies. The Howards had a four-bedroom house and part-time servants in the San Borja section. Leonard Yaeger, the AID mission director in Peru at the time, remembered him as "quiet, hardworking, and diligent. He was not a flamboyant type."

Helene Kaufman, who served in the mission with Howard, had a similar recollection of Howard. "At parties the guy was a wallflower. You would have missed him unless someone introduced you."

Peru is a leading producer of coca leaf, from which cocaine is produced. In Lima, as in Colombia, drugs are easily available. Howard, according to CIA records, also used drugs in Peru, although the extent is not clear. In the Budapest interviews he claimed: "[In Lima] I did not do drugs, except one time I had a pipeful of marijuana."

While Howard worked for AID, Mary did odd jobs, for the most part teaching piano. Again, there is no evidence that Howard had any intelligence role while he was with AID, although the CIA has sometimes used that agency for cover. He did become friends with a woman who was the intelligence assistant to the CIA chief of station. But Mary Howard said her husband had no connection to the CIA when he served in the U.S. embassy in Peru. "In fact," she said, "it was a big game in Lima to figure out who the agency people were."

In March 1979 Howard resigned from AID. "I guess I had dreams of parlaying my business background into a big job in Washington or New York and making more money," he said.

Helene Kaufman went to his going-away party. "He told me all about the benefits AID has when you leave, like storage space for up to a year." She remembered her surprise that "someone had actually bothered to read through all that stuff. He had that kind of meticulousness."

Kaufman formed the impression that Howard was moving to the Midwest. "You know, for a nice, quiet life. It seemed appropriate for him."

With six years of government service behind him and an M.B.A., Howard began looking for a job in the private sector. In June he was hired by James H. Lowry and Associates, a management consulting firm in Chicago. The Howards bought a house in Barrington, a suburb northwest of the city.

The following spring he interviewed with Ecology and Environment, a Buffalo-based firm that held federal contracts to identify hazardous waste sites. E&E liked what it saw, and in May 1980 he was hired to manage the company's regional office in Chicago. At the time Congress was pushing to clean up toxic waste sites around the nation, an effort that later evolved into the multimillion-dollar Superfund program. The Environmental Protection Agency contracted with E&E to help it identify the sites to be cleaned up. The EPA had a hot line for the public to call in with reports of suspected hazardous sites. Howard's job was to select from the reports flowing to Chicago the most likely targets for investigation.

Trish McGuire, the administrative coordinator in the company's Buffalo headquarters, got to know Howard when he came in for meetings to plan work on the toxic waste contract. "Ed managed our biggest office, in Chicago," she said. "There were probably fifty-five people in the office. He was also responsible for the Kansas City office.''

McGuire, a chubby, bespectacled, and single young woman from a South Buffalo Irish ward, was a year younger than Howard. She liked him and became one of his closest friends in the environmental firm. "He was very mellow, easy to listen to, projected concern for other people," she recalled. "He could let you know he was there for you without coming right out and saying it. He often called me on the phone to talk out a problem."

Howard impressed others well. On the day that he waited in an anteroom at E&E headquarters in Buffalo for his job interview, he fell into conversation with another nervous candidate. James Lockwood, a short, muscular man who had been a champion college wrestler at Montana State, in Bozeman, was hired to run E&E's Washington office in Rosslyn, Virginia. The acquaintance that began in the waiting room flourished into friendship.

Lockwood, now an attorney for a large engineering company in Washington, said Howard had performed well in Chicago. "He was fun to be around. Everybody liked him without exception. He was poised and had a lot of grace under pressure. He didn't lose his temper when things went awry." The two men stayed in touch, Howard visiting Rosslyn periodically and Lockwood traveling to Chicago.

In October 1980, on a business trip to the Kansas City office, Howard went out for drinks and a steak dinner with Trish McGuire, who had flown in from Buffalo, Fred Bauer, of the Chicago office, and Bauer's wife. "After we dropped Fred and his wife off, we went out for a few more drinks," McGuire recalled. That was when Howard opened up and began telling McGuire his troubles.

"He didn't seem to be a philanderer, but he gave me the impression he wasn't overly happy in his marriage, although a lot of men that age feel that way. Like his in-laws were too domineering and too much an influence in his life, both in terms of money and their influence on his wife. They had more money and could provide more money for her than he could. Maybe he just felt insecure about it.''

McGuire thought Howard's wife had influenced him to leave AID and Peru and settle in Chicago ''because that was near where her parents were.'' At the same time Howard spoke warmly of Mary. ''I got the impression she was a very nice lady and he liked her a lot,'' McGuire said.

Howard also talked at length about the Peace Corps that night in Kansas City. What he confided was startling. ''He said the whole Peace Corps thing was such a sham. He loved the work, but all he was in South America was a drugrunner and a pimp. Those aren't the exact words he used, those are my words, but that's what it amounted to. He said he was responsible for getting women and drugs for visiting dignitaries. Those were almost his exact words.''[2]

McGuire said Howard also talked about his own drug use in Colombia. ''I knew he had been involved with drugs when he was in the Peace Corps because he told me that,'' she said. McGuire formed the impression that the drugs Howard used in Colombia were ''frequent and potent.'' But ''grass and hash are the only two he mentioned. I don't think he was into hard drugs. I can't see Ed shooting up.''

Howard, according to McGuire, was still using drugs in Chicago: ''He would make an occasional comment that he got ahold of some good grass or some hash.''

By the fall of 1980 Howard, at age twenty-eight, was outwardly doing well. He was married, owned a home, and appeared to be a successful young executive. But beneath the surface there were problems. Even in Barrington Mary and Edward Howard argued about his drinking. It was a subject that was to cause continual stress in their

---

[2]Howard acknowledged McGuire's account, at least in part. ''We were trying to get U.S. businessmen, garment manufacturers from New York, to invest in Colombia,'' he said. ''They would cut the materials in New York, and the girls in Cali would sew. These guys would come down, and I'd work with them all day, and some of them wanted to meet Colombian woman. I wasn't a pimp. I never got them drugs; they were older guys, not interested in drugs.''

marriage. Although Mary Howard said she could not pinpoint when her husband's alcohol abuse had become a problem, "we discussed it in Chicago."

Howard managed to conceal his drinking, however, presenting a very different picture to the world. "E and E liked to party," James Lockwood recalled. "Ed drank less than anybody. I've never seen him even a little bit out of control. And no drugs whatsoever. No marijuana, coke, nothing." Trish McGuire knew about the drugs but never saw Howard drink too much. "I would never have considered him an overdrinker," she said.

But Howard was bored in Chicago. That fall he found time for a brief extramarital affair, not his last. He also decided there was more to life than looking for toxic waste dumps. Months before, he had applied for another job with the government.

"He just mentioned one day that he had," his wife, Mary, said. But Howard confided to his wife that the decision had formed gradually in his mind.

"What I've wanted to do for a long time," he told her, "is work for the CIA."

4

The Hiring

"As a kid I used to see the James Bond movies. Great. The guy steals; he gets away with things, like any of us would like to do."

We were sitting in a booth at the Kisbuda restaurant on Leo Frankel Street, on the Buda side of the Danube, having dinner. Howard, chain-smoking Marlboros, kept glancing around the restaurant, to see if we were under surveillance. He did not doubt that we were. Over steaks and beer, however, he seemed to relax a little.

"The first screening interview was in Chicago in June or July of 1980," he said. "I got a call. Go to a hotel room. I met two guys and had two interviews, one with each of them. One was white-haired, distinguished, lively, and funny. A personnel type. The other guy was DDO. Old, looked like he'd been through the wars. He wouldn't say a lot, and he kept flicking the blade of his pocketknife all through the interview. I didn't like him very much.

"Then I got a phone call in October. Come to Washington for a week. It was a very intensive week. They put me up at the Holiday Inn in Rosslyn. They paid plane fare, the hotel, and per diem. I had psychological testing, the medical exam, test battery. Crazy stuff. Questions like 'Do you prefer showers or baths?' "

Howard didn't know whether he had passed. But by the end of the week he realized he was at least a serious candidate for the agency.

* * *

In the early days the Central Intelligence Agency recruited officers for the Clandestine Services almost exclusively from Ivy League colleges. And even then those tapped were very carefully selected.

"Nearly all of us were brought in by someone who knew us," a former station chief, now retired, explained. At Yale, Allen "Skip" Walz, the crew coach, was the agency's quiet talent spotter. William F. Buckley, Jr., the columnist and author, was recruited off the Yale campus in 1950, for example, and served in the CIA's Mexico City station. There were dozens of others who moved from the best prep schools to the Ivy League to the agency.

The elite easterners ran the DDO for years somewhat like a private social club. By the late 1970's, however, the old boys were getting older, and Admiral Stansfield Turner, President Carter's director of Central Intelligence, decided it was time to remove the barnacles. As a navy man Turner had no background in the Clandestine Services and no vested interest in protecting its members. On October 31, 1977, a day of infamy in the DDO that became known as the Halloween Massacre, Turner with a stroke of the pen eliminated 820 positions in the Clandestine Services.

While the survivors in the agency and many former DDO officers still grumble about Turner's action, the truth is that several other factors combined with the cutbacks to create personnel problems for the CIA's covert branch. The Vietnam War had made the military and the CIA unpopular. America's youth, many wrapped up in the counterculture, regarded the CIA as about the last place they would look for a job. During the 1970's the CIA had difficulty enlisting college graduates. Its recruiters were forced by campus protests and the political climate to interview students furtively in motels on the edge of campus.

The conservative tide that elected Ronald Reagan in 1980 was also reflected in the colleges. The CIA became more welcome, and protests for a time died down. But young people had also become career- and business-oriented. By the 1980's the CIA was faced with the growing problem of competing with private industry. It simply could not pay what the banks and large corporations were offering college graduates. In 1987, for example, a young CIA recruit might be offered a starting salary of just under twenty-two thousand dollars, but the same graduate might be able to land a job with a brokerage house at thirty-five thousand dollars.

It had also become a more dangerous world. CIA officers and installations and, more broadly, American diplomats and embassies were sometimes the target of terrorist attacks. The agency was not as safe a career choice as IBM.

By 1980, when Edward Howard applied to the CIA, the agency was struggling with all these factors in its efforts to attract and keep good people. Casting aside the total secrecy of the past, the agency was advertising in major newspapers in large displays that featured the CIA eagle. The directorate of operations had long since abandoned its preference for the Ivy League. Ohio State was now as likely a breeding ground for a DDO officer as Yale. The fact that Edward Howard had been educated at the University of Texas and American University was no barrier to his recruitment for the Clandestine Services.

The CIA has a set procedure for handling applicants, and Howard went through it. The screening interview he had in Chicago was the first step, the meeting where the agency gets an initial look at a prospect.

If that goes well, the candidate is asked to fill out a sixteen-page Personal History Statement in two parts. Part One, known as a Position Application, asks for physical data, marital status, education, business skills, military service, knowledge of foreign countries and languages, the names of relatives who live abroad, employment history, and whether the applicant has ever been convicted of a crime or belonged to a group seeking to overthrow the government. It also asks about alcohol and drug use.[1]

Part Two, the Clearance Application, asks for employ-

---

[1] Applicants are also asked verbally whether they have ever had a homosexual encounter. Officially the agency denies that it automatically bars homosexuals, but in practice it does not knowingly hire gay men or women.

ment data, family history, including details about parents, siblings, and in-laws, places of residence since age seventeen, financial status, and references.

If these initial hurdles are passed, the candidate is asked to take an all-day series of tests known as the Professional Applicant Test Battery (PATB). The package, which includes timed and untimed tests, is in form not unlike the SATs or Graduate Record Examination familiar to legions of students. There is a considerable difference in content, however. The test was designed by an educational testing service especially for the CIA, and it includes such questions as how the applicant would break into a locked building after hours and remove something from a desk.

The tests are followed by a second and much more detailed interview. Typically, for someone whom the agency sees as a possible candidate for the DDO, the interview would be conducted by an older case officer or former station chief. The applicants are warned that if they opt for the life of a spy, their friends will think they have been stuck in a minor embassy post for years, making no headway in the "State Department." They are bluntly told that they will probably earn less money than their friends and may have to endure hardships.

By stressing the down side of life in the Clandestine Services, the recruiter attempts to spot and weed out those who are unsuitable for covert work. The applicant who is discouraged by the recruiter's recitation is marked down as not DDO material.

If the in-depth interview goes well, the clearance process is begun, and the applicant is subjected to a full field investigation by the CIA's Office of Security. The investigation covers the applicant's life history. Friends, neighbors, relatives, and business associates are questioned.

Applicants are also told they will have to take a polygraph examination and are advised in writing that there is "no need" to reveal this fact even "to your immediate family." Others should certainly not be told, the CIA warns, because only the CIA and the National Security Agency use lie detectors to screen prospective employees; telling a friend about a lie detector test would therefore reveal that the candidate had applied to either the CIA or the NSA. Finally, applicants must take a medical examination that includes psychological and, for certain posts, psychiatric tests.

To the CIA Howard looked like an ideal recruit. The agency does not hire ex-Peace Corps volunteers for a period of five years, but that was no barrier; Howard had been out for six.[2] He had a graduate degree and work experience, including managerial responsibilities in his current job. Both he and his wife were accustomed to living overseas, and both had worked for the government previously. Howard was fluent in Spanish and could get along in German. He had lived in Germany, England, Colombia, and Peru. He was a smooth, well-spoken man who collected guns and knew how to use them. At the age of twenty-eight he was older than the typical applicant from a college campus, but young enough to learn the tradecraft of intelligence.

"He tested well," one former CIA officer said. Indeed, Howard seemed almost made-to-order for the agency.

Except for one problem. The CIA Personal History Statement that Howard filled out contains a section called "Personal Declarations." It asks whether the applicant uses alcohol and, if so, to what extent. "I think I put either normal or moderate consumption of alcohol," Howard said. Whatever his reply, it did not alarm the agency. Question 6, however, reads: "Do you use or have you ever tried such items as marijuana, hashish, cocaine, LSD, amphetamines, heroin, or drugs of a similar nature?" Howard admitted that he had.

For those who answer yes to Question 6, the next ques-

---

[2] While it is well publicized that the Peace Corps will not knowingly hire ex-CIA officers, it is not generally understood that the agreement is two-way: the CIA hires former Peace Corps volunteers only after a five-year waiting period. Even then the pertinent CIA regulation requires that the employment of any former member of the Peace Corps "must have the specific prior approval of the deputy director concerned." Howard said this was done in his case.

tion requires a listing of each drug used, how taken, the dates taken, the circumstances, the first time used, and the last time used. Howard filled in the details of his drug use.

In the Budapest interviews Howard spoke in some detail about drugs. At various times, he said, he had used marijuana, cocaine, hashish, LSD, and Quaaludes. He insisted he was never more than a "recreational user" of drugs.

"In college, maybe once a week at the University of Texas at Austin, maybe I'd try some marijuana. In the Peace Corps I did marijuana and cocaine. In Cali I met an old guy, a Marxist lawyer. Some of his clients couldn't pay him, so they paid him in cocaine. He would sell it to me for four, five dollars a gram. In the States it was a hundred dollars a gram.

"Maybe once a week, on Saturday night, I'd buy a gram just for recreational use. My peak period was Cali. We'd get high with a gram apiece. One person can do a gram in the course of a night. We used straws to snort it, maybe every twenty to thirty minutes. You get a rush for fifteen or twenty minutes, and then you use more, and again, until you have none left. We'd do a gram of coke, then go down to the bar and have a couple of beers. That was our Saturday night."

Howard said he had used LSD once, during his sophomore year in college, had used hash "a couple of times" while a student in Munich, and had taken Quaaludes once in Colombia. "I have definitely not used opium, heroin, PCP, or crack," he said.

As part of the screening process Howard had to take a polygraph test, as do all candidates. In CIA jargon, he was "fluttered." Howard passed his entrance polygraph with no difficulty. During the test, he said, "the operator wrote a list of drugs down the left-hand side of the page and the years along the top; he made a matrix. He filled the matrix from the preinterview, and then during the polygraph he asked, 'Except for the times you told me about, have you ever used drugs?' I said no. That was it. I passed the polygraph."[3]

---

[3] In a telephone interview with the author on November 27, 1985, Patti Volz, a CIA spokesperson, said that Howard's entrance polygraph had indicated "some drug use." But many applicants use marijuana, she

Although the polygraph, or lie detector, has been widely criticized as an imprecise and invasive tool, the CIA sets great store by it. Like other candidates, Howard was told that he would face a second polygraph after three years and at periodic intervals thereafter.

A former CIA man intimately familiar with the details of the Howard case, interviewed on the condition that he not be identified, said, "Howard had a very serious drug abuse problem for four years, daily use, while in the Peace Corps and AID." He had been "clean" for about two years before joining the CIA, the former official said.[4]

"They knew when they hired him that he had used hard drugs," he said. "They didn't find out afterward. They knew from the start."

In 1987 the House Intelligence Committee officially concluded: "The CIA hired Edward Howard despite an extensive history of using hard drugs."[5] The Intelligence Committee, which held a closed-door investigation of the Howard case, tried hard to pin down the extent of his

---

added. She did not mention cocaine or the other drugs Howard's entrance polygraph had disclosed.

[4]Although Howard said he had used drugs only once in AID, he continued to smoke pot and hashish in Chicago, according to Trish McGuire, at the very time he was being screened for employment by the CIA.

[5]The term "hard drugs" is a colloquial, rather than a legally defined, expression. Most authorities would certainly include addictive drugs, such as heroin, within that term. Increasingly experts are classifying cocaine as a hard drug. Apparently the House Intelligence Committee did so as well.

There is no complete agreement on the extent of Howard's drug use. Howard's parents said they were unaware of any drug use by their son. Howard's own description of his drug history is given in this chapter. His wife disputes the House Intelligence Committee version. "They make him sound like a heroin addict or something," Mary Howard said. "He wasn't." Asked about the list of drugs, including LSD, that the CIA admitted to the House Intelligence Committee that Howard had used, she said: "It's not true. That's a bunch of baloney. Maybe there was experimental use in college like a lot of people. If he had used LSD for years, his mind would be completely spaced out."

It is clear, however, that Howard used a variety of drugs over a period of more than ten years, including regular and frequent use of cocaine while in Colombia.

history of drug use. With a great deal of waffling the CIA reluctantly provided a list of drugs used by Howard to the panel.

How could the CIA have hired Howard, given his history of cocaine and other drug use? A thoughtful former senior official of the intelligence agency, a man wise in the ways of its bureaucracy, sketched in the historical background. "The agency for years was death on drugs," he said. "We'd gone through the flower children, and how do you get anyone to work for the agency who never smoked pot? We had to persuade OS [the CIA's Office of Security] to drop its categorical opposition to drugs, to anyone but Jack Armstrong. 'Look at the whole person' became the new euphemism for taking potheads. It was nothing but a recognition of reality of the world. With the Turner firings and passage of time there was a significant recruitment problem for ops officers. A strenuous effort was made to hire them."

What the new policy amounted to was that CIA candidates who admitted to smoking pot would not be automatically barred if they promised to stop once employed by the agency. In theory admission of hard-drug use—cocaine, for example—would raise a red flag, but again, not lead to automatic rejection.

John P. Littlejohn, the CIA's deputy director of personnel for employment, conceded that many applicants today have used marijuana. "That in itself isn't going to disqualify you. Hard drugs would raise questions, but we look at the circumstances and whole person. Someone who uses drugs at a frat party and now as an adult isn't using—that says something to us." But once an applicant is accepted, no drugs are permitted. "You can have a martini," Littlejohn said, "but you can't have a joint."

In 1980, when Howard was applying to the CIA, the director of the Office of Personnel (OP) was Harry E. Fitzwater, a veteran naval aviator who had previously run the agency's computers and then its training program. His deputy was Dr. Lawrence G. Woodward. Neither official personally screened Howard's application. That was done by lower-level "processing assistants" in OP.

On his Personal History Statement Howard had listed hashish, marijuana, and cocaine. He added LSD to that list on his entrance polygraph. Despite Howard's other qualifications, the list of drugs he provided, both on the statement and in his lie-detector examination, could not be ignored. The personnel officer whose job it is to decide on what the agency calls hard cases scrutinized Howard's application, including his drug use, and made the decision to hire him. Later he told associates he wished he hadn't.

How could it have happened? The former CIA official who studied the Howard case provided the answer: "He was quick, sharp-witted, well educated, had a good background, overseas service; he wasn't young and inexperienced. They wanted him. So they waived the drugs."

Howard's file was stamped "E.O.D.," which meant he was "Entered on Duty." If he did well and passed a second polygraph at the end of three years, he would be moved into unrestricted status.

In January 1981 Howard reported to headquarters in Langley, Virginia. For the moment Mary remained behind in Barrington. But Howard was ecstatic. His long-standing secret ambition was at last fulfilled. He was an agent of the Central Intelligence Agency.

5

Farmhand

CIA headquarters is a secluded, spooky place. The grayish white concrete building, seven stories high, is set, deliberately, in the middle of the woods, about a half mile inland from the Potomac. It is heavily guarded, closed to the public, and surrounded by a ten-foot-high chain-link fence.

In the winter, when Edward Howard reported in, the CIA may be glimpsed through the trees from the parkways nearby. In the summer it is completely hidden by foliage. To the north of the front entrance is a domed auditorium, rather Martian-like in appearance and irreverently known as the Tastee-Freez.

A bronze statue of Nathan Hale, Yale, Class of 1773, the nation's first spy, stands in front of headquarters. His hands are manacled behind him, and the inscription on the base proclaims: "I only regret that I have but one life to lose for my country."

Howard's first weeks at the agency were taken up with the usual round of training classes and orientation. He was issued his security badge and familiarized with the rules for locking safes and placing unwanted materials in burn bags at the end of each day. He was told to disguise his true employment to the outside world, even to friends and family.

Mary Howard knew, of course, but his parents did not. "We didn't even know it was CIA," his father, Kenneth Howard, said in an interview. "He told us he worked for the State Department, to relieve our mind, I'm sure."

More than four years were to go by before Howard's parents realized their son had worked for the Central Intelligence Agency.

Howard's immediate problem in January 1981 was to find a place to live. He asked one of his instructors, a woman, whether she could help. The instructor said she knew someone—another agency employee, of course—who had a room and put Howard in touch with him.

And so that month Howard moved into an apartment in Arlington, Virginia, with William George Bosch. It was located in a high-rise condominium on Pimmit Drive, in Falls Church, not far from CIA headquarters. Bosch became Howard's closest friend in the agency.

The son of a German-born yard conductor on the Long Island Rail Road, Bosch, then thirty-two, had grown up in Westbury, Long Island. He spoke of his mother, who still lived there, a brother who worked in New York City, another brother in California, and a sister in Texas. He had served in an Army intelligence unit in Vietnam, then joined the agency in 1973 while finishing college at the American University.

At six feet three and just over two hundred pounds, Bosch was several inches taller than Howard, who was two years his junior. Bosch was blond, balding, and gangly; Howard was dark-haired and compact. But Bosch shared Howard's taste for adventure. Bosch like to drive expensive, fast cars, and he had an eye for attractive women. And both men very much wanted to be spies.

For seven years Bosch had toiled on the clerical level in the administrative side of the Clandestine Services. He had been sent overseas for a time, to Saudi Arabia. But his real ambition was to become a case officer. He kept pushing, hoping that one day he would be rewarded.

In the meantime, Bosch was working in the Latin American division of the DDO as an intelligence assistant, a status somewhere between a secretary and a case officer. In March Bosch got exciting news. He was being sent to the Farm, for training as a real spy. Guns, secret writing, shaving-cream cans with secret compartments for messages—the whole works. With any luck he would be posted overseas, where his potential as a secret agent could at last be fully realized.

Howard knew that he, too, would soon get his chance to go to the Farm. For the moment he had to be content with a series of less interesting assignments. To familiarize him with the operations of the directorate, he was rotated around headquarters, first on the Swiss desk, then the covert-action desk of the international activities division (IAD).

That winter and spring he was able to see his wife on the weekends. Sometimes he flew to Chicago; sometimes Mary came east. Howard also began looking for a house in northern Virginia that would be convenient to CIA headquarters.

He contacted Dwight Avis, a real estate broker with Century 21 in Vienna, Virginia, a Washington bedroom community of modestly priced houses. Avis knew just the place—a development of brand-new attached town houses arranged in a quiet square that was secluded from the area's busy highways. And in a few years the Orange Line of the Washington subway system would reach Vienna.

"I was strong on Country Creek," Avis recalled, "because I knew it was going to be close to the Metro." Avis remembered Howard. "He came in by himself. He told me he was with the State Department."

The Howards selected a town house at 9654 Scotch Haven Drive in the Country Creek development, obtained financing, and purchased it in May for $98,234. For the moment they held on to the house in Barrington; Avis advised them that real estate prices were down, and they would do better to wait.

The new two-story house on Scotch Haven Drive was the last in its row, so there was open space next to it. A wooden fence enclosed a small backyard which overlooked a jogging path that ran along a stand of pines. The house had an unfinished basement, a sunken living room that overlooked the woods, and three bedrooms upstairs.

The Howards' next-door neighbor was John Matejko, a television tape editor for the Washington bureau of ABC News. A Navy lieutenant commander, Douglas M. Arendt, and his wife lived on the other side of the Howards, across the open space. When the Howards first moved in, Matejko, his wife, Marianne, the Arendts, and another couple were invited over for a housewarming.

"Mary and Ed were making homemade ice cream," Matejko recalled. "We had a few drinks. I asked, 'What do you do?' Mary said, 'We met in the Peace Corps, and Ed now works for the State Department.' Ed said he had been an AID officer in South America. The furnishings were nice, with a distinctively Spanish accent, a lot of dark woods. It had obviously been bought in South America. He seemed a very pleasant, intelligent guy." But on other occasions Matejko thought he detected an intense, brooding side to his new neighbor. "He seemed to be more aloof as time went by."

Otherwise, however, the Howards blended into the neighborhood. The young State Department officer was frequently seen jogging on the path behind the houses. The couple had a large German shepherd that they had purchased as a pup in Lima. Howard named the dog Whisky.

Mary Howard's parents came to visit the young couple on Scotch Haven Drive, and on one trip Evar Cedarleaf, who was handy with tools, helped Ed finish the basement. Evar used light wood paneling, and when he was through, the basement, with its cozy fireplace, had expanded the house by a whole floor. With Howard's future apparently bright and the couple settled in, their new home seemed an ideal place to start a family. By July Mary Howard had exciting news for her husband: she was pregnant.

About the same time Bill Bosch completed his training at the Farm and returned to headquarters. Howard kept up his friendship with Bosch; they saw each other once a week, sometimes in the cafeteria on the ground floor of CIA headquarters or occasionally Bosch came to the Howards' new house.

And then, in August, it was Howard's turn. It was time for the real espionage training to begin. At long last he would be sent south. To the Farm.

STOP. RESTRICTED AREA. ENTERING THIS FACILITY SIG-
NIFIES YOUR CONSENT TO THE SEARCH OF YOUR PERSON
& PERSONAL PROPERTY INCLUDING VEHICLES. TURN ON
INTERIOR LIGHT.

The setting looks exactly like the entrance to a military
base. The sign, in bold letters, the searchlights, and the
aggressive, armed guards are there to discourage a wrong
turn by any of the millions of tourists who drive by each
year en route to colonial Williamsburg, only a few minutes
away.

A larger sign, above the guardhouse, purports to identify the site. It reads: ARMED FORCES EXPERIMENTAL
TRAINING ACTIVITY, DEPARTMENT OF DEFENSE, CAMP
PEARY. The installation is on the left-hand side of the highway as motorists head south for Williamsburg. It stretches
over ten thousand acres between Interstate 64 and the York
River.

Despite its markings, Camp Peary is not a military
base. It is the training facility of the Central Intelligence
Agency, better known as the Farm. Although former employees have written about the Farm, the CIA, even today, does not acknowledge its existence. All officers of
the Clandestine Services receive their principal training
there.

The heavily forested site is, of course, closed to outsiders and protected by a chain-link fence. It had previously been a training base for the Navy's Seabees and,
during World War II, a prisoner of war camp for cap-
tured German soldiers. Aerial photographs taken by local authorities for tax purposes show clusters of
barracks, a huge warehouse, a gym, target ranges, and
a private airstrip with a large *R* (for ''restricted'')
painted on it. Deer are abundant, and there are stocked
lakes for fishing.

At the Farm Howard, like all career trainees of the
DDO, received intensive instruction in espionage tradecraft, including recruitment of agents, communications
with agents, surveillance and countersurveillance, and escape and evasion. He spent four months at the Farm and

later received specialized training at other locations in the Washington area.[1]

Some of the members of Howard's class at the Farm were instructed in weapons assembly and handling, paramilitary operations, parachute drops, sabotage, and martial arts. Howard did not take the paramilitary course; the trainees who did were destined for duty in places like El Salvador, where such skills might be necessary.

The communications courses that Howard took at the Farm included training in radio, codes, secret writing, the use of one-time code pads, dissolving paper, microdots, dead drops, and signals. The dissolving paper, Howard explained, was for quick destruction of sensitive material. "Suppose you take notes at an agent meeting. Just throw them in the toilet, or spill your drink on them, and they're gone."

A dead drop is a favorite device of spies, both East and West, because it is a means of passing messages without the risk of personal contact. An agent leaves a message at an agreed location, behind a loose brick in a wall, for example, and his case officer clears the drop and perhaps leaves a new message and money for the agent.

Often the CIA communicates with agents by radio. Howard was trained in how to instruct an agent to tune in on the exact frequency and listen for the code numbers to decipher with the help of the one-time pads. "We pretended to be agents and copied down number groups," he said.

Howard lived dormitory-style in the BOQ, the bachelor

---

[1] CIA trainees receive specialized courses, on a selective basis, at places other than the Farm. For example, trainees have been instructed in explosives and detonation at Harvey Point, near Elizabeth City, North Carolina. For certain surveillance exercises, trainees sometimes stalk each other on the Mall that runs between the Lincoln Memorial and the Capitol or are taken to Harpers Ferry, West Virginia. Courses in locks and picks, flaps and seals (how to open letters clandestinely), and photography have been given at the CIA's Blue U, an eight-story office building at 1000 North Glebe Road in Arlington, Virginia. "Blue U" gets its unusual name from the fact that the exterior of the modernistic building is a checkerboard pattern in two shades of blue.

officers' quarters at Camp Peary. There was constant pressure on the trainees; Howard and his classmates knew they were being tested and evaluated. Still, he found some of the training exhilarating.

"I liked the process, the mechanics," he said. "At the Farm my best grade was breaking and entering. I had a perfect score. Get in, take pictures of documents, and get out. I loved that shit. They had a house. It was dark, at night, and you had to get in, take the pictures, and get out without anyone knowing. We had a team of four to break in."

And once while at the Farm, quite unexpectedly, Howard came upon the house where Yuri Nosenko, the controversial KGB defector, had been confined by the counterintelligence chief James Angleton. It made an unforgettable impression. "I saw Nosenko's cell in the woods in Camp Peary," Howard recalled. "It's in a house with barbed wire around it and spotlights. It was eerie."

While Howard concentrated on courses in agent handling, the paramilitary training was going on around him. The paramilitary courses at the Farm include instruction in border crossing at a mock border, complete with guards, watchtowers, and dogs, and infiltration by boat, sometimes at night. The paramilitary training also includes climbing obstacles, long marches, setting up tents, and nights in the field. In the martial arts courses the trainees learn to kill with their bare hands.

One graduate of the Farm remembers a hairy exercise with hand grenades. "You pull the pin, throw the grenade, and duck," he said. "Not all were live, but some were, and you never knew which ones were. It was a bit like Russian roulette."

"Some of the training was a little nutty," a former staff official of the Farm recalled. "For example, we demonstrated the snatch technique for exfiltrating agents. If you infiltrate agents into a Soviet-bloc country, there may come a time when you have to exfiltrate them. They set up two poles with a bungee between them and attached a line to the bungee with a sort of seat. The agent sits in the seat between the two poles. A light aircraft moving slowly hooks the line and snatches the agent into the sky while someone in the plane with a crankshaft literally winds him in. When the young trainees would see this, they were in awe. I doubt the agency ever really used it, but it sure impressed the trainees.''

Although Howard never hung from a bungee, he did spend a good deal of time learning countersurveillance, the techniques of detecting and evading surveillance by others. The CS training is provided by FBI instructors, not only at the Farm but also in a city to which the trainees are taken (Richmond or other cities in the South are often favored). The CIA men and woman are taught how to spot a tail and how to ''dry-clean'' themselves by going in and out of crowded department stores, for example, or other places where it would be difficult for anyone to follow them.[2] Howard seemed to have a knack for this aspect of espionage work; according to one CIA source, he scored number one in his class in countersurveillance, although Howard himself said he was never told this.

Howard also had a day of disguise training at the Farm, learning what he needed to know about wigs, makeup, and fake mustaches. He kept one of the wigs he was issued.

After almost four months at Camp Peary the career trainees are given their final exam. Typically the CTs are taken to a major U.S. city for a live exercise, with CIA instructors as role players. ''The group split up into teams housed in different motels,'' a former CIA officer who went through the training at the Farm explained. ''You would be given the location and description of an agent to contact in a restaurant or bar. At the bar the agent would have signaled if he felt he was under surveillance, either with a gesture or by wearing a certain colored jacket. You would debrief the agent or your might 'task' him to get further information. The guy had his own 201 file, and you had read it.[3] He

---

[2] The term ''dry cleaning'' to evade surveillance is also used by the KGB.

[3] The CIA opens 201 files on any person of interest to the agency.

might be in the foreign ministry of the host country, for example.''

As part of the final exam the trainee must usually recruit an agent whom he or she has been assessing during a series of meetings at or near the Farm. The purpose of the half dozen meetings is to make sure the agent has access to the information he claims he can provide and is not a provocation by an opposing intelligence service. In the final meeting the trainee makes the ''pitch,'' as a recruitment attempt is termed.[4]

Sometimes the instructors would spring the unexpected, the ex-CIA man recalled. ''One instructor I had, playing the role of an agent, got loud and boisterous in the restaurant. 'I've been telling you people for a year about my medical bills. What are you going to do about it?' Other instructors demanded more money or asked the agency to exfiltrate their family if they were arrested. You had to know how to respond. I had one who suddenly said, 'I'm being posted to Ouagadougou.' So you have to make a recontact plan on the spot. It was a nervous time. You wanted to do a good job; you were being graded.''

Howard's final examination followed the customary pattern. ''We had the final exercise in a southern city,'' Howard said, ''meeting agents we had recruited. We worked in groups of four. Each of us had four or five agents. We tried to determine which ones to recruit to save the U.S. from a big mistake. It was all going on in a mythical country, like Atlantis. It was supposed to be an island in the Atlantic.

''One agent would be head of the secret police, another in the foreign ministry, and so on, and we had to decide which were the best ones to recruit.''

Howard apparently did fairly well. He claimed that he ranked in the top 25 percent of his class at the Farm.

---

[4]Trainees at the Farm also learn the always dangerous cold pitch, the approach to a potential agent—a Soviet diplomat, for example—without any warning or previous meetings. And they learn about a false-flag recruitment, in which the recruiter pretends to represent a country other than his own.

Even while in training at the Farm, Howard was able to spend some of his time at home on Scotch Haven Drive, and he renewed his friendship with James Lockwood, the onetime college wrestling champion who ran the Rosslyn office of E&E, Howard's former employer.

"We ran together all the time he was in Washington," Lockwood said. "He got me into distance running." At the time Lockwood was running a mile or two, but Howard was jogging three or four miles at a clip. The two men often met and jogged together around the Iwo Jima Memorial in Rosslyn. "Ed said he'd gone to work for the State Department. He never mentioned CIA."

That fall the Howards invited the Lockwoods to dinner at their house in Vienna. It was a very mundane evening, Lockwood recalled, "talking, eating dinner, and then they showed us their slides from the Peace Corps. They were proud of that experience. We had them back to our house in Springfield."

One night at a bar in Rosslyn, however, Lockwood was surprised to discover that his friend was a political conservative. After law school at Syracuse Lockwood had joined a combat battalion of the Army Engineers, and had spent a year and a half in Vietnam, where he was shot at during the Tet offensive. The experience helped shape his views; Lockwood came back from the war a liberal. At the bar "we had a philosophical conversation. I was to the left politically. Here's a guy in the Peace Corps, and he goes and votes for Ronald Reagan. The conversation got heated. Ed felt money is best spent on defense, not social programs. He was a strong Reagan supporter."

Just as Lockwood had misgauged his friend's politics, there were other perceptions of the Howards that did not reflect the reality. Their next-door neighbor Kit Arendt thought that Mary Howard worked for a bank. John Matejko, their other immediate neighbor, believed Mary was "teaching at a school or working at a bank."

They were wrong. Mary Howard, in the fall of 1981, had joined the CIA. "I felt if I was going to work anywhere," she said, "it would be logical to work in the agency." Like her husband, she was assigned to the directorate of operations, where she worked, initially, as a secretary at the CIA's language school in an unmarked building in Arlington.

The DDO is a tight-knit organization whose members tend to socialize together and on occasion to intermarry. CIA couples are not unusual, and often, as in the case of the Howards, a DDO officer's wife will be recruited by the "Company." From a security point of view the agency finds the arrangement convenient. Like all couples working for the CIA's covert side, the Howards lived a double life, in which concealment from family, close friends, and neighbors gradually became the norm.

The neighbor who knew them best, John Matejko, agreed to take care of the dog when the Howards were away, and that seemed to be often. He would go into the Howards' house to feed him. "Gaines pellets," Matejko said. "She had about two hundred rawhide chew sticks that Whisky liked. If I wanted to get the dog to go down to the basement, where he was kept, all I had to do was throw one down the steps. One weekend they said they were going down to Williamsburg. 'We haven't seen it yet,' Mary said. They brought us back a present.''

In December, his training at the Farm over, Howard was temporarily assigned to the German Democratic Republic (East German) desk of the European (EUR) division. There are several geographic divisions within the DDO, and some are more prestigious than others. Although Howard spoke some German, he was fluent in Spanish. With his knowledge of that language and his previous work in South America, Howard might have expected he would be assigned to the Latin American division. But within the DDO, LA division is regarded as something of a dumping ground, not the very best path to rapid advancement.

Thus, Howard was pleased to learn that he was being prepared for an assignment in Austria. "I wanted to go to Vienna," he said. "It's the spy capital of the world. It's where a lot of things go down. It's a big station for such a small country.''

Then something even better, and totally unexpected,

happened. In January 1982 the woman who was personnel officer for the Soviet/East European division asked Howard and his wife to come to her house.

Over coffee the woman gradually worked around to the reason for her call. She asked Howard whether he might be interested in going to Moscow for SE division. Yes, Howard replied quickly, it would be interesting, yes.

"Moscow!" Howard recalled. "I was dumbfounded. To become a Soviet target officer in the CIA was like being top gun." He could scarcely believe his good fortune.

Howard was thirty years old. He had made it through the CIA selection process into the Clandestine Services. Mary, too, had been accepted into the ranks of the DDO. And now, having excelled in his rite of passage at the Farm, he had passed through yet another closed door into the agency's inner sanctum. He had made it to the fourth floor. To the most coveted division of all, SE.

6

SE

"SE is the holiest of holies," the former Far East division case officer said. "It's a closed, cliquish, incestuous bunch of people. Nobody looks over their shoulders."

That created a problem, he said. "SE screens their own and thumbs their nose at anybody else. But once you're in, you're in. It's a club. The irony is, they don't take a good, close look at the people they bring in."

The division, the most secret in the directorate of operations, is responsible for the clandestine collection of intelligence and for covert operations in the Soviet Union and the Communist-bloc countries of Eastern Europe.[1]

The officer of the chief of the SE division is located on the fifth floor at Langley headquarters. The division is organized into a number of branches and sections, which occupy offices on the fourth, fifth, and sixth floors. Among the important branches are SE/USSR, the Soviet branch, to which Howard was assigned, SE/PCH, for Poland, Czechoslovakia, and Hungary, a separate branch for Romania and Bulgaria, and SE/SS for support staff.[2]

Approximately three hundred people work in SE division at headquarters. They customarily use the blue ele-

---

[1]The one exception is the German Democratic Republic, which remains part of the DDO's European (EUR) division.

[2]SE/SS houses the division's administrative sections, including SE/B&F, for business and finance; SE/PEMS, for personnel employee management system, the unit in charge of assigning case officers to various overseas stations and bases; and SE/personnel.

vator in the southwest corner of the CIA lobby to reach their offices.

When the Howards were approached by the Soviet division, it was made clear to them that SE was interested not only in Edward Howard but in Mary Howard as well. Although up to now Mary Howard had worked at the agency as a secretary, the CIA planned a very different role for her in Moscow.

The Howards were to be a husband-and-wife spy team.

Before their special training for Moscow could begin, there was another hurdle to pass. Once tapped by SE division, Howard and his wife were required to meet with CIA psychiatrists, both separately and together. Moscow is a stressful post, where case officers must work under the nose of the KGB, and the psychiatric screening was an important step before their selection could be made final. The Howards passed the psychological evaluation and reported in to SE in February 1982. They were assigned to the SE/USSR branch on the fourth floor.

Like all DDO officers, Howard was given a pseudonym, consisting of a first and last name and a middle initial. His was Roger K. Shannon. In all CIA cable traffic pseudonyms are used whenever there is a reference in the text to a CIA officer.[3]

At the Farm Howard had been assigned another name, Edward L. Houston, which was technically his alias and was distinct from his pseudonym. Among other purposes, he used the alias to sign his cables. So complicated is the agency's secrecy system that its employees sometimes give false names even to each other; when Howard first reported in to the Soviet division, he gave his name as Edward L. Houston.[4]

---

[3]Pseudonym files, keyed to true names, are kept in the divisions at headquarters and at stations overseas so that case officers can figure out the references in the cable traffic.

[4]Howard had a third name that he used for operational purposes in the CIA: Patrick M. Brian, which he sometimes varied as Patrick Brian or Patrick M. Bryan. Howard had served in the Peace Corps in Cali with Patrick M. Brian and borrowed his name. "I was allowed to choose this name and deliberately selected the name of an old friend with

He revealed his true name only as he was taken upstairs
to meet the division chief, David W. Forden. A handsome, if somewhat short, man of fifty, with prematurely
silver hair, Forden was a popular division chief who played
tennis with his secretary and related easily to his staff. He
was born in New York, was graduated from Wesleyan University in 1952, earned a master's degree in public administration the following year, and then joined the CIA under
Army cover. In the early days Forden ran operations into
Czechoslovakia from Germany. By 1965 he was in Warsaw under State Department cover as a political officer.
After putting in time at headquarters, he was sent to Mexico in 1970, again under embassy cover. He climbed the
ladder as a field officer and finally got his division.

Although Howard was unaware of it, in early 1982 Forden had a problem. The woman case officer who had been
selected for the Moscow station had flunked her psychological evaluation. Someone else was needed, and right
away. Moscow was too important a station to leave a slot
unfilled. That is how Howard came to be chosen for SE
and Moscow.

Hannah Arendt has called bureaucracy "rule by nobody." The CIA officials who made the initial decision to
hire Howard, and those who selected him for the sensitive
Moscow post, did not rush forward later to claim credit.
The bureaucratic mists have closed in to mask those decisions. But clearly the division chief would have had to
approve Howard's selection for Moscow. The choice of a
new CIA officer to operate at the very center of Soviet
power was too important to be left to underlings.

The former CIA official who closely studied the Howard
file confirmed this. "Dave Forden approved him," he said.

In SE Howard would certainly have been reminded of
the agency's elaborate security precautions. Before leaving
each night, employees are warned to make sure that all
classified trash is stapled in brown bags labeled "Top Secret" and put down the chute. Deep in the basement of

---

whom I'd lost contact," Howard told me. "It was not a joke but simply
an easy way for me to remember my cover."

the CIA, powerful machines shred the documents into a fine pulp. Passwords were needed to access the files in SE's computers, and even innocuous files required them.

Despite the tight security, there were frequent office parties in the division, and alcohol was plentiful. Howard's drinking, which he managed to conceal from friends like Jim Lockwood, was still a subject of marital discord between Howard and his wife.

The agency did not, apparently, discover that Howard had an alcohol problem when he was hired. It was not picked up on his entrance polygraph in 1980. But his CIA colleagues knew; on a couple of occasions he had been seen drinking heavily. The incidents were not reported officially, but Howard's problem was known around headquarters.

According to the former CIA official who studied the Howard file, both Forden and the Soviet division were aware that Howard had an alcohol abuse problem at the time he was brought into the division and chosen for Moscow; the bureaucratic pressures to fill the job were such that Howard was selected for the Moscow station anyway.

Certainly, by February 1982, when Howard began work in SE division, the CIA knew about his drinking because he had consulted the agency's alcoholism counselor after leaving the Farm and *before* reporting in to the division that month.[5]

Howard conceded that he had a drinking problem at the

---

[5]The extent of the agency's knowledge of Howard's drinking problem at the time he was brought into SE division and simultaneously chosen for Moscow is obviously a sensitive issue and was never clarified even in later, rather limited closed-door congressional investigations of the affair by the House and Senate Intelligence committees. One congressional source said that the CIA may not have known "officially" about Howard's drinking when he was selected for Moscow, but "the people who knew him knew he had a problem." A senior member of the House Intelligence Committee told the author that "there were several instances of drunken conduct [by Howard] while he was at the CIA." The congressional sources agreed that the agency did become aware of Howard's drinking problem, while he was still employed. Howard himself said that when selected for SE, "if they knew I drank too much, I never knew that."

agency, one that bothered him to the point that he consulted the counselor. He spoke about it in considerable detail on the first full day of our conversations in Budapest.

"My first year in the agency I was under a lot of pressure," he said. "At the Farm I'd go with the guys to the club on the base. We'd drink beer and wine. On a Friday night I'd have a bottle of red burgundy." After Howard had left Camp Peary in December 1981 and begun work for a period of six weeks on the East German desk, "the drinking started to bother me. There are signs in the halls with pictures of beer bottles. 'If you drink a lot of beer, you drink a lot. Come see us.' So I went to see the alcohol counselor, in the Office of Medical Services. He was a retired case officer."

The alcoholism counselor apparently did not regard Howard's case as too serious on the scale of alcohol problems at the agency.

"I've got people who sit in the parking lot at headquarters, drinking," the counselor complained to him. "I've got one lady who filled her windshield wiper dispenser with vodka and rigged the line so the hose comes inside the car. When she's caught in traffic, she can turn on the wipers and squirt herself."

The counselor shook his head and fixed Howard with a kindly gaze. "You'll settle down," he said. "If it gets worse, come and see me."

Howard described his drinking while at the CIA as "average case officer drinking." But he added that "case officers drink more than average Americans" because of the pressure of their work. "In Langley people had bottles in their desks. One division chief had cognac in his safe."

Howard confirmed his wife's account of arguments over his drinking even in Barrington, before he joined the CIA. Part of the problem was her teetotaling midwestern background, he said. "Her parents don't drink. On New Year's Eve they have sherry.

"Working as an ops officer in the Soviet division," Howard said, "maybe three times a year I had more than

I should. At the agency I never drank on the job. But I drank in the top twenty percent of case officers.''

Howard's immediate boss on the fourth floor was Thomas J. Mills, the chief of the USSR desk, a balding, slender man of fifty-one with gray hair, blue eyes, and glasses. A veteran CIA operator and Michigan native, Mills had served in Belgrade and Berlin and spoke Serbo-Croatian and excellent Russian. Howard established a good rapport with Mills, who became the senior agency official closest to him.

Howard had now been designated by the CIA for its most sensitive operation, the Moscow station. The plan was to send him in under embassy cover. Why did the agency choose for such a crucial post an untried newcomer who had no previous experience working as an intelligence officer overseas?

The reason, Howard was told, was that he had a ''secure past.'' Since there was nothing in his Peace Corps and AID background to suggest that he was an intelligence officer, the Soviets might not realize he was CIA. ''They told me they wanted someone who was clean, who had not worked for the agency overseas,'' Howard said.

It is true that the agency often does try to send a ''fresh face'' to its overseas stations. Later CIA Director William Casey privately defended the decision to send a rookie to Moscow as a common agency practice. ''We do that all the time,'' he said.

''The problems you have working in the bloc are unique,'' a former DDO officer explained. ''You have constant electronic surveillance. They [the KGB] have a very good data base. They know who's been posted where. It doesn't take them long to figure out that Joe Blow, who was posted in Kinshasa, Prague, and Warsaw, is CIA. So the problem is to find someone they don't know. We often send out junior officers to Moscow on their first tour.''

Whether the risk of using an inexperienced officer is worth the possible temporary gain in anonymity is debatable, however. Once a CIA agent starts to operate in the Soviet capital, it does not take the KGB very long to spot him. "There is so much KGB coverage," the former DDO officer said, "that anytime one of our guys leaves the embassy the KGB agents are practically lined up on the street waiting for him."[6]

Although Howard had received basic training in espionage at the Farm, he would need specialized tutelage for Moscow, where the CIA operates under difficult conditions. Agents of the KGB's Second Chief Directorate closely monitor the movements of CIA officers in the Moscow station. "They [the KGB] have ways to identify you," Howard said. "They look at the odometer on your car. Why is this guy driving so many miles?"

In addition to Howard's special training, Mary Howard, who had thus far received no education in the tradecraft of intelligence, would have to be prepared for her role as a spy in Moscow.

Mary Howard's primary job, it was explained to her,

---

[6]Although the CIA attempts to disguise the identities of its rank-and-file officers in Moscow, the KGB knows who the station chief is—because it approves him in advance. Under a little-known practice the chief of the CIA's Moscow station is, in effect, subject to an *agrément* by Moscow, in much the same fashion that a new American ambassador must be approved before being dispatched to the Soviet Union. In turn, the CIA approves the KGB resident in Washington.

Sometimes the two intelligence agencies exercise their veto power. In July 1985, as the CIA station chief in Moscow was leaving, the KGB vetoed Langley's first nomination for his successor. Moscow's delay in approving a new COS was linked to the fact that the FBI objected to the officer the KGB wanted to send to the Soviet consulate in San Francisco. The FBI eventually withdrew its objection, and the KGB accepted Murat Natirboff as the CIA chief of station, although it held up his visa, delaying his arrival in Moscow. Natirboff, a heavyset man with gray hair, dark complexion, and dark eyebrows, looked rather like a Russian. In September 1986, after the KGB had arrested *U.S. News & World Report* correspondent Nicholas Daniloff on charges of espionage, Moscow surfaced Murat Natirboff's name, publicly identifying him as the COS and claiming he gave Daniloff instructions. Natirboff, listed as an embassy counselor, had already left Moscow that summer.

The arrangement between the CIA and the KGB creates an anomaly: the name of the CIA's Moscow station chief is concealed, normally, only from the American public. The CIA has already provided it to the KGB.

would be to provide countersurveillance for her husband when he was en route to a meeting with a Soviet asset or to the site of a dead drop. She would watch for the KGB.

Mary Howard, an attractive and intelligent women in her mid-thirties, now lives in seclusion with her young son near St. Paul, Minnesota. She broke her long silence and agreed to be interviewed for the first time by the author. In a series of conversations that took place over a year's time, she spoke in detail about her life and her husband but was reluctant to describe her work for the CIA. When asked, however, whether her training might have prepared her to sit in a car and act as a lookout for her husband, she replied, "It could have been something like that." She also said she had received special instruction to prepare her for her CIA assignment in Moscow.

Howard confirmed that Mary was to act as his espionage partner in the Soviet capital. "They almost always send case officers with wives," he said. "Four eyes are better than two."

Late in April 1982 the Howards' Moscow training began. For a period of six weeks Howard and his wife enrolled in the CIA's Denied Areas Operations Course.[7]

The work was rigorous, and the hours long. On some days the trainees started at eight and ended at midnight. When Howard enrolled in the denied areas course, he knew he would have little time to take care of his dog. He gave Whisky away to his relatives in New Mexico.

The headquarters for the highly secret Denied Areas Operations Course was the CIA's Ames Building on North Fort Myer Drive in Rosslyn.[8] But the Howards spent most of their time on the streets of Washington and in suburban Alexandria, Arlington, and Bethesda, training in identifi-

---

[7] The CIA uses the term "denied areas" for the Soviet Union and other Communist countries where it must operate against hostile intelligence services.

[8] The ground floor of the Ames Building houses the agency's overt, walk-in recruitment office where persons interested in CIA employment can pick up brochures and applications.

cation of surveillance, countersurveillance, and escape. In most of the exercises the CIA trainees played the role of agency officers and the FBI played the part of the KGB. Sometimes CIA teams posed as the KGB. On occasion Howard and the other trainees ducked in and out of buildings and stores as they tried to elude FBI counterintelligence agents on K Street, the main thoroughfare of Washington's downtown business district.

"We ran exercises against the FBI," Howard said. "The training was to detect and evade surveillance, to dry-clean yourself in a department store, for example, by going in one entrance and out an exit. The point was to learn to detect surveillance on the way to a meeting or a drop site."

The basic approach, Howard explained, "was to have a cover, a reason for traveling to a particular neighborhood. Shopping for food, for example. You look for the same people in different locations. At first you go to obvious places like department stores. Then to more provocative places. For example, you might end up in a park where you force the surveillance to show itself. You're in the car on the way to a meeting. Maybe toward the end you make a U-turn. Perhaps you get out and take a twenty-minute walk, even if it tips them to what you are doing. It's better to do that than to go to a meeting under surveillance."

At an actual meeting in Moscow, the Howards were instructed, Mary would be perhaps two hundred yards away. "She would be out of sight of the Soviet agent so as not to alarm him," Howard explained. "She might be feeding the birds or eating a sandwich. Everything is planned down to the last detail, including the route to take to the meeting, the recognition signals, everything."

In addition, the Howards learned such basic escape techniques, familiar to any moviegoer, as entering a restaurant and slipping out the back way. As part of the denied areas course, Howard was also taught how to resist KGB interrogation, in case something went wrong and he was seized. Howard heard a lecture on the subject by Martha Peterson, a blond, slightly plump woman who, as a CIA officer in Moscow, had been caught by the KGB five years earlier.

Peterson, a thirty-three-year-old officer in the Clandestine Services under cover as vice-counsel of the embassy, was grabbed by the KGB on July 15, 1977, while placing a hollow rock in the bridge that spans the Moscow River at the Lenin Hills. The rock, the KGB claimed, contained two poison capsules, cameras, gold, and a microphone. Peterson was expelled and then declared persona non grata.[9]

The advice on how to resist interrogation was to prove valuable sooner than Howard could have anticipated. One morning that spring the Howards were instructed to clear a drop at the marina on Maine Avenue, along Washington's Potomac River waterfront. It was to be a routine training exercise, like dozens they had done before. The Howards were told to pick up a carton of half-and-half on the wharf; it would presumably have a microfilm or a document inside.

"We were running against the FBI," Howard said. "We went to the marina. We listened on the radio. No FBI activity. We go down to the wharf. As I pick up the carton, a woman runs up screaming, 'You've got to pay me.' Suddenly two FBI agents appear, slam me against the wall, and pull a gun. The gun was stuck against my head. Mary starts crying.

" 'Don't move, you son of a bitch!' The FBI agent says. They slapped the girl, who was busted with us. The FBI men show us a white powder in the carton. They said, 'This is cocaine.' They drive us to the FBI's Washington field office. They put us in separate rooms."

---

[9]The Soviet government, through its newspaper *Izvestia*, charged that Peterson had provided the poison used to murder "an innocent Soviet citizen," but it gave no details to back up the claim. Her expulsion took place with no publicity. But almost a year later, on June 12, 1978, the Soviets chose to surface the case with major fanfare. It released a photograph of Peterson in custody sitting in front of a table on which the contents of the hollow rock were spread out. At the time two Soviet spies were on trial in New Jersey for stealing U.S. naval secrets. Both were convicted. The KGB obviously publicized the Peterson case as part of a number of measures it took to retaliate for the arrest of its spies in the naval secrets case.

The CIA officers taking the ops course were told at the outset that some of the exercises might become jarringly realistic. But was this only a drill? "Mary, I learned later, broke down and told them everything. All I said was I wanted to see a lawyer. Finally they found my CIA credentials, they take me out, and there's Tom Mills. They had been watching the whole time on closed-circuit TV.

"The FBI man said it was just a fake. Then he sits down and tells me what we did that was good and bad." Howard had realized early on it was a mock arrest. Why weren't you more worried? the FBI agents asked him. "I said I could see that the FBI agent's gun wasn't loaded. He held it against my head, but then in front of me, and I could see there were no bullets in the chambers. When I said I saw the gun wasn't loaded, they were amazed."

It was toward the end of the denied areas course that Howard learned to jump from a moving car into a blind spot to elude surveillance. If done at night as the car rounded a corner, for example, a pursuer in a car some distance behind might not realize his quarry had vanished. The FBI instructors who demonstrated the technique taught Howard well.

"Mary and I did the jump against surveillance," Howard said. "There's a place in Georgetown where you go under the K Street Bridge and then turn right toward the Kennedy Center on Rock Creek Parkway. I jumped there, onto a grassy area with bushes. Mary was going fifteen miles per hour. There were no problems."

The jump may not work, however, if the person tailing the car notices that the passenger in the auto under surveillance has suddenly disappeared. For that reason CIA officers receive dummy training as well.

Howard's dummy training took place in a separate, special course. The dummy that CIA agents use in escape maneuvers, and that Howard used in training, was developed by the agency's technical boffins. It is spring-loaded and carried inside an attaché case that is placed on the front seat of a car. When the case is unlatched, the dummy pops up.

The device, which operates on the same principle as a

child's jack-in-the-box, is known for that reason as a jib. Howard was intrigued with the dummy. "It even has little knobs inside the briefcase," he said, "so the driver can reach down and turn the head of the dummy, so it looks like they are having a conversation."

Howard found the CIA's dummy useful in other ways. To get from his house on Scotch Haven Drive to head-quarters, Howard normally took I-66, which has restrictions that ban single-passenger cars during rush hours. "A couple of times, when we were doing training, I used the dummy on I-Sixty-six," he said.

Although Howard had been brought into the most prestigious of the CIA's clandestine divisions, he sensed that spring that he was not yet fully accepted by his colleagues or privy to all their operations. Once he passed the denied areas ops course, he could feel the change. He was accepted now. Everyone knew where he and Mary would be going. As Howard put it, "I was in the pipeline."

Howard had already received his basic education in tradecraft at the Farm, and in the ops course he had mastered the techniques of detecting and eluding surveillance in the Soviet Union.

Now he was ready to be inducted into the most rarefied, exquisitely secret level of the entire agency, a level that even within SE was closely guarded. He would learn the CIA's operation in Moscow.

7

Moscow Rules

Because of the controlled nature of Soviet society and the omnipresence of the KGB, it is very difficult for the CIA to recruit agents in Moscow.

As a result, Soviet citizens who agree to work for the CIA; M16, the British service; or other Western intelligence agencies, are almost invariably recruited in the West. The Soviet scientist in a delegation visiting California, the KGB man assigned to the Soviet embassy in Burundi, and the economist from Leningrad attending a conference in Rio de Janeiro—all are possible targets for recruitment by the CIA.

If a Soviet with access to secret information is recruited or volunteers information, complex methods must be worked out for communicating with the agent and for transmitting the information to the CIA, all in great secrecy.

Normally it is outside the Soviet Union that an agent, once recruited, is given this communications plan. A CIA case officer in Moscow cannot simply pick up the telephone and tell an asset when and where to meet; all that must be decided in advance or communicated to the agent in some other secure fashion.

A communications plan, or commo plan, as it is called in the CIA, tells the agent the signal for a meeting with a case officer—when they will meet, where, and the parols, or passwords, they will exchange. It also enables the agent, in turn, to alert the case officer that he wants a meeting.

A former CIA case officer with long experience in Moscow explained that a communications plan, once established, "can be amended by one-way voice link. A transmitter is set up in Germany or even at headquarters in Langley. The agent knows that at certain times on certain nights you will transmit to him, normally in five-digit groups. He is given an OTP [one-time pad], of which only one other copy exists, which the sender has."

The pages of a one-time pad consist of different, random five-digit groups of numbers that are used to encipher messages with the aid of a matrix, or number grid, that can be read much like the coordinates on a road map. Each page is destroyed after use. Since only one other copy of the pad exists, the code is unbreakable. The agent uses his copy of the one-time pad to decipher the message.

The old Moscow hand explained what happens next. "The OTP is on edible paper. Once he deciphers the message, he tears the pages out, burns them, flushes them down the toilet, or eats them—however he's been instructed. You can use voice link to confirm or change a meeting." He paused and smiled. "Sometimes we would broadcast code groups just to make the Soviets think we had a lot of assets even if we didn't."

Howard learned the communications plan for Moscow in part by reading the cable traffic on the Soviet desk and the SE division files. "First there is a signal between an agent and his case officer," he said. "The signal tells you where and when to meet. They may vary to indicate a different where and when. A blue thumbtack instead of a white. Or the commo plan would be, perhaps, look for a chalk mark of a number five on an electrical box. It means I meet someone at a park. Or maybe an embankment on the Moscow River, where people are fishing."

The plans included preselected meeting places, as well as backup times. If for example, Howard were to meet an agent briefly on crowded Gorky Street on a Tuesday at 11:00 A.M., there would be a backup time, perhaps Thursday at 3:00 P.M., if the agent failed to appear. A thumbtack on a telephone pole or a chalk mark in a hallway might also signify danger or perhaps confirm that a dead drop has been successfully emptied and the information retrieved.

In a nonhostile environment, such as a Western country, a case officer and an agent might have only one meeting place. In the Soviet Union communications plans are much more complex, and meeting sites are constantly varied. In Moscow the CIA will sometimes keep the same contact plan for two years because the station might lose touch with an agent. If contact is maintained, the plan is changed only once a year.

"We meet an agent two or three times a year in Moscow," Howard said. "They are short meetings. You pick up the information on microfilm, and it goes to Washington."

At the actual meeting, Howard said, "first you have a visual signal. The agent is carrying a key chain or a newspaper. You are smoking a pipe. Usually the case officer speaks first. 'Oh, I see you're reading *Evgeny Onegin.*' 'Yes, I'm halfway through.' "

It is because of the extensive KGB surveillance that face-to-face meetings with agents are rare in Moscow. The most common mode of passing data in Moscow, according to veteran CIA case officers, is the brush contact. By prearrangement, the CIA officer and the Soviet asset brush by each other on a crowded boulevard on in a department store, and a roll of film or a note is passed in a twinkling, so fast that a watching countersurveillance agent cannot be sure that any material has changed hands.

The CIA officer with long experience in Moscow explained how fast the brush contact must work. He snapped his fingers. "Like that," he said.

Naturally this takes practice; the two parties executing the brush contact cannot drop the film or fumble around in their pockets. The brush contact or brush pass is an espionage ballet, and it must be carried off skillfully. Howard, for reasons that are unclear, was never trained to do brush contacts; he was taught to handle face-to-face meetings and to clear drop sites.

According to Howard, "there were maybe forty operational sites in Moscow on file, both dead drops and meeting places. All of the operational sites were coded. Boris, Katya—Soviet names."

Finally there were the agents.

The CIA has relatively few assets in the Soviet capital. The former CIA case officer, a veteran of the Moscow operation, when asked how many agents the station ran, replied, "We would be lucky to have two to three important ones and a few low-level."

Howard agreed with that assessment of the number of agents in Moscow. At various times in our interviews he spoke of "five or six." Each agent is given a code name beginning with two letters, known as a digraph. He declined to reveal the digraphs or code names.

His job, Howard was told, would be to service these agents, all of them previously recruited, to collect information from them, to provide them with necessary espionage equipment, and to request, or "task," them to provide additional intelligence.

"I would have been a street man in Moscow," he said. "Once a week I would have met with the chief of station (COS) to get my instructions: where, when, to meet. The COS would say, 'Go to Gorky Park; here's his code word; here's yours.' The true names of the agents go to the basement in a black envelope"—Howard said they are literally black—"and no one has access to them after that."

For the fifteen months that he was assigned to the Soviet desk, Howard read the cable traffic. Gradually he came to know the details of all of the agency's operations in Moscow.

Because Howard was taking training and language courses to prepare for Moscow during almost all his time in SE, he made a habit of dropping by headquarters on weekends to catch up. "Saturdays during the whole year I could come in and try to read the cable traffic. This was general traffic, in the general reading file. The special reports on agents' meetings would only be available if I saw the case officer during the week and got into his file."

Even during the week Howard often could get out of his training courses long enough to spend time at headquarters. "I would come in and ask, 'How's Agent X doing?'

'Oh, we had a meeting last week.' 'Who met him?' Or one agent might complain he was not getting enough money or have some crazy request like he wanted pornographic material.

''I don't know whether I knew everybody, all the assets in the station,'' Howard said. But, he added, ''Every case officer knew eighty percent of the assets in Moscow.

''During the summer of 1982, they said, 'Here is a specific number of cases.' Let's say they said, 'Here are four cases.' I would see the reports come in. JKJones was met Tuesday at site Boris. Those are made-up names. He got his package; we got his.''

Asked whether he was actually assigned certain agents for whom he would act as case officer, Howard replied: ''It's not like anyone sat down and said, 'Here are the agents you will handle.' Our number one asset might be handled by three or four officers; whoever has the least surveillance will meet him.''

According to intelligence sources, however, one of the most important assets revealed to Howard, although perhaps only by his code name, was Adolf G. Tolkachev, an electronics expert at a Soviet aviation institute in Moscow. For a period of several years, as far back as the Carter administration, Tolkachev passed information of enormous value to the CIA.[1] The data described Soviet research in aircraft technology, electronic guidance, and countermeasures, sophisticated radars, and, above all, Soviet stealth technology—the techniques of designing and building aircraft to avoid detection by radar. Howard would be taking over the Tolkachev ''account,'' the sources said. He was to become Tolkachev's new conduit for handing over Soviet secrets to the Moscow station of the CIA.

Howard confirmed that Tolkachev ''very well could be one of the assets I would have handled. I knew broad categories of information. There was one person working

---

[1] Admiral Stansfield Turner told the author that as CIA director under President Carter he was aware that Tolkachev was a major agency asset in Moscow. He declined to say precisely when Tolkachev had been recruited, however.

on military electronics. Tolkachev could fit the description of a couple of people in the agents' reports I saw. A couple of people were giving us defense information.''

Howard consistently sought to minimize the extent of his knowledge about the CIA's operations in Moscow. He said he did not know the true names of Soviet agents, since these were coded, or the locations of the operational sites, also coded. He conceded he knew the communications plans but said these were frequently changed.

However, it is clear that while serving at the heart of the CIA's Soviet operations, Howard was in a unique position to acquire vital information. Although it is probably accurate that he knew only the code names of the agency's assets in Moscow, not their true names, he readily admitted that he knew the type of information that these assets were transmitting to the CIA. Intelligence specialists say that such knowledge, if acquired by Moscow, would allow the KGB to pinpoint the Soviet sources and arrest them.

Knowing the details of the CIA's communications plans might also have enabled the KGB to roll up the CIA's assets. If an agent was to signal a meeting by placing a chalk mark on a particular telephone pole, for example, the Soviets could watch the pole.

On the Soviet desk, in sum, Howard had access to the code names and contact procedures for the CIA's assets in the Soviet capital. He knew the nature of the information being transmitted to the CIA by each agent. He knew the passwords. He knew the code names of the operational sites and might have gained access to the actual locations. "He was," one knowledgeable official said, "shown everything."

Most of the news reports about Howard have focused on damage to the CIA's network of human assets in Moscow. But perhaps equally important is the fact that Howard had access to the CIA's technical operations in the Soviet capital. In Moscow, as in other stations, the CIA plants bugs, puts in wiretaps, and intercepts communications to the extent that it can.

Some years back, for example, the CIA was able to listen in on the conversations of Kremlin leaders as they spoke on the radiotelephones in their limousines. The secret intercepts were code-named Gamma Gupy. But the agency's technical operations in Moscow ranged far wider than that; the Moscow station is a major listening post for the collection of ELINT, or electronic intelligence, inside the Soviet Union.[2]

Howard was briefed on these technical assets and operations as part of his training for Moscow. "Station officers do these ops," a CIA source said, "they don't just meet with agents, so he had to know about them."

Information is normally compartmentalized in intelligence agencies, and need-to-know is a cardinal rule. That way, if something goes wrong, if secrets are betrayed, the mole will be able to give away only the information he has personally handled. In theory he will not know information contained in any other compartment.

Why was this precaution not taken with Howard? How could he have been inducted into the secrets of the entire Moscow operation? The question has baffled many people, both in and out of the government. The answer lies in the nature of the CIA's Moscow operation.

When members of the House and Senate Intelligence committees asked the CIA why Howard had been shown everything, one source said, "The answer they gave is that the Moscow operation is so difficult, everyone is a sort of jack-of-all-trades, everyone has to know everything."

A senior member of Congress who had access to the secret findings of the congressional inquiry into the Howard case explained: "You don't compartmentalize a HUMINT [human intelligence] officer in Moscow. He has to know it all. Who he has to contact, and how."

An ex-DDO man confirmed the special operational problems in Moscow. "Normally, in any other station,

---

[2]From Soviet installations in the United States the Russians pluck millions of telephone conversations out of the air as they travel along microwave circuits. Computers, programmed to recognize key words of defense or intelligence interest, then select those conversations to be analyzed in Moscow. The CIA and the NSA attempt to do the same inside the Soviet Union.

they would not tell Howard the whole operation, but Moscow is a special place. There are a limited number of assets. Howard would have been the street guy. The place is so limited that the street guy who meets agents in Moscow has to know who they are.''

Another former CIA agent in Moscow, who rose to a high level in the Clandestine Services, shed further light on the problem. The Moscow operation is so small, he said, in effect there was nothing to compartmentalize.

There was another factor in Howard's case that led the SE division to open up the Moscow files to him. He was "going in clean" as a "black" officer under deep cover. There are degrees of clandestineness cloaking CIA agents serving in embassies overseas. Howard was to be assigned to the Moscow embassy as a political officer. A former CIA official explained: "He had to know everything in advance because it would have been hard to take him up to the seventh floor to the CIA station." He meant that Howard would have been quickly spotted, considering the number of Soviet employees, many of them KGB agents, who worked in the embassy at the time.

Mary Howard continued to work in SE during the summer of 1982, then went to language training to learn Russian. Howard, too, began studying Russian in preparation for his Moscow assignment, enrolling in classes at Georgetown University.

From June to August Howard became a college student again. His cover story was that he was a recently dismissed employee of the Labor Department, caught in a budget cutback. "So I sat with the eighteen- and nineteen-year-olds, and here I am thirty."

Howard did not realize just how severe the generational gap was until he left class one day humming "Open Wide for Chunky," a jingle that had been popular in the late 1960's, when it appeared in a TV commercial for a candy bar. A student asked him what the tune was. "I told her and got a blank look."

Howard told Jim Lockwood he was getting ready to go to the Soviet Union for the State Department; at Howard's request, they switched their jogging to the towpath along the canal in Georgetown. That way, Howard explained, he could go to his Russian class afterward.

From September to the end of the year Howard continued his language training at the agency's own language school on North Fairfax Drive in Arlington. About this time the Howards began casually letting other friends and neighbors know that they would be leaving for Moscow. Ed, the young "State Department" officer, had been selected for the embassy there.

John Matejko, Howard's next-door neighbor, noticed that Howard had begun jogging with a headset on the path behind the houses and assumed he was listening to Russian-language cassettes.

Every six or eight weeks, while he was training for Moscow, Howard called Trish McGuire in Buffalo to chat. He gave her his telephone number at the CIA and noted that Mary worked in the same office. "He was really looking forward to going to the Soviet Union," McGuire recalled. "He was real up. He told me he was in the State Department; he never mentioned CIA. He said he was in intensive training, learning the language and habits of the Russian people, and he was thrilled. He was really happy, and you could hear it in his voice."

Although the day the Howards would be spying together in Moscow was approaching, they apparently did not dwell on the dangers that might lie ahead. Had Howard and his wife ever discussed the risks?[3]

"Only once," he said, "When I was being interviewed in October of 1980, at first they wanted me to become a NOC [pronounced 'knock'], a CIA officer under nonofficial cover. Like a businessman, with no diplomatic pro-

---

[3]Both the CIA and the British MI6 have used wives to assist their husbands in sometimes risky operations in Moscow. For example, Colonel Oleg Penkovsky, who was regarded by both the CIA and MI6 as one of their most valuable Soviet assets, passed information to Janet Anne Chisholm, the wife of a British MI6 officer stationed in Moscow. With her children playing in a sandbox nearby, Chisholm met with Penkovsky, who handed over film, concealed on one occasion in a box of candy. Penkovsky, an officer of the GRU (Soviet military intelligence), was arrested in 1962 and tried and executed the following year.

tection. I thought, *My God, I thought I'd always have diplomatic protection.* I was a little anxious, and I think it got to her. But I wanted to be a case officer from the beginning. That's what we both wanted.''

The agency dropped its suggestion that Howard work as a NOC, and, Howard said, ''In Moscow it was my understanding that my immunity would cover Mary. She had a diplomatic passport.''

As a CIA officer under embassy cover Howard would have had diplomatic immunity in Moscow. If something went awry and he was apprehended by the KGB, his immunity would protect him from arrest and imprisonment. About the worst that could happen was that he would be detained, declared persona non grata, and expelled. Although Mary Howard would not have had a job in the embassy, under the Vienna Convention of 1961, she would also have been protected by her husband's immunity.

Meanwhile, Howard's friend Bill Bosch had good news. He was getting married, and the agency was sending him to Bolivia for his first tour as a case officer in the Clandestine Services.

The marriage was all in the family. Bosch had met Vicky Ringland, his bride-to-be, in the Latin American division, where she was working as a secretary. Victoria Ringland was in her mid-twenties and several years younger than Bosch. Her parents warned her not to act hastily. But she was highly impressed with Bosch; he wore Armani suits and looked sharp.

Vicky was the daughter of Peter Ringland, who, as it happened, was an old SE division hand, fluent in Russian, who had served in Iran, Berlin, Athens, Geneva, and Istanbul. Ringland and his wife, Valentina, were an agency couple; normally they might have been expected to welcome a son-in-law who was in the Clandestine Services, but they were not thrilled with their daughter's choice of Bosch, whose social credentials matched his lackluster agency career.

Nevertheless, the Ringlands did not stint on the wedding reception at their home in Chevy Chase in the early fall. There was caviar, Russian salmon, and violin music.

Howard met Peter Ringland there, although he had seen him at the language school in Arlington. Ringland was a short, intellectual man, with graying brown hair, who smoked cigarettes with a holder.

Just after Thanksgiving of 1982 Howard flew out to New Mexico to attend the funeral of his maternal grandmother in Reserve. On the return flight from Albuquerque on November 30 the woman sitting next to Howard left her cosmetic bag behind when she got off at Denver. "I reached over and grabbed the bag," Howard recounted. "It had some makeup stuff and two twenty-dollar bills. I pondered for almost an hour what to do. There was no ID, no driver's license. So I kept the forty dollars. Maybe a good, moral person would have called the stewardess. I felt so bad about it I gave the money to charity, to the public television station in northern Virginia. I pledged forty dollars to WETA."

In January 1983 Edward Howard took another step to build his cover as a Foreign Service officer. He enrolled in a full-time six-and-a-half-week State Department course at the Foreign Service Institute in Rosslyn. The course, which is given continuously, teaches diplomats about local customs, cross-cultural differences, and the nuts and bolts they need to know about living overseas. There were forty-five students in Howard's class.

Because Howard was going in "black" or "clean," as a deep-cover officer, the CIA went to unusual lengths to insert him into the normal Foreign Service channels. After the Rosslyn course he took a three-week course to learn to be a State Department administrative officer, then a six-week course in budgeting. That training was necessary, Howard was told, because he would be the embassy budget officer. He was instructed not to let his fellow students in the State Department know that he really worked for the CIA.

The Howards bought a new car and told the neighbors they would be taking it to Moscow. The automobile, a blue Chevrolet Celebrity, was actually a CIA car; Howard had purchased it and been reimbursed by the agency.

On the morning of February 11, 1983, Washington was

blanketed with the worst snowstorm in years. Howard set off for work but had to turn back. John Matejko encountered him around 11:00 A.M. and Howard told him he couldn't get his car back into Scotch Haven Drive. Matejko gave him a hand and cracked: "Christ, Ed, this is a hell of a car to take to Moscow. It can't even deal with the snow in Virginia."

The Howards were told they would be going to Moscow the third week in June, as the summer began. There were still many weeks of preparation ahead, but the pieces were falling into place. The next month Howard was issued an impressive document, printed in elaborate script in the style of a diploma. It was headed: "The President of the United States of America," and it read: "To Edward Lee Howard, a Member of the Foreign Service of the United States of America, Greeting: Reposing special trust and confidence in your Integrity, Prudence and Ability, I have nominated and, by and with the advice and consent of the Senate, do appoint you a Consular Officer and a Secretary in the Diplomatic Service of the United States of America."

The commission was dated March 11, 1983. It was signed by George P. Shultz, the secretary of state, and by Ronald Reagan, the president of the United States.

It was an exciting time for Howard. Eight days later his son, Lee, was born. On a cold Saturday morning John Matejko saw Howard coming home from the hospital. He was very happy, really beaming, Matejko remembered.

"I have a son," Howard said. "Mary just gave birth."

Howard said he had been up all night at the hospital, and he looked a little haggard. Matejko invited him in, and his wife, Marianne, brewed some coffee. Howard talked about his son and said his wife was doing fine. "It was the most excited I ever saw him," Matejko said.

The neighbors remembered Mary happily pushing Lee in the carriage that April. Howard's mother came up from Texas to help with the baby. It is a time of year when the area around Washington is never more beautiful. The bright yellow forsythia burst out; the dogwoods bloom. Forsaking the barren limbs of winter, the oaks and maples turn suddenly pale green. For the Howards that spring the future looked bright.

In late April, almost at the last minute, Howard was informed that he would have to take another polygraph. It was true, he was told, that it was several months short of the three years when he would normally have been due for another lie detector test, but Howard would understand that it was necessary because he was going overseas to a particularly sensitive post. There was, however, nothing to worry about. It was all part of the predeparture routine.

Howard was not concerned, and neither were his superiors in SE. After all, he had passed the first polygraph test without difficulty. There was no reason to think anything would be different this time.

8

The Firing

In the CIA in 1983, but certainly nowhere else in the world, a strange phenomenon could be seen. On top of the candy and drink machines scattered around the building in Langley, Virginia, quarters appeared from time to time. The coins just lay there, unclaimed.

At the time, everyone at CIA knew, there was a threshold amount of money that might be taken without the agency's Office of Security regarding it as a theft. But no one knew what that threshold was. If, by accident, a coin came back from a machine along with a candy bar, was pocketing the money a form of stealing? CIA employees feared that it might be and that the transgression would be picked up on their next polygraphs. The safer course of action was just to leave the coin on top of the machine.

The odd business of the unclaimed quarters was a small but telling indication of the pervasive fear of the polygraph, or lie detector, that exists throughout the intelligence agency. That very belief in the omniscient power of the polygraph to unmask deception was the strongest weapon possessed by the Office of Security.

The use of the polygraph is designed, in part, to intimidate and instill fear in the subject who takes the test. If the device is successful in detecting lies, it does so to a great extent because the subject *thinks* that it works. That is because the lie detector does not measure lies; it records changes in four physiological areas: breathing, blood pressure, heartbeat, and sweat. The theory of the polygraph is that when people knowingly lie, the stress will cause physiological changes that can be measured.

Various ancient cultures have thought that guilt can be detected by physical changes. In Europe and Asia authorities believed that a guilty man had a dry mouth. A suspect's mouth would be stuffed with bread or rice. If he could swallow, he was judged innocent; if not, he was put to death. In the third century B.C. the Greeks believed that deception could be measured by changes in a suspect's pulse. In the sixteenth century Galileo invented a device that kept time with a person's heartbeat. The modern lie detector traces back to the turn of the twentieth century. Its strongest proponent in the federal government is the Central Intelligence Agency.

The CIA clings to its faith in the polygraph even though scientific studies have shown that a person who takes four hundred milligrams of meprobamate, a common tranquilizer sold under the name of Miltown, before a polygraph examination will probably be able to lie successfully.[1] Other suggested methods of "beating the machine" range from physical actions, such as biting the tongue or squeezing the toes against the floor, to mental conditioning.

In 1983 John F. Beary III, acting assistant secretary of defense for health affairs, said in a memorandum: "I am told the Soviets have a training school in an eastern bloc country where they teach their agents how to beat the polygraph." The unnamed country is reportedly Czechoslovakia. "The polygraph," Beary, a longtime foe of the device, has argued, "detects excitement, not lies." According to Beary, the polygraph rests on the false premise that there is a "Pinocchio effect," or "a body response unique to lying."

Polygraph findings are not admissible in court, and it is easy to see why. A 1983 study by the Office of Technology Assessment, a congressional agency, reported that lie de-

---

[1] This was the conclusion of a study at the University of Pennsylvania reported in 1981. Of volunteers who took meprobamate and lied, the polygraph was able to detect only 27.2 percent, which meant that nearly three-quarters of those lying were able to do so undetected.

tectors singled out as deceptive 19 percent of persons who were actually telling the truth.

Although it is not generally understood by the public, the interview that takes place before the subject is strapped into the lie detector is as important as the test itself.

A former CIA man who had been through the polygraph test, and who had reviewed the Howard case, explained the procedure. "They interview you first and tell you the questions they will ask you. Then on the polygraph they ask a general question, such as: 'Have you ever stolen anything or stolen anything since your last polygraph?' Then they ask a question they have not previously told you: 'Was what you told us before, in the interview, true?' That question is on the second list of questions, the list they don't show you."

For his polygraph in April 1983 Edward Howard reported to a room just behind the badge office, on the lobby floor at CIA headquarters, to the right of the main entrance. First he was interviewed by the polygraph operator. Is there anything you want to tell us? the operator asked. There was. Howard related the November 1982 incident aboard the airliner. He admitted he had taken the forty dollars from the woman's cosmetic bag.

An official who had access to secret files on the Howard case said that Howard also sought to invoke the "threshold" defense over the incident, claiming that he believed the amount taken was, in any event, below what the agency would consider a "theft." The theft, he argued, was insignificant.[2]

There were more questions. Howard was asked if he had used drugs since going to work for the CIA, and he said he had not. Then the operator strapped a corrugated rubber tube around Howard's chest. Called a pneumograph, it would expand and contract to measure his respiration rate. The technician then wound an inflatable pressure cuff around Howard's arm, a cardiosphygmomanometer that records blood pressure and pulse. Finally, the

---

[2]As a result of the Howard case, there is no longer a threshold below which theft is tolerated by the CIA.

most scary objects of all, two metal electrodes, were attached to his fingertips with surgical tape. The device, a psychogalvanometer, would measure Howard's galvanic skin response (GSR) to electric current. The reading would vary with how much he perspired as he was questioned. All these instruments were hooked up to a recording device that would measure his responses as squiggly lines on a roll of moving graph paper.

The polygraph operator, a young man about twenty-five, seemed satisfied with Howard's answers. "Afterward," Howard said, "the guy shook my hand."

But the Office of Security, studying the results of the lie detector test, apparently decided that Howard's answers had showed deception. "Two or three days later," Howard said, "a man from OS says 'We have a problem, we want to check on some specifics.' " Howard was called in for what was to be the second of four polygraphs administered to him during April and May.

"The second polygraph operator was about forty-five and acted like some sort of chief," he said. "On the second polygraph the man didn't believe me. I was surprised. They said, 'When you react to questions on crime, you show a big response. Go home and write down everything you've ever done.' I went home and wrote down everything I could possibly think of. A beer behind the wheel of a car. Maybe six times. Maybe I spit on the sidewalk. So I came in with the list."

The CIA already knew that Howard had, as a college prank, stolen a bubble gum machine. He had admitted the theft when he joined the agency. "As a freshman in college," he said, "we got drunk in the dorm, and on a bet I stole the Lions Club bubble gum machine and took it to the room. The next morning I brought it back. I woke up, saw a bunch of beer bottles on the floor and this stupid bubble gum machine. On my first polygraph in October 1980 I admitted that. Also on the first polygraph I admitted that when I was eight or nine, I stole some carrot seeds, and my father found out and spanked me."

The CIA's Office of Security stepped up the pressure on Howard. "After the second polygraph they took me to OS on the fourth floor. They said, 'We're going to give you the Hammer.' That's what they called this guy. He was thirty years old, brown hair and eyes, mustache, very physically fit. He looked tough.''

Howard was so nervous before the third polygraph, he said, that he took a tranquilizer. ''After I got my security badge, about half my class was called in for a conference,'' he said. We were told, 'If you ever use drugs, you're out.' When I worked for the CIA, I used zero drugs. But when I took the third polygraph, I was very nervous. My mother-in-law is a doctor. She was visiting, like always. She gave me a mild tranquilizer, like a blue pill, maybe twenty or thirty in a little bottle.

''The Hammer asked, 'Have you taken drugs?' I said, 'Yes, I took a tranquilizer.' That's when they hit the roof.

''They kept saying, 'You've committed a major crime. Did you rape someone, hit someone with a car? I kept saying no. 'You're lying,' the Hammer said. 'If you don't tell me the truth, I'm going to turn off this machine and you are going to walk out of here, that's it.' ''

The fourth polygraph was administered on Friday, April 29. Howard had seen a story in the Washington *Post* two days earlier quoting John Beary, the Pentagon's foe of polygraphs, as saying that the tests brand ''innocent people as liars.''[3] He clipped out the article and brought it in with him to the test. He showed it to the polygraph operator.

''Bullshit!'' said the Hammer.

But after the fourth polygraph, to Howard's surprise, ''they said everything's okay. The Hammer shook my hand. I went to the International Safeway in McLean and got a bottle of champagne and hors d'oeuvres and went home. My in-laws were there, Mary's parents, and I said everything's OK. So I relaxed for the weekend.''

While the Howards were drinking champagne, the CIA was in turmoil. The predeparture polygraphs may have

[3]George C. Wilson, ''Polygraph Tests Are Unreliable, Pentagon Told,'' Washington *Post*, April 27, 1983, p. 1.

been routine, but the findings were not. The results of the Howard lie-detector tests reverberated through Langley headquarters with the force of an explosion.

Howard was poised to go to Moscow, primed to handle the agency's most secret and most highly prized agents in the Soviet capital. Now, in the rarefied upper echelons of the CIA, word circulated among a handful of officials that Edward Lee Howard had flunked his polygraph.

The theft that Howard admitted, when he dipped into the cosmetic bag of the woman passenger on the airliner, was not in itself what was so troubling to the agency. Rather, according to intelligence officials, it was that his polygraphs indicated deception on the subject of theft. "It was the deception that bothered them more than the theft," a former CIA official said. "It is always the deception."

Three senior officials with knowledge of the Howard case insist that when Howard was polygraphed in 1983, he also admitted breaking into vending machines at CIA headquarters, a statement which Howard denies making. He implied that the officials may have been thinking of the episode with the bubble gum machine.

There is some disagreement about whether, or to what extent, the polygraph also uncovered any continuing drug use by Howard after he had joined the CIA. "As a result of the second polygraph, the agency became aware of the drug use in the period between the two polygraphs," one intelligence official said. A CIA spokesperson, Patti Volz, said in November 1985 that Howard's second polygraph "picked up drugs and petty theft." Another intelligence official insisted that drugs were not an issue at this point. Howard himself denies that he continued to use drugs when he worked for the CIA.

Although the CIA attributes something close to divine powers to the polygraph, it seems unlikely in retrospect that the lie detector results alone could have caused the dilemma in which the agency now found itself. By this time Howard's drinking had come under closer scrutiny. There is evidence on the polygraphs that Howard was questioned repeatedly about his drinking.

Moreover, Howard's stability and his psychological fit-ness for the rigors of Moscow appear to have been cause for concern within CIA. It is possible that the agency had, even earlier, begun to have second thoughts about sending Howard to Moscow. Against that background the polygraph results triggered a crisis.

Something had to be done about Edward Lee Howard, and done quickly. But what?

Ultimately, everyone knew, the decision would have to be made by John H. Stein, then the DDO, the chief of the Clandestine Services. Stein, a trim, dark-haired man of medium height, with an easy, pleasant manner, fit the traditional image of the DDO. A fifty-year-old Yale graduate, he had joined the agency in the 1950's. He was sent to Brussels in 1959, spent two years in the Congo (now Zaire) in the mid-1960's, and then moved to Cameroon until 1968. In the early 1970's he was in Cambodia, then Tripoli, Libya, and Washington. Stein became the deputy chief of operations in the Soviet division and then the chief of station in Brussels, where he impressed President Carter's CIA director, Stansfield Turner, who brought him back to headquarters as assistant DDO. William Casey promoted him to DDO in 1981.[4]

---

[4] In 1980, when Howard was hired, the DDO was John N. McMahon, although he did not personally oversee Howard's selection. But McMahon had been appointed by Admiral Turner during the Carter administration. Early in 1981 William Casey shunted McMahon aside in favor of a remarkable choice: Max Hugel, a sewing machine importer from New Hampshire by way of Brooklyn who had toiled in the 1980 Reagan presidential campaign that Casey had managed. Then reporters Bob Woodward and Patrick E. Tyler of the Washington *Post* revealed charges that Hugel had engaged in improper or illegal stock market dealings. According to the *Post*'s revelations, Hugel had threatened to kill a lawyer who got in his way, warned a business associate that he might be found "hanging by the balls," and in effect admitted, in an unpublished biography, that he was a liar and an informer and had cheated in business deals. To top it all, he apparently beat the CIA lie detector; when the charges broke, Hugel claimed he had been "blackmailed" by two business associates, but his CIA polygraph test, which he passed, included questions about whether he had ever been subject to blackmail. Hugel said he had not. The outcry over his appointment—

"Stein had been in Africa and got lucky," an old agency hand said. "He had two Soviet walk-ins and got them out. It was easy, but it helped him get the DDO job under Casey."

In trying to decide what to do about Howard, Stein had to take into account the views of others in the CIA bureaucracy. Howard had been selected by the Soviet division; SE and its chief, David Forden, were under Stein in the CIA hierarchy. But there were other important players on the stage. The office of Security (OS) reported to Harry Fitzwater, the deputy director for administration, who was equal to Stein on the organization chart and who had been the chief of the Office of Personnel (OP) when Howard was hired. Robert Magee, by then the director of the Office of Personnel, also reported to Fitzwater.

As far as William R. Kotapish, the CIA's director of security, was concerned, the answer to the problem was clear: Howard should be fired. Kotapish, a gregarious six-foot man in his fifties, had no reservations about the accuracy of the lie detector; he had been one of the agency's first polygraph operators. He had risen to director of OS in 1979. As the security chief of the CIA Kotapish had a threefold job: he was responsible for investigating the backgrounds of prospective employees, for making sure they did not engage in any disloyal or compromising activity after being employed, and for protecting the physical security of the agency. It was the job of the counterintelligence staff to protect the CIA from hostile penetrations by foreign powers, so there was some overlap between the two offices.

Although an old polygraph operator, Kotapish was not a Neanderthal security type with a "house dick" mentality. Compared with some previous security chiefs, he was more intellectual and practical, his supporters within the agency said. It was Kotapish who altered the CIA's view on marijuana. "Bill was the fellow who changed the policy to look at the whole person," one of his CIA col-

---

led by the DDO old boys—was such that Hugel had to go. Casey reached down into the ranks and chose Stein.

leagues said. "He was the one who brought the agency into the twentieth century on pot."

But the Howard case was something of an embarrassment to Kotapish since Howard, a user of pot and a great many other drugs, had breezed into the agency. Howard did not look like a shining example of the results of the new, liberalized drug policy sponsored by the OS chief. Now, faced with the disturbing Howard polygraph results, Kotapish pushed for his immediate dismissal.

Robert Magee, the head of personnel, sided with Kotapish, concluding that something drastic had to be done about Howard, and quickly. Harry Fitzwater, the CIA's deputy director for administration (DDA), to whom both men reported, agreed.

Magee then drafted a recommendation to John Stein, the DDO. It set forth the position of the directorate of administration: Edward Lee Howard should be dismissed.

But the powerful SE division—panicked at the thought of antagonizing a case officer who now knew all its most vital secrets—argued that Howard could not be fired. David Forden, the chief of the Soviet division, advocated that Howard be transferred to another job outside the division. It would be the safest course of action, Forden insisted.

The debate never reached the point where a specific less sensitive job for Howard was discussed. Forden wanted to keep him somewhere in the DDO, but as far as possible from SE. Howard could be parked in an innocuous job somewhere in the agency, and security could keep an eye on him. The main point, he argued, was to put him where he could be watched.

But there was an equally powerful counterargument. If Howard were ever to betray the secrets he knew to the Soviets, he would be even more valuable to the KGB inside CIA headquarters, as an agent in place. SE might be creating a mole by keeping him. And if Howard were discontent with a new, minor job, what was to keep him from resigning?

The agency's administrators were adamant that whatever was done, it had to be done immediately. The agency was deadlocked as the bureaucratic tug-of-war was fought out. On the one side was SE division. Arrayed against it were the Office of Security, the Office of Personnel, and the directorate of administration.

John Stein was thus in a difficult position, caught between the competing pressures from his own SE division and the agency's administrators. His loyalties were instinctively with the operations directorate that he headed and in which he had served from the start.

It was a tricky business, putting a spy out in the cold, and one could never predict the result. Despite the risks of firing Howard, would it not look worse if he were kept and developed into a security risk? In the end Stein overruled Forden and decided that Howard must go. CIA Director William Casey, as the law required, signed off on the decision.[5]

On Monday afternoon, May 2, Howard got a call from the Office of Personnel. He was told to come in. Howard was busy that day, taking a one-day course in counterterrorism at the State Department. He did not report in at CIA headquarters until Tuesday.

Two personnel officers were waiting. "What, are you going to screw around with my Moscow assignment?" Howard asked.

"I don't think you're going overseas," one of the personnel men replied.

Howard was aghast. "They shoved a paper at me. Form for Resignation. They said, 'We want you to take some psychological tests.'

"I said, 'What happens if I don't sign? What are my rights?'

---

[5]Unlike most other government agencies, the CIA has arbitrary power to dismiss its employees. Under the 1947 law creating the agency, the director "may, in his discretion, terminate the employment of any officer or employee of the Agency" whenever he deems it necessary "in the interests of the United States." In the rest of the government it is almost impossible to fire anyone; hearings, appeals, and excruciating paperwork discourage most bureaucrats from dismissing incompetents. It is usually preferable to fob off unwanted employees on some other unsuspecting division or branch.

"They said, 'We had a panel meeting, and it was decided you should resign.'

"Can I appeal to the panel?" Howard asked.

"No."

"What if I don't sign?"

"If you don't sign, it will take three or four days and the director will fire you. We'd like to have your resignation."

Howard signed.

"I'm dumbfounded," he said, remembering that moment. "I call my wife, and she's crying on the phone. They were convinced I was lying. Nothing was said about drugs or theft. They took me into the SE administrative office, and a secretary was already preparing my résumé."

The résumé could not indicate that Howard had worked for the CIA. "What do you want to say your job was at the State Department?" the secretary asked.

"Economic specialist," Howard replied.

"OK," she said. "This is the telephone number. If anyone calls, it rings here."

The telephone number on the résumé, Howard explained, "was a backstopped State Department number that rang in Langley."

Two security officers appeared and walked Howard out of the building to the blue Chevrolet. "I handed them the keys. I was not even given a chance to clean out my desk. They told me at first a driver would take me home, but then they asked if I would mind taking the bus."

Howard was allowed back inside, to get a pass for the Blue Bird, the special CIA buses that shuttle to the Ames Building in Rosslyn and other agency installations. He called Mary at the language school. "I took the bus to Rosslyn and the Metro to Arlington. I got off and met her, and then we drove home."

The former CIA official who studied the Howard case described the drama at that point: "Howard is angry and upset because he thinks he's done nothing wrong. The polygraph results are never explained to you, so no one is telling him what's going on. No one in SE will see him. He is frozen out. No one is telling him why."

Howard shook his head as he remembered that day. We were talking over coffee at the Kisbuda restaurant, near the end of dinner. "If I had committed a crime—but I hadn't," he insisted. "It was their stupid needles. Their stupid needles on a machine."

So the polygraph was the villain? I asked.

"They certainly fucked themselves," Howard replied.

9

Cover-up

"It all happened on a weekend, very fast," Mary Howard said. "They met in a closet, then told us by Tuesday that he was out."

Although fired and no longer able to go to his office, Howard was kept on the payroll for several weeks and instructed to see the agency's senior psychiatrist, Dr. Bernard Malloy. He was also told to report for a physical examination.

At the age of thirty-one Edward Howard for the first time in his life had experienced failure. As Howard perceived it, up to now, his career had been totally upwardly mobile. From modest roots he had completed college, become a Peace Corps volunteer, earned a graduate degree, joined AID, landed a good job as manager of an environmental firm's Chicago office, been accepted by the CIA, and then been selected for an exciting, highly secret, and extremely sensitive job by its most elite division.

Now the rug had been pulled out from under him with minimal explanation. The evidence suggests that Howard could not handle what had happened to him.

He began acting strangely. Right after he was fired by the CIA, but while still on the payroll, he placed the first in what officials say was a series of bizarre telephone calls to the United States embassy in Moscow, using a special circuit. Howard did not have to be in Langley headquarters to make the calls. He dialed a local number in Washington that gave him a direct line to the embassy in Moscow.

It was 7:00 P.M. in Washington and 3:00 A.M. in Moscow. Using the special circuit, Howard was connected to the embassy and got a marine guard.

"My name is Ed Howard," he said. "Tell Carl Gebhardt I'm not reporting in for my physical."

Although he had been drinking, Howard knew exactly what he was doing. Carl E. Gebhardt was the chief of station in Moscow, the man who would have been Howard's boss had he been dispatched as scheduled to the Soviet capital. The KGB knew who Gebhardt was, since the Soviets had approved his selection as station chief under much the same kind of *agrément* with Washington that is required for ambassadors.

And, as Howard realized, the mention of Gebhardt's name would galvanize the KGB wiremen who were listening in to the call. It would also alert the KGB that something very odd was going on with Ed Howard.

There were other implications that Howard knew would not be lost on the KGB. He had already applied for a visa to come to Moscow, so the Russians knew that an Edward L. Howard, supposedly a political officer, was being sent to the Soviet Union. Now that Howard had mentioned the name of the chief of station, it was obvious that Howard worked for the CIA and was not a diplomat.

"I'd had a few beers," Howard said, in recounting the call. "But I wasn't heavy drunk. They were still trying to control me. I found a way to let them know I was pissed off. He [the marine guard] took the message down and said 'Yes, sir.' He didn't know where the call came from."

Howard, of course, had no need to tell the chief of station in Moscow that he was not going to report in for a physical forty-eight hundred miles away at Langley. "I was pretty hacked off," he said. "It was a revengeful joke call to the embassy. Yeah, I knew the Soviets would be listening.

"A day or two later I'm called in by a security officer for SE, and he gives me a lecture for twenty minutes: 'We know you called the embassy. You didn't need to pass a message to Moscow.' I said I realized that."

Howard said he made only one other call to the embassy. About six months later, he said, he telephoned John

Beyrle, a friend from the State Department who was serving in Moscow.

A senior intelligence official insisted, however, that Howard had placed a series of calls on the special embassy circuit. In one, the official said, Howard asked to talk to a female KGB colonel who was known to be on the embassy staff. Howard, he said, had been briefed about the woman during his preparation by SE division for the Moscow assignment and asked for her by name.

Until October 1986, when the Soviets pulled out their nationals from the American embassy in Moscow, the embassy had for years employed Soviet citizens in a variety of jobs. It was understood that the KGB planted its agents among these employees, and sometimes, as in the case of the female KGB colonel, their precise identities and ranks were known. Although security officials argued against the arrangement, the State Department found it convenient; the Soviet employees not only spoke Russian; they knew how to deal with the Soviet government bureaucracy. So the risks were tolerated.[1] What Howard told the female KGB colonel if he got through to her is not known; the U.S. embassy does not bug itself. And the National Security Agency, which monitors overseas calls, does not listen in on the special circuit. "We don't know what he told her," a highly placed intelligence source conceded ruefully. "We never got an intercept of that conversation."

The CIA, of course, has never publicly admitted that Howard may have talked to a KGB colonel inside the U.S. embassy in Moscow after he was dismissed by the agency. However, the CIA had identified an attractive woman on the embassy staff, known as Raya, as a KGB colonel.

Raya, whose real name was Raisa, was not easily forgotten, once encountered. At six feet one, the statuesque,

---

[1] Although it was not generally known, until the Soviets withdrew their nationals, the number of Soviet employees working for the American embassy in Moscow almost equaled the number of Americans. According to State Department figures, 200 Soviets worked for the embassy, and 225 Americans.

blond KGB colonel, known around the embassy as Big Raya, towered over Carl Gebhardt, the five-foot-six CIA station chief. Her job was to send the passports of American diplomats to the Soviet Ministry of Foreign Affairs to be registered. She also handled the hiring of Soviet employees for the embassy and was the contact point with the UPDK, the Soviet "service bureau" that administers foreign embassies. One American diplomat described her as "voluptuous."[2]

Howard actually reached the CIA station chief in Moscow, an agency source said, using the same special circuit. "The conversations with the station chief were trivial, nothing of substance," the official said. "But the fact that he made them was bizarre, of course. There were a total of four or five conversations using the special circuit."

Howard insisted that he never talked to a woman KGB colonel and "was never told in Washington there was a KGB colonel on the embassy staff." He said he did not know the name Raya. He also denied that he had talked to the CIA station chief. But he readily admitted his 3:00 A.M. call to the marine guard and his anger at the agency that had prompted it.

The CIA is responsible for its own security. Once an employee has been dismissed, however, any potential security risk falls under the jurisdiction of the FBI. By law the CIA has no law-enforcement or internal-security functions in the United States. Foreign counterintelligence, apprehending spies inside the United States, is the responsibility of the intelligence division of the FBI.

---

[2]During the marine spy scandal at the Moscow embassy that surfaced in 1987, lawyers for Sergeant Clayton J. Lonetree produced a picture of Raya at a party with other Soviet women and male embassy employees. The photograph was taken at a marine ball at Spaso House, the residence of the American ambassador to Moscow, in 1985. The picture was produced by the lawyers to demonstrate that socializing with Soviet women was commonplace at the embassy. Raya was seated next to the commander of the marine detachment, Master Sergeant Joey E. Wingate. Michael V. Stuhff, one of Lonetree's attorneys, said he had been informed that Raya was a KGB colonel.

The CIA did not advise the bureau that Howard, an employee with knowledge of its most sensitive secrets, had been abruptly fired. Nor was the FBI told he had made one or more bizarre telephone calls to the Moscow embassy and was being seen by the CIA's senior psychiatrist.

Edward O'Malley of the FBI, and the intelligence division he headed, were not notified. Jay Aldhizer, the bureau's liaison man with the agency, was also blissfully unaware of the dismissal and Howard's troublesome actions.

The CIA cover-up of the Howard case had begun.

The agency had, by now, made a series of crucial decisions to contain the Howard case within the confines of Langley. Yet its officials knew how risky that policy was.

Even as the CIA moved to conceal the Howard affair from the FBI, the agency's psychiatrists were quietly assessing the dimensions of the potential threat to the agency posed by Howard. That delicate task was assigned to Dr. Malloy, an old war-horse who could hardly be better suited for the job, from the CIA's point of view.

Bernard Mathis Malloy, the agency's senior psychiatrist, known to his intimates as Barney, had already proved his mettle. He had survived Watergate unscathed, navigating the perilous path between President Richard Nixon's Plumbers and the White House burglary of a fellow psychiatrist that sent John Ehrlichman, the president's assistant, to jail.[3]

---

[3] Malloy had been brought in by the White House to prepare a psychological profile of Daniel Ellsberg, the man who leaked the Pentagon Papers to *The New York Times*. The CIA psychiatrist met with E. Howard Hunt and G. Gordon Liddy in the Plumbers' basement headquarters to discuss the profile. Liddy told Malloy that their goal was to turn Ellsberg into "a broken man." The White House, dissatisfied with Malloy's first draft, told him to try harder. After the break-in at the office of Dr. Lewis Fielding, Ellsberg's psychiatrist, more information was sent to Malloy, who prepared a second profile. Malloy said he could not remember whether the Plumbers told him Ellsberg had been under a psychiatrist's care, but he was sure there was no discussion about obtaining Ellsberg's medical record. The director of CIA medical services said that "no psychiatric information" had been sent to Mal-

A tall man in his sixties, with graying reddish hair, a distinct southern accent, and a reedy, high-pitched voice, Malloy saw Howard four or five times at CIA headquarters in May 1983, after his dismissal. Howard agreed to see the CIA psychiatrist because he had little choice. "They kept me on the payroll until mid-June, so I felt, OK, play their ball game."

Howard concluded that the agency officials wanted him to see Malloy "to protect themselves, to see if I had any hard feelings or wanted revenge. I would go back to headquarters, and since I had no badge, I had to be met." At one of the sessions with Dr. Malloy, Howard's boss, Tom Mills, showed up. "He seemed very concerned about me," Howard said.

Clearly the CIA was worried about what Howard might do, but not worried enough to alert anyone outside the agency. CIA headquarters, of course, knew about Howard's contact with the Moscow embassy on the special telephone circuit because the station chief had reported that back to SE division.

Throughout, SE division was at the center of the Howard affair. It knew of Howard's alarming behavior. But the Soviet division shared this knowledge with William Kotapish, the chief of the Office of Security, whose representative lectured Howard about telephoning Moscow. And SE apparently shared its concerns as well with the counterintelligence staff, then headed by David H. Blee, Gus Hathaway's predecessor.

A Californian, a Harvard Law School graduate, and an OSS veteran, Blee at sixty-six was one of the oldest of the old boys in the CIA. He had been stationed in Karachi and New Delhi in the early days, then had become head of the Near East and the Soviet divisions and deputy director of the DDO before taking over the CI staff.[4]

---

loy. The burglars said they never found Ellsberg's file; Dr. Fielding said a file cabinet had been broken into, and the file removed.

[4]In 1976, as national intelligence officer for the Middle East, Blee had written a prescient paper warning that the CIA did not have a clear picture of the regime of Mohammad Reza Pahlavi, the shah of Iran. A

A former intelligence officer with knowledge of the Howard affair said that all three divisions—SE, OS, and CI—participated in the decision to conceal the case from the FBI. "As soon as Howard made the phone calls," he said, "SE talked to OS and CI, and it was determined it was not something to go to the FBI on." That decision maintained the pattern of the agency's actions in the Howard case; at all costs the matter was to be contained. The agency would continue to wash its own linen in-house.

Besides, there was always a chance that Howard would not do anything.

---

little more than two years later the shah was overthrown. The CIA had provided inadequate warnings of the Islamic revolution that toppled the Iranian ruler.

10

New Mexico

Curtis Porter liked to play basketball to relax. He had the build for it. He was a beanpole, six feet five and slender, with wire-rimmed aviator glasses, brownish blond hair, and an easygoing style.

At thirty-six Porter was in his second year as director of the Legislative Finance Committee of the New Mexico legislature. In May 1983 he was looking around for an economic analyst for his staff, someone who could estimate revenues flowing into the state, especially taxes on oil and gas. He placed an ad in the Albuquerque *Journal*.

He was surprised a few days later to find an applicant waiting in his office in the state capitol in Santa Fe. The man hadn't telephoned in advance.

"He just showed up," Porter said. "It was a cold call. I decided I would see him anyway, for ten minutes or so." Porter asked Philip M. Baca, a senior analyst, to sit in on the interview.

The two officials quickly realized they had no ordinary walk-in on their hands. The soft-spoken young professional had impressive credentials. He worked, he said, for the State Department in Washington. He was a Foreign Service officer with a background in economics and finance.

But the State Department wanted to send him to Moscow, he explained, and he had decided to leave because he did not want to bring up his child there.

"He interviewed well," Baca recalled. "He had a nice speaking voice. He was pleasant, not vivacious, but not

97

introverted, either." The visitor not only had the right credentials; he had the added advantage of being a native of New Mexico. Oddly, in a state where Spanish origin can be an advantage, especially in the political world, Howard never mentioned, either then or later, that he was half Hispanic.

The résumé he handed to Porter and Baca listed "U.S. Department of State, January 1981–June 1983 to present," and it explained that his duties were "monitoring economic relationships with major countries." It also listed, accurately in this case, his experience in AID and the Peace Corps and in the private sector in Chicago.

It was not every day that an ex-State Department officer applied for a position with the New Mexico legislature, and within a short time, after interviewing several other applicants, Porter hired Ed Howard at a starting salary of thirty thousand dollars.

The Howards packed up their household goods and, with their new baby, moved to Santa Fe. En route they stopped off to visit Howard's parents in Garland, Texas. While they were there, three diplomatic passports arrived in the mail for Howard, Mary, and their baby, Lee. Howard kept them.

Since the house on Scotch Haven Drive could not be sold right away, they decided to rent it for a time. Their tenant that summer was Van A. Harp, who, with his family, was renting while waiting to move into a new house. There was mild irony in the tenant's occupation in view of later events: Van Harp was an agent of the Federal Bureau of Investigation, a supervisor at FBI headquarters. He was paying rent to a man who was to become the central figure in a major national security case, a fugitive accused of espionage, and the object of a worldwide search by the FBI.[1]

In August the Howards sold their house in Virginia for $111,000. They purchased a one-story brown stucco mock-

---

[1]"I never met him [Howard]," Harp said. He added that he was "completely unaware" of the identity of his landlord until the author made inquiries of Dwight Avis, the rental agent, whose partner alerted Harp.

adobe house in El Dorado, a development twelve miles
out in the desert south of Santa Fe.

It was a place of great natural beauty, albeit rather des-
olate. The house was surrounded by desert flora and fauna,
from the golden snakeweed that grew everywhere to
prickly pear and walking-stick cactuses, juniper trees, and
Russian olives. Piñon jays chattered by day and ruby-
throated hummingbirds darted among the blossoms. Children growing up in El Dorado did not have to worry much
about traffic, but there were tarantulas and rattlesnakes.

The sunsets in the desert were spectacular. In the evenings the Howards would watch the sky change to pink,
red, and orange. At dusk the Sangre de Cristo Mountains
turned purple, then swiftly black. The first stars appeared,
and after that the night belonged to the coyotes, the chirp-
ing toads, and the owls.

The houses in El Dorado were set far apart, so what the
residents gained in privacy and space they lost in intimacy.
The Howards lived at 108 Verano Loop. As the term
"Loop" implied, the road on which their house was sit-
uated formed an oval. The eastern end led out to the highway, but many of the residents of Verano Loop preferred
a shortcut called Moya Road, a bumpy, heavily rutted
stretch just to the west of the Howards' place.

Howard had a twenty-minute commute along Interstate 25
to his office on the first floor of the capitol. Mary Howard took a part-time job in an orthodontist's office to supplement her husband's salary.

By all accounts, Howard quickly ingratiated himself with
his colleagues, legislators, and the executive branch staff
members with whom he dealt. "He did his job and did it
well," Curtis Porter said. "My feedback from the legislature was all very positive."

The Howards made friends, among them Bob and Kate
Gallegos, who initially worked on the committee staff with
Howard and later became neighbors in El Dorado. Kate
Gallegos, a tall, straight-haired woman, had grown up in
Ohio. Her husband, a soft-voiced, pudgy man, was a na-
tive of New Mexico. They had a son, Jason, several years

older than Lee, but the two families spent a fair amount of time together.

Kate Gallegos remembered an evening when Howard had been drinking heavily. "One night I had to drive him home," she said, "after he'd had maybe eight to ten scotches. That's the night I learned he had been in the CIA. He said he'd quit."

David Abbey, the chief economist of the state Department of Finance and Administration, was the official with whom Howard had perhaps the most contact in his job, and the two became friends. When they were drinking together, Howard's mood would change; he would become maudlin and slur his words. And Howard drank a good deal; he was spending a lot of time at the Bull Ring, a bar a block from the capitol that was a hangout for the state's politicians.

But none of this seemed to affect his work. Howard continued to make a good impression in his career, and he began traveling extensively for the committee. In August he went to Los Angeles for a conference sponsored by Data Resources, Inc. (DRI), a worldwide economic consulting firm.

Then, on October 20, 1983, Howard returned to Washington for the first time since being ousted by the CIA. Later the same week he went to Williamsburg, Virginia, for a Federal Energy Regulatory Commission conference. Perhaps it was the thought of journeying to Williamsburg, so close to the Farm, or just being back in Washington, but the trip apparently triggered, or intensified, the anger that had been building up inside him.

For it was while in Washington on this trip that Howard, by his account, took an action that later became a pivotal, crucial event in the entire case for both Howard and the CIA.

"Slowly that summer a feeling of anger and resentment built up," Howard said. "I was so upset that when I took a business trip to Washington in October of 1983, I found myself on Connecticut Avenue. I walked up Connecticut, doing some shopping. I walked into the park opposite the Soviet consulate.

"From my training I know there is surveillance on the embassy and residence, but they don't have it on the consulate. I thought about going in and talking to them. Then I thought, *You can't do that.*"

"To tell them what?" I asked.

"I had no plan, no documents. I thought they're going to think, *You're a crank or an FBI provocation.* They're not going to believe you. Then I thought, *Regardless of how they [the CIA] treated you, this is not the right thing to do.*"

It was not only the morality; there was a question of price. Howard also said he was unsure of what the Russians would be willing to pay him for secrets. "I thought, *If I go in, they'll give me five hundred dollars and kick my butt out the door.* I felt the Soviets were cheap."

"You were going to give them information?" I asked.

"Of course. If a former CIA officer goes in the embassy, that's what they want."

Howard apparently spent hours hanging around the Soviet consulate, debating whether to go inside. He said he did not go in.

But at some point in 1983, perhaps that day, Howard in fact made his first contact with the Russians. He went into the consulate and left a letter identifying himself as a disgruntled former employee of the CIA.[2]

At the time the FBI did not know that Howard had entered the consulate because Howard was right: there was no surveillance of the building. From time to time a Washington motorcycle police officer or a patrol car is parked in front of the consulate. But it is not the job of the local police to watch the people going in or out or to photograph their faces.

The Soviet embassy is located on Sixteenth Street in downtown Washington, four blocks from the White House. A new embassy complex, of which only the residential

---

[2]Much later the FBI learned that Howard had gone inside the consulate. The FBI believed it was either on his October trip to Washington or even earlier, after he had been dismissed by the CIA in June and before he had moved to Santa Fe.

portion is occupied, has been constructed on Mount Alto, just above Georgetown on Wisconsin Avenue. The building that Howard described is the Soviet consulate, a three-story sand-colored brick mansion at 1825 Phelps Place, a narrow, quiet street one block west of Connecticut Avenue near the Washington Hilton.[3]

Howard told his wife what he had done. Mary Howard said her husband had disclosed the "embassy contemplation" to her. She said he had described how he lingered outside the building and how he had wanted to go inside and sell secrets to the Russians. She said she could not recall how soon after the incident he had revealed it to her.

About a month later Howard placed another call to the Moscow embassy on the Washington telephone number. This time he telephoned his friend John Beyrle, the Foreign Service officer with whom he had taken a course early in 1983. Beyrle was a genuine State Department officer, not a CIA man under diplomatic cover.

Beyrle, then twenty-eight, was a Michigan native fluent in Russian who was preparing for his first State Department tour at the same time that Howard was getting ready to go to the Soviet Union. In the Foreign Service course they were drawn together when they discovered that they were the only two members of the class who expected to go to Moscow. Twice the Howards had Beyrle over for dinner at their house in Vienna, and Howard showed him

---

[3]Months afterward, when CIA officials learned that Howard had sat in a park and contemplated going inside a Soviet embassy installation in Washington to sell secrets, there was confusion because officials thought that Howard had loitered near the Soviet *embassy,* and there is no park opposite. It was speculated that Howard might have sat in Lafayette Park, but that is three blocks south of the embassy, directly in front of the White House. The answer to the mystery, apparently, is that Howard hung around the consulate, not the embassy. There is a park, around the corner on S Street, not far from the consulate on Phelps Place. The park, which is not even marked on most maps, is known as Mitchell Park. It has some benches. It is, in fact, almost opposite the consulate but cannot be seen from the entrance to the Soviet building, because of an intervening row of town houses, known as Kalorama Square.

his gun collection in the basement den. One Saturday, Howard took Beyrle shooting at a range in Winchester, Virginia. The two men fired Howard's pistols.

But Beyrle did not suspect initially that Howard worked for the agency. One member of the class had gotten up the first day and declared himself as a CIA man. Howard, a deep-cover officer, did not.

When it came time to discuss overseas postings, the class was told there was only one slot open in Moscow. With his background in Russian studies, Beyrle took it for granted that he would get the job and join his wife, Jocelyn Greene, who was being sent to Moscow by the United States Information Agency (USIA).

But Beyrle became alarmed when personnel was evasive about whether he would go. At a weekend training session at Harpers Ferry, Howard overheard Beyrle arguing with a personnel officer about the Moscow assignment.

Howard took him aside. "Let's go for a walk," he said. Out of earshot of the others, Howard broke cover. He felt bad, he said; Beyrle was just married and of course he wanted to be with his wife, but he had best make other plans. "I'm going to Moscow," Howard revealed. He explained he was going in under deep cover; it had been approved at a high level in the State Department. Howard made it clear he was an undeclared CIA officer.

Beyrle warned Howard that the agency's plan wouldn't work. Why was Howard, with no Soviet background, being sent to Moscow and Beyrle posted elsewhere? It would fool no one.

Howard said he shared Beyrle's concerns and would talk to his superiors at the CIA. Soon afterward the class was told that there would be two slots opening in Moscow after all. One for Beyrle, one for Howard.

Beyrle arrived in Moscow in April, and later heard that Howard's assignment had been canceled.

He was surprised when Howard reached him at his office in Moscow early in the morning. It was late evening in Santa Fe, and it took Beyrle a few minutes before he realized that Howard was drunk. Howard asked how Beyrle and his wife were.

Beyrle said they were fine.

"Well, tell Frank I said hi," Howard said, and hung up.

The only Frank whom Beyrle knew in the embassy happened to be a CIA man under cover as a political officer.

Soon afterward he encountered his colleague in the hall. "Ed Howard says hi," he said.

Frank, looking stricken, pulled Beyrle into one of the embassy's secure rooms, a place known as the bubble and supposedly immune to electronic eavesdropping by the KGB.

He asked Beyrle a barrage of questions about the call. Where had it been placed from? Did it sound like long distance? What did Howard say?

Later that day Carl Gebhardt, the station chief for whom Howard had left the strange, middle-of-the-night message six months earlier, summoned Beyrle to his office and peppered him with more questions. The diminutive COS, a man with a perpetual tan and deep set eyes, confessed that they were "having some problems" with Howard. "Let us know if he calls again," he said.

In mid-December Howard had lunch with two officials of the Los Alamos National Laboratory, a major nuclear weapons research center. But both officials said Howard was interested in the impact of high technology on the state's economy and did not ask about classified matters.[4]

Howard never called the Moscow embassy again, but he did get in touch with his good friend Bill Bosch in the embassy in La Paz.

"What the hell are you doing in New Mexico?" Bosch asked.

----

[4] New Mexico has an extraordinary number of highly secret military and scientific installations, not only Los Alamos but the Sandia National Laboratories, which also design nuclear weapons, and Kirtland Air Force Base, home of the Air Force's Space Technology Center. Officials said there is no record of Howard's ever having visited those sites. Howard's direct knowledge of CIA operations in Moscow, not his proximity to the classified labs in New Mexico, is what interested the Soviets.

It was a long story, Howard said. He would explain the next time they saw each other. As it happened, that was sooner than either man expected.

Within a few months Bosch, too, was forced out of the agency, his career as a spy in ruins, his marriage shattered. He resigned from the CIA in January 1984.

The following month he got another call from Ed Howard. Howard was going to be in New Orleans in March for a conference. Could Bosch drive down and meet him there?

The call could not have come at a better moment psychologically. Bosch was feeling low. Unemployed and with time on his hands, he quickly agreed. There would be a grand reunion of the two old friends in the French Quarter in New Orleans. They would have a few drinks and a little fun.

And they would have some stories to swap about the agency.

11

Strike Three

From the start things had not gone at all well for Bill Bosch in Bolivia.

There was, to begin with, the matter of several bad checks. At the time the American ambassador to Bolivia was Edwin Gharst Corr, a shrewd career diplomat from Oklahoma with a down-home style. He left the administrative chores to the deputy chief of mission, William G. Walker, another veteran of the Foreign Service. Walker had earned a reputation as a careful administrator, a man who brooked no nonsense. And he looked the part, with his red hair and trim mustache, gold-rimmed spectacles, and precise manner. It was Walker who was responsible for the smooth functioning of the embassy.

It soon came to Walker's attention that the cambio, or money-changing office, near the embassy had received several bad checks, totaling somewhere around two thousand dollars from one William Bosch, of the United States mission. Walker's red eyebrows went up. Inflation was rampant in the country, and most embassy employees wrote small checks so as not to be stuck with wildly plummeting Bolivian pesos.

He called in Bosch, who explained there had been a computer foul-up with his bank in Washington. Walker talked to the CIA station chief, Bosch's boss. He asked him to make Bosch cover the bounced checks.

And how was Bosch doing? Walker inquired casually of the COS. "Not too well," the station chief replied. "He's slow to pick up the tricks of the trade, and his wife doesn't like Bolivia—the people, the dirt, the isolation. It was not what she expected in an overseas post.''

Next, the airline that had handled Bosch's luggage contacted Walker. It seemed that the luggage had been broken into or lost, and Bosch had put in a claim that the airline considered unusually high. The airline representative showed Walker a list of clothing that added up to thousands of dollars.

What's going on here? Walker wondered. *This guy wears expensive clothes, and he's bouncing checks. And the chief of station says he doesn't have the knack of being a case officer.* To Walker it all seemed rather odd, but it was an agency problem, not his.

La Paz is built on a mountain. The airport is on the top at thirteen thousand feet, and the road goes down to the city. The lower suburbs are the most expensive. With his new bride, Bosch settled into one of the moderately priced suburbs.

Victoria Ringland Bosch was attractive, although unusual; she made an indelible impression on those who knew her. She had a distinctive, squeaky voice and believed she and her identical twin sister, Missy, enjoyed a bond of extrasensory perception. When Missy, who lived in Dallas, felt pain, Vicky told friends, she could feel it; when Missy had her baby, Vicky went through it with her.

In the insulated embassy community, however, word soon circulated that the marriage was in trouble. Vicky Ringland came from a close-knit family, and her parents had strongly opposed the marriage, she told people in the embassy.

Bosch, although married only a few months, was seeing other women, apparently including one who appealed to his strong ethnic ties. Bosch wrote his name with an umlaut and identified proudly with his German background. His grandfather had been a German carpenter who came to New York with his son, Bosch's father, in the 1920's. Bosch remembered his father, the railroad conductor, taking him, as a boy, to Yorkville, on Manhattan's East Side, where they would not hear a word of English spoken.

In Bolivia Bosch seemed to spend a lot of his time at a

Swiss-German restaurant called the Swiss Chalet. Walker noticed that every time he took his wife to the restaurant, Bosch was at the bar. He wondered about it but thought that since Bosch was a spy, maybe that was where he met his contacts. Finally, he asked someone and was told that Bosch was mooning after a German waitress at the restaurant.

In September Bosch took Vicky back to the United States, and they separated. Bosch then returned to La Paz. They were later divorced.[1]

Bosch, who had made no previous public statements, agreed to be interviewed at length by the author, although he declined to be photographed. He proved an affable, articulate man, although sometimes emotional when he discussed his relationship with Edward Howard, and his problems in Bolivia, both professional and personal. "Did I have marital problems?" he asked. "Yes. Was I unhappy? Yes. Did I date? Yes."

Bosch explained away the bad checks in Bolivia as the result of a mix-up; he had borrowed money from the agency, but the check for the loan went back and forth between La Paz and Washington and did not, somehow, get credited to his account. He also defended as reasonable his insurance claim for the pilfered luggage.

Although Bosch declined to discuss the specific nature of his work in the La Paz station, he indicated it was highly sensitive. In fact, Bosch was targeting Cuban intelligence officers, and later, Soviets. "Two gentlemen who had my job were fired," he said. "I used to kid and say I wasn't going to be strike three." He paused and said in a flat voice, "I was strike three."

Vicky Bosch also worked in the La Paz station, sometimes typing up her husband's operational reports. In Bosch's off hours he was frequently seen socializing with a Peruvian diplomat. According to one intelligence official, Bosch got into trouble with the CIA station in Bolivia when he took an unauthorized person, reportedly a foreign

---

[1] Vicky married a Dallas lawyer whose brother, also a Dallas lawyer, was already married to her identical twin sister, Missy.

national, into a safe house. The CIA is rather touchy about outsiders' learning the location of its safe houses.

Bosch blamed a clash in personalities for some of his difficulties in Bolivia. "I had a deputy chief of station who did not like me."

The situation was more complicated than that, however. There were, in fact, three CIA station chiefs during the year that Bosch served in the La Paz station. The first COS was not enchanted with the young case officer Langley had sent him, but he was wary of doing anything about Bosch. He had already been burned once; another young officer in the station had been sent home, and the station chief had been reprimanded for failure to document the case as well as he should have.

The second COS tried to work with Bosch, calling him in for fatherly lectures that gradually grew sterner. But the second station chief, a man in his late forties, died suddenly after cancer surgery. The third station chief decided to send Bosch home, according to an embassy official.

It was at that point, in November 1983, that Bosch became involved in a currency dispute with the embassy beside which his earlier difficulties paled.

In most American embassies the ambassadors permit diplomats to sell their cars and household effects, if they wish to, before leaving. The diplomats are then permitted a one-time "accommodation exchange" at the embassy to convert the local currency they receive for their goods into dollars at the official rate.

At the time Bolivia was, in the words of Ambassador Corr, "practically a basket case economically." Because of the runaway inflation, the Bolivian peso was constantly dropping in relation to the U.S. dollar.

In Bolivia in 1983 the official rate was about 211 pesos to the U.S. dollar, but the more realistic black-market rate was 2,000 to a dollar. It meant that enormous profits could be made, in theory, if the embassy went along with it, by a diplomat who sold personal property at inflated Bolivian prices and converted the millions of pesos into dollars at the highly favorable official rate. And it was all perfectly legal.

Early in November Bosch informed his station chief that he intended to sell his worldly goods for pesos worth somewhere between $150,000 and almost $250,000 at the official rate. A few days later the station chief apparently told him to go ahead.

On November 14 Bosch submitted a list of the items he sold that totaled just under 40 million Bolivian pesos—$189,000 if converted at the embassy rate. The original cost of the items was approximately $40,000.

The most costly item on the list was a used BMW that Bosch had bought for a little over $15,000 with a loan in that amount from the CIA credit union. He had paid back only $2,800 and defaulted on the balance. He now proposed to sell the BMW for $96,000. The list also included a nineteen-inch Sony color television, for which Bosch wanted $4,000; a Betamax, for slightly more than that; a Head tennis racket, for $428; and windshield wiper blades, for $192.

When the list reached the desk of William Walker, the deputy chief of mission, he stared at it in disbelief. To Walker, it was a flagrant abuse of the exchange rate. Walker turned thumbs down on the sale; Bosch was told that Ambassador Corr would not approve it. He was forced to revise the list downward and eventually was permitted to cash in pesos amounting to about $40,000.

For Bosch it was the end of the line. When he left to go back to Langley, the station chief warned him never to set foot again in South America. If he ever tried to do so, the station chief threatened, he would do everything in his power to stop him.

In January 1984 Bosch resigned from the CIA. He said the decision was his, but a former senior agency official with direct knowledge of the case said Bosch was told to resign or he would be dismissed. "He was allowed to resign as a courtesy to him," the former CIA man said. "That's what we usually do so his résumé doesn't say 'fired.' " Bosch was forced out, the ex-official said, as a result of the currency dispute and incompetence.[2]

Bosch stayed in Washington for a time, then moved to New York to live with his sister. He had finally been given his big chance by the agency, with calamitous results. His scheme to sell off his possessions in Bolivia at an enormous profit had been thwarted, leaving him stuck with a check for more than nine million pesos, over forty-three thousand dollars, that he could not cash. The agency had frozen his retirement pay because of the unpaid car loan. Troubles and woes were piling up, one after another.

A colleague who knew Bosch in La Paz sympathized with his plight. "Bill had romantic visions of becoming a big-time spy. He perhaps hoped for Berlin, he saw himself in a trench coat at Checkpoint Charlie, but he ended up in, forgodsakes, Bolivia. It's hard to be James Bond in Bolivia."

By early 1984 the string had run out. Bill Bosch, late of the CIA's La Paz station, a man who liked expensive, fast cars, designer clothes, and beautiful women, faced the reality. He applied for unemployment insurance.

---

[2]Bosch, through his attorney, Victor B. Kenton, insisted he was not asked to leave the CIA. He claimed that he was caught in a crossfire between the station chief and the deputy, who often disagreed on operational matters. Bosch's troubles with the CIA were not over even when he left the agency, however. The CIA kept $9,500 in leave and retirement contributions that would otherwise have been payable to Bosch to offset the $12,200 balance on the car loan from the CIA credit union.

12

Shoot-out

Howard's drinking had been getting worse. "In Santa Fe I moved into hard liquor, gin and tonics, and got into trouble," he said.

On Sunday evening, February 26, 1984, about a month before Howard was due in New Orleans, he planned to top off the weekend by going shooting at a target range. Howard not only collected guns and liked to shoot and hunt but was also a federally licensed dealer who bought and sold weapons.

In November 1982, while still employed by the CIA, Howard applied to the Treasury Department's Bureau of Alcohol, Tobacco, and Firearms for a license to deal in rifles, shotguns, pistols, revolvers, and ammunition. He got the license, as of January 1, 1983. While preparing for his Moscow assignment, Howard bought and sold a Browning automatic and two revolvers. He continued to deal in guns in Santa Fe.

"I abused alcohol once a week in Santa Fe," Howard said. On that night in February, he recalled, before leaving the house, he drank "a couple of big Australian beers. I'd say I had the equivalent of six beers."

He had tucked a silver-chrome .44 Magnum under the seat of his red Jeep. Realizing that he was not in any shape to go shooting, Howard abandoned that idea and drove off instead to a bar-restaurant in a motel on the outskirts of Santa Fe.

In the parking lot outside the bar that Sunday night, Howard encountered another Jeep, a yellow Toyota Land Cruiser, driven by its owner, Peter Hughes, then twenty-four. Hughes and his buddy, Conrad Hayas, twenty-three, and their girlfriends were out on a double date.

"My girlfriend was real good-looking, with long blond hair," Hughes said. "He [Howard] looked over, and we exchanged glances. I'm sure he was looking at my girl, blatantly staring at us. There were no words exchanged." Hughes and his friends pulled out of the parking lot. "Next thing I know he's on my tail, turning high-low beams on and signaling right, as if to get us to follow.

" 'He's tailgatin' us,' I told my friends. I said, 'Conrad, open the door and see if we know this guy.' " At that point, according to Hughes, Hayas "flipped him off"— that is, gave Howard the finger. Hughes, aware by now that he had trouble on his hands, dropped off the two young women at Hayas's house, backed out, and drove to his own place, with Howard still in close pursuit.

Hughes lived in an apartment complex set back from the street on West Santa Fe Avenue, not far from the capitol. He turned into the driveway. Hughes and Hayas, now joined by another friend, Bob Martinez, were waiting as Howard got out of his Jeep and walked into the courtyard of the building.

"Suddenly from his back, he pulls out this *cannon*," Hughes said. "I mean a silver-chrome forty-four Magnum. An awesome gun. He said, 'This is a Magnum, and I don't give a fuck.'[1]

"He holds this gun on us, me and Conrad and Bob. He's backing us off with a gun. He's looking a little buzzed, with slurred speech. He says to me, 'Get back in the Jeep.' Edward Lee Howard was totally freaked out and was expecting to see some girls. He couldn't understand where the girls had gone. He didn't say anything, but I just kind of read it. I'm sure that's what was going on.

---

[1]The Smith & Wesson .44 Magnum is a double-action six-shot revolver, with a strong recoil, that fires a heavy bullet at very fast velocity. When developed in 1955, it was termed the "world's most powerful handgun." It is also known, from its frequent appearance in the movies and on television, as the Dirty Harry gun, a reference to the character made famous by actor Clint Eastwood.

"He makes me get in the Jeep. I'm thinking it isn't worth losing my life over a silly thing like this. I said, 'No problem.' I got back in the Jeep and closed the door. I'm inside the Jeep, and he's pointing the gun at me. His eyes get this blazing look, and he starts walking toward me with the gun, pointing at my head. I think, *He's about to pull the trigger. He's going to shoot.* The barrel of the gun is coming in the window. So I duck. I grabbed for the gun and his wrist, and it fired, putting a hole in the roof.

"I got his arm under the steering wheel and forced it down to my feet. He's wedged in there. Meanwhile, my friends had seen the muzzle flash. Bob comes running around, grabs him in a headlock, and pulls him out of the jeep. I get the gun from his hand.

"Bob had him on the ground. He's hitting him pretty good. I mean, everyone was pissed." With Howard disarmed, the three youths beat him up. Finally, as Hughes held the gun on him, they forced him to walk out to the street to his car.

"Then he starts acting really weird," Hughes said. " 'Lemme have my gun,' he says!

"I said, 'You just tried to kill me, you sonofabitch. Get the fuck off my property.' "

One of the youths threw a rock, hitting Howard on the head. As Howard, his face bloodied, tried to get into his Jeep, Martinez repeatedly kicked the door on the driver's side, trapping Howard between the door and the steering wheel so that he could not climb in. Finally they let him go.

"We go back in the courtyard and find his wallet," Hughes said. "I'm thinking, *This isn't so bad. We got this nice forty-four Magnum and the guy's wallet.* We looked through it, but there was no cash. We looked at the jeep and saw the hole in the roof. I thought, *Holy shit, this guy could have killed us.* So we called the cops."

Patrolman John Martinez and Sergeant Ray Rael of the Santa Fe police force were dispatched to the scene at 7:04 P.M. En route they heard the details on the police radio; Peter Hughes had reported he was assaulted by a man with a gun who was driving a red Jeep. Three minutes later the officers spotted the Jeep and stopped it.

In the language of the police report, "The male subject had blood on his face and also on his clothing . . . he advised that he was assaulted on Santa Fe Ave. by a group of male subjects. He also went on to say that he had met the subjects at a bar and had followed them home as they had promised him a girlfriend for the night and a good time." Howard was advised of his rights and placed under arrest for aggravated assault with a deadly weapon. He was taken to St. Vincent's Hospital, where he was treated for lacerations on the head and face, and then put in jail overnight.

Howard claimed after his arrest that the kicking of his Jeep door is what touched off the trouble. That happened at the beginning, he said, not at the end, as Hughes related it.

He persisted in this version in the Budapest interview. He said the incident began in the parking lot of the bar when Hughes's passenger opened his car door "and hit my Jeep door." Howard said he registered a mild protest. The passenger got out, Howard said, and "Then he kicks my Jeep. He kicked it on the driver's door in a high kick. They drove off. I lost my cool and proceeded after them. I used poor judgment."

He pulled his gun, Howard claimed, only after he noticed that one of the three youths "had something in his hand, like a stick or a pipe." While talking to Hughes, he said, "all of a sudden I get hit hard with something on the back of the head. As I stagger from the blow, four or five hands grab for the gun. It goes off. I did not plan to fire the gun. Then I just get beat silly to the ground. These guys proceed to kick the shit out of me. Basically their background is cooks and bottle washers at pizza restaurants. All I wanted to do is get out of there.

"I run to the Jeep and circle the block and say, 'Oh, my God, those guys have my gun. I got to go back and get it.' I paid good money for that. So I drove back to their house, and a police car pulled me over."

The shooting incident and arrest were a watershed for

Howard. Up to that point his drinking, and his private rage at the CIA, had been carefully hidden from friends and associates. Now, charged with a felony, he was caught in the machinery of justice. His problems could no longer be concealed from the community.

It was almost as though there were two halves to his personality. The world knew Howard as a highly intelligent, successful young economist and former Foreign Service officer. The other half of Howard was an angry alcoholic who packed a gun and acted irrationally. The two pieces did not fit, and now both were visible for the first time.

Although the Santa Fe *New Mexican* carried only a five-paragraph story the next day reporting Howard's arrest, his appearance betrayed the fact that he had been in a serious brawl. Howard had been badly beaten, and his face showed it. He told friends, neighbors, and co-workers that he had been "hassled" in a bar and gotten into a fight.

For Santa Fe District Attorney Eloy F. Martinez, the case was a problem. On the one hand, there was Howard. "He looked," Martinez said, "like a respected citizen, with a good education." In a supposedly classless but actually highly class-conscious society, Howard's respectability was his strongest asset. He was an economist with a graduate degree, married, a father, and a state employee. On the surface, his accusers were footloose youths. Peter Hughes worked at El Patio restaurant, and Conrad Hayas at the Pizza Hut.

It was more complicated than that, however. DA Martinez knew Peter Hughes—he often ate at the restaurant where he worked—and was aware that the youth came from a prominent family. His father, James Lindberg Hughes, was a fighter pilot shot down in Vietnam, who spent six years as a prisoner of war. When he returned a hero, the whole town turned out for the parade, and Hughes had run, albeit unsuccessfully, for the Republican nomination for Governor.[2]

---

[2]Hughes lost the 1974 Republican primary to State Senator Joseph R.

Martinez decided to reduce the original charges. "We dropped the deadly weapon count because it didn't seem consistent with his background. Otherwise, if convicted, he would have gotten a one-year mandatory jail sentence. It didn't seem consistent that a person of his caliber would resort to that kind of action."

The district attorney disclosed, however, that he had at least briefly considered lodging an attempted murder charge against Howard. "There was pressure from his [Peter Hughes's] mother that we would pursue an attempted murder charge, the most severe charge. We felt that there was some evidence he was under the influence of alcohol, so attempted murder would have been difficult to prove, and we took that into consideration, along with his background and the fact that he had no prior record."

Martinez turned the case over to a relatively new assistant district attorney on his staff, Nilda Pabon Balderston. Howard, after all, had nearly blown Peter Hughes's head off. "We talked about the possibility of attempted murder and went down to three counts of aggravated assault," she recalled. "I didn't recommend attempted murder because it didn't make any sense to me that a man in a responsible position would go around the town and then pull a gun on these kids. And he had been beaten up. That made us a little sympathetic. It was a mystery; it still is."

But Howard had more than respectability; he also had political clout. In his work he had come to know a number of important state legislators, a fact that was not lost on the DA. One of the lawmakers, Max Coll, the powerful chairman of the Taxation and Revenue Committee, referred Howard to a Santa Fe attorney, Morton S. Simon, a transplanted New Jersey resident who had grown up in South Orange.

Howard told Simon something he had not yet confided to his employer: that he had worked for the CIA. Mary Howard also told the attorney that she had been employed by the agency.

Skeen, who in turn lost the gubernatorial race that year to the Democratic candidate, Jerry Apodaca. Skeen was elected to Congress in 1980.

The CIA very quickly knew about the shooting incident. If it did not learn of the case through its own sources, it was advised by Howard himself. "When I had the problem with Hughes," he said, "I called the agency and talked to a young, smart lady on the legal staff. She said to say I had been employed *at* the State Department. She emphasized the word 'at.' "

One former CIA official insisted that the agency had intervened in the case to make sure it was handled in a low-key manner, with minimum publicity and a favorable outcome for Howard. Simon said he was never contacted by the intelligence agency. The district attorney, Martinez, said he was unaware of Howard's CIA background. "I don't think that was ever brought to our attention," he said, although Morton Simon "could have mentioned it." Nilda Balderston said she was "not aware of any pressure from Washington." District Judge Bruce E. Kaufman, before whom Howard appeared, denied as "mildly incredible" a published report that the CIA had made representations to him. "I never heard from anybody," he said.

Howard did solicit letters of support, which were filed with the court, from a number of officials in Washington, as well as from several members of the New Mexico legislature and friends. Among those who wrote were Leonard Yaeger, Howard's old boss in Lima; Carl H. Leonard, who had supervised the AID office in Peru and who said he had always found Howard to be "honest, calm, and level headed"; State Department officials Katherine H. Peterson and James H. Morton, who ran the Foreign Service course that Howard took; and his jogging partner, Jim Lockwood.

Meantime, Morton Simon was massaging the case nicely, pushing Martinez hard for a plea bargain. Because Simon waived the preliminary hearing, there was no grand jury and no indictment. Simon, as a result, managed to keep the proceedings almost entirely out of the newspapers. Since he had no prior record, Howard hoped for leniency; but the charges were serious, and he faced a possible maximum sentence of twelve years on the three counts.

Frightened by what was happening to him, Howard, acting on his own, contacted the state assistance program, which provides drug, alcohol, and psychological counseling to New Mexico state employees. In March he started seeing the program's director, Neil Berman, a clinical social worker from Brooklyn. He continued to meet with Berman on a regular basis until September 1985. On occasion Mary Howard accompanied her husband to the sessions.

Berman, a short, thin, mustached man with an informal, relaxed manner, was sympathetic toward the young economist who presented himself in his office. The facts of the shooting incident were confused, Berman felt, and Howard had, after all, been beaten up by his accusers.

Berman counseled Howard for alcoholism. He did not regard Howard as a psychiatric basket case, a man who was coming apart emotionally. Rather, he considered Howard cool and calculating, a capable employee of the state and a valued staff member of a powerful legislative committee.

By late that month Morton Simon and the DA had worked out the plea bargain. Howard would plead guilty to the three counts of aggravated battery and receive five years' probation, provided he underwent a psychological evaluation by Dr. Elliot Rapoport at his own expense, followed any recommendations for continued treatment, and paid Peter Hughes seventy-five hundred dollars in compensation, plus the cost of repairing the car. In addition, Howard would be restricted under the terms of his probation from leaving the state without the approval of the court, except on business trips.

Howard had talked on occasion of a political career, of running for the state legislature himself. Now that he was about to be convicted of a felony, he knew he would have to give up that ambition.

On March 27 Howard appeared before Judge Kaufman to plead. Peter Hughes was in the courtroom. Simon explained to the judge that both parties thought the plea bargain was appropriate because of Howard's background. He had been, Simon assured the court, "a certified foreign service officer with the State Department for a number of years."

Assistant DA Balderston said that "Peter was very frightened by the incident," but that the district attorney felt the arrangement would compensate Hughes and at the same time ensure "that Mr. Howard essentially isn't destroyed." A felony conviction on more serious charges, she added, would probably preclude Howard from ever getting work as an economist.

Judge Kaufman wondered if Howard would be able to come up with the seventy-five hundred dollars. "Your Honor, yes," Howard replied, "not only with my finances; but I have my in-laws who would loan me some money, and I could repay them."

Howard then pleaded guilty to all three counts. Kaufman questioned Peter Hughes, who said he had come through the evening's events with only a scratched finger but with a bad case of nerves. He had not been able to sleep normally since the incident, he said, and he spoke of "post-trauma stress." The judge asked Hughes whether the seventy-five hundred dollars would be adequate to cover any necessary therapy, and Hughes thought it would.

The sentencing was put off until the following month, but for Howard, the worst was over. He had beaten the rap, and he still had his job. He knew he would get probation. He would not have to go to prison.

That afternoon he left for New Orleans. It was time to keep his rendezvous with Bill Bosch.

13

Bourbon Street

Bosch, three months out of the CIA, drove to the airport in New Orleans to pick up Howard. He had not seen him since Howard had been dismissed by the agency. Bosch was shocked when Howard got off the plane; half his face was still bandaged from the beating he had received.

Howard quickly gave his version of the fracas. They drove back to town and checked into the Hotel Monteleone in the French Quarter. Howard, who had an expense account since he was there on state business, let Bosch share his room.

The two old friends soon adjourned to a bar on Bourbon Street, in the heart of the Vieux Carré, where they began a night of serious drinking. There was a lot to tell. Bosch filled Howard in on his misfortunes with the agency in Bolivia; Howard in turn described the polygraph tests that had ended with his abrupt dismissal on the verge of his departure for Moscow.

According to Bosch, Howard said the trouble over the polygraphs had centered on his alcohol problem, not on theft. Howard had been asked about petty theft, but that was not the primary concern. "He said they were asking him about petty theft and drinking," Bosch recalled. "They kept on saying he was lying. And they kept pushing the drinking problem. Everything was revolving around the drinking problem."

In the bar Howard confided to Bosch that after his dismissal he had been totally depressed and was drinking heavily. "He told me he had contemplated getting revenge," Bosch said, "and drinking, he would sit for hours in the vicinity of the Soviet embassy or consulate." Howard was obviously referring to the episode the previous October, when he had loitered near the Soviet consulate on Phelps Place, wondering how much he might get for the CIA's secrets if he went inside. But Bosch said Howard "swore up and down to me he did not do anything" on that occasion.

Suddenly Howard broached an idea to his old buddy. "He said, 'Let's both of us get together. We could really do a job on the agency. Let's you and I go to Mexico City.' "

Sometime during the evening Howard made clear where he wanted to go in Mexico City. "He discussed going to the Soviet embassy," Bosch said.

Bosch declined, on the advice of his counsel, to say whether he had agreed to go to Mexico City with Howard. But he telephoned his sister in Houston that night with an invitation. "I said, 'Hey, let's go to Mexico City.' " Bosch said his sister "knew I'd been drinking" and did not accept his invitation.

Bosch insisted, however, that this took place before he understood that Howard had more than a pleasure trip in mind. "When he first talked about Mexico," Bosch said, "I thought it was a social trip. He had a friend down there."

Howard, according to Bosch, tried that night to telephone his friend Richard Marchese, the general manager of Dentsply Caulk, a dental supply company in Mexico City.[1] Bosch said it would be logical to assume they would have stayed with Marchese had the trip taken place. He said Howard also checked on plane flights to Mexico City.

[1] About ten days earlier Howard had received a letter from Marchese, a Peace Corps volunteer whom he had met in Cali, attesting to his "good moral character." Howard had solicited the letter for the court appearance.

"I think he may have called a travel agency to find out about flights," Bosch said.

"The trip was supposed to be the following weekend," Bosch said, "but it never took place." Bosch asserted that he did not take seriously Howard's proposal that they visit the Soviet embassy in Mexico. "I was not serious, and I didn't believe Ed was," he said. Howard never specifically proposed that they go inside the embassy and offer secrets to the Russians, Bosch claimed. "I had no intention of ever doing anything like that."

Bosch nevertheless found listening to Howard an exhilarating experience. "I'm down," he said, recalling that night on Bourbon Street. "My life just ended with the agency. But being with Ed, I felt high. I said, 'This guy is more fucked up than I am.' I had my head together."

Howard, too, sought to minimize his proposal to Bosch. "We were two old buddies who had been screwed by the agency," Howard said. "In New Orleans we were joking. We were in a bar on Bourbon Street. We had a couple of beers. I told Bill I had a good friend in Mexico City, Richard Marchese, and if we went there we could see him. We [Bosch and Howard] could go to the Soviet embassy. Wouldn't the surveillance freak out to see me and a Latin American [division] guy going into that embassy? What would the surveillance team think if we went to the Soviet embassy together in Mexico City? There were no plans to go, no plane reservation."

According to Bosch, some of the conversation and telephoning took place in the bar, some in the hotel room. A great deal of alcohol flowed. "Later that night we both got a little loaded, and we got separated," Bosch said. "I went to the hotel, and there was Ed, sound asleep." It was that kind of night.

In the morning, Bosch said, things looked different. "The next day I said I don't have the money to go to Mexico. It just got dropped."

But a seed had been planted. Bosch indicated that he began to worry about what his friend might do. "I truly did not believe Ed had done things, but he might be stupid enough when he got drunk to do something stupid. I did not want to see my friend screw his life up.''

Howard and Bosch spent the rest of the week in New Orleans, with Howard attending the energy conference at the Monteleone during the day and spending his evenings in the French Quarter with Bosch. With the trip to Mexico no longer on the agenda, a new plan evolved. Bosch would drive his friend back to Santa Fe, stopping off in Garland, just outside Dallas, to see Howard's parents.

Bosch called his sister in Houston, the morning after that first night on Bourbon Street, and this time invited her to meet them in Dallas. She agreed.

On the drive to Dallas, and again on the way to Santa Fe, the two friends had hours together to talk about their troubles and the way the agency had treated them. Bosch later told the FBI that on the long drive they spoke again about how, if they ever wanted to, they could hurt the agency. Bosch talked about his CIA work in Latin America. I could tell them this, Bosch said, drawing on his experience in Latin America. And I could tell them that, Howard said, referring to his own work in SE division.

It was getting to be a heavy trip for Bosch. In a Dallas nightclub his sister and Howard suddenly disappeared, and Bosch found himself face-to-face with his estranged wife; his two traveling companions had conspired to arrange for her presence, apparently in the hope of a reconciliation. It did not happen.

Bosch and Howard stayed with Kenneth and Mary Howard, in their one-story ranch-style house on a quiet street in Garland. He then drove on to Santa Fe with Howard. When Bosch hugged Mary, he could sense all was not well with the couple. ''I knew they were under a lot of stress.'' Bosch stayed with the Howards at their desert home on Verano Loop, then drove to Washington.

By now, Bosch said, he had decided that ''Ed needed help.'' In New Orleans he worried that Howard might be ''capable of suicide.''

Bosch now knew that Howard said he had lingered near a Soviet embassy building, thinking about going inside to sell CIA secrets, something the CIA did not yet know. He also knew that Howard had proposed that the two men go to the Soviet embassy in Mexico City to "do a job on the agency."

Bosch had no legal obligation to report this information to the authorities. Contrary to popular opinion, there is no requirement that a citizen with knowledge of a crime, or a contemplated crime, share that knowledge with a law-enforcement or intelligence agency.

Yet Bosch faced a dilemma. He had to choose among conflicting obligations to his friend, to the agency, and to himself. It was a tricky situation, not without potential dangers to Bosch.

Whatever moral duty Bosch might have felt to report Howard's actions to the CIA was presumably tempered by the unpleasant circumstances of his own departure from the agency. He must have worried as well that by reporting the Mexico City proposal, he might open himself to an investigation on suspicion that he had conspired with Howard to commit espionage.

Nevertheless, Bosch insisted that he came forward and took steps to warn the agency that his friend was flirting with espionage. He did so, he said, through an indirect channel to Langley.

Early in April Bosch drove to Washington and, he said, had dinner with his former sister-in-law Tanya Ringland. "During my conversation with Tanya I said, 'I'm really worried about Ed.' Tanya suggested I talk with Peter." At sixty-two, Peter Ringland, Bosch's ex-father-in-law, was no longer a regular employee of the CIA, but he had been teaching courses on contract and still had close ties to the agency, Bosch knew. As an old SE hand he would know exactly whom to talk to.

Ringland was away from Washington at the time, Bosch said, so he postponed his departure, waiting for him to return. When he did not, Bosch left for New York. "Two days later Peter called me at my sister's house in New York," Bosch said.

"What's with Ed?" Ringland asked, according to Bosch.

"I said, 'Ed needs help.'" Bosch said he believes he

informed Ringland about Howard's hanging around outside the Soviet consulate in Washington, but he replied, "I don't know," when asked if he also told Ringland about the proposed junket to the Soviet embassy in Mexico. Bosch said he did tell his former father-in-law that Howard had gotten into a shooting fray in Santa Fe.

"How much I told Peter I don't remember," Bosch added. "But Peter said the whole Ed Howard case was handled poorly, and he would take care of it."

Now Bosch convinced himself that he had solved his dilemma. He had at least warned the government indirectly. "I do believe I shared enough information with Peter Ringland to bring it to the attention of the people who would take care of it. I had no more direct link with the agency. They won't believe Bill Bosch." By contrast, he said, "I knew that my ex-father-in-law had a direct plug back into the agency." He said he believed that Peter Ringland still worked for the CIA at the time.

Peter Ringland declined to comment on whether Bosch had warned him about Howard in the spring of 1984 or whether he had relayed that information to the CIA. His daughter Tanya was almost equally unwilling to be drawn into a discussion of the events that Bosch described. She would not confirm his account, although she did not deny it, remarking at one point that she found the whole subject "distasteful."

Sometime in 1984, probably in May, Bosch said he met Howard in Philadelphia and disclosed his warning to Peter Ringland. "I told him I had told Peter," Bosch said. "Ed was pissed off. He just looked at me."

At times Bosch appears to take credit for attempting to tip off the CIA, as he claims he did. At other times Bosch flagellates himself for not having kept silent. "I told Ed we had a special relationship," Bosch said, "that I was his friend. I betrayed that friendship," he said mournfully, "because I told Peter."

For his part, Bosch said he assumed that Peter Ringland had passed on his warning to the CIA. If Bosch did, in fact, warn Ringland, as he insists he did, he had now protected his flanks; in the event of later trouble he could say he had tried to get word to the agency. He had done his best to warn Langley of the gathering storm.

14

Decision

What Edward Lee Howard needed, concluded Dr. Elliot "Sonny" Rapoport, Ph.D., the court-appointed psychologist, was "deep breathing exercises."

That, along with other "stress reducing techniques," including "deep muscle relaxation" and "self hypnosis," would undoubtedly help in resolving "this most unfortunate matter."

Dr. Rapoport, a respected figure in Santa Fe clinical circles, included these recommendations in the treatment plan he sent to the prosecutor in May.

Judge Kaufman had ordered the evaluation when he sentenced Howard on April 25 to five years' probation. The conditions imposed by the judge fulfilled the terms of the plea bargain that had been worked out by Howard's attorney and the DA. Howard would pay Peter Hughes seventy-five hundred dollars, pay to repair the bullet hole in the car roof as well, and remain in the state except for business trips.

Dr. Rapoport saw Howard three times in April and early May. In his report he noted that Howard had worked for the State Department in Washington but, after being assigned to Moscow, had decided to seek "more stable employment" in this country. He also reported that Howard had admitted to "a period of apparently problem drinking for about six months prior to his arrest."

While he found that Howard displayed signs of considerable anxiety and stress, he manifested no symptoms of any mental or personality disorder. His test results showed no signs of "brain dysfunction or any organic deterioration secondary to alcohol consumption." Howard, he reported, had "good contact with reality." His Rorschach test and interviews "suggest that Mr. Howard is neither mentally ill, nor depressed and/or suicidal.

"Of particular interest," Dr. Rapoport added, "are scales which assess antisocial or criminal orientation which, in Mr. Howard's case, do not indicate that he is inclined to act out in an antisocial manner and that he is not otherwise criminally oriented."

Howard had obviously made a good impression on Sonny Rapoport, as indeed he did on most people. The young professional appeared to have had a regrettable misunderstanding with three youthful citizens. The criminal charges, Rapoport concluded, were "totally out of character for Mr. Howard. . . .

"In evaluating this incident," Dr. Rapoport wrote, one should remember that "Mr. Howard had experienced a change in career, a change in residence, the birth of his first child, the stress of his new position, the death of his grandmother, the economic burden of holding mortgages on two homes and domestic problems resulting from a three month visit by his in-laws in his home. As these stressors increased, Mr. Howard found himself using alcohol to help cope with these problems. . . ." As for the incident itself, Dr. Rapoport suggested it had begun with an exchange of words, and the action by the victims in "apparently kicking his new car was simply and literally the last straw that broke the camel's back."

The psychologist urged that Howard remain in treatment with Neil Berman, the state alcohol counselor whom he was already seeing, to "work through" the events of the shooting episode and learn to cope with stress without resorting to drink. It was "highly unlikely," he concluded, that Howard would ever again display such poor judgment.

The same month that Howard received this glowing report from the psychologist, he was sent to Washington on business to attend a tax conference. En route he stopped in Denver and spent several hours at a motel with the woman whom he had been seeing when he lived in Chicago five years before. Around midnight he left to take the red-eye to Washington. It was almost exactly a year since he had been fired by the CIA.

One evening after the day's meetings were over, he visited friends in Vienna, Virginia. Howard drank that night and was well along when he decided that the thing to do was to pay an unannounced visit to his old boss at the agency, Tom Mills. Mills, too, lived in Vienna, near Tysons Corner, about three miles from Howard's old house.

Howard pulled into the driveway of the CIA official's home and demanded to see Mills, who came outside. Mills, he said, explained it was not a convenient time to chat; he was entertaining an Eastern-bloc diplomat, who was inside having dinner. Howard recalled the conversation this way:

"I can't talk to you," Mills said.

"They really fucked me."

"I understand that."

Eventually Mills was able to disengage and go back to his dinner party. What he said to the Eastern-bloc diplomat to explain the scene in the driveway is not known.

According to CIA sources, a shouting confrontation had taken place in the driveway. Howard denied that, insisting "there was no shouting match." But Mills reported the highly unorthodox encounter to the CIA, which could not have been pleased to learn that Howard was still acting unpredictably. On the same visit to Washington Howard went to CIA headquarters and met once more with Dr. Malloy. Tom Mills was present in the psychiatrist's office.

There had been more unauthorized calls to the Moscow embassy, Mills said. "They're blaming you." Mills was undoubtedly chiding Howard for his call to John Beyrle, which had so upset the Moscow station.

Dr. Malloy, Howard said, then suggested that the Labor Department might be willing to pay for a psychiatrist for Howard if he filed a claim. The idea of filing a grievance that might embarrass the CIA appealed to Howard, who said he contacted the Labor Department and got the necessary forms. "Malloy said to send the forms to him," Howard said, adding that he did so.

Some correspondence ensued. "The letters from the Labor Department didn't even have my name," Howard said. " 'Dear Sir, re claim number so-and-so.' It was just a number, like a Swiss bank account. All my communications went to Malloy. But nothing really happened with the claim."[1]

Howard's visit to Malloy after the driveway encounter was an indication that the agency was still very worried about Howard and keeping tabs on him. It also showed that the CIA still believed that Howard could be managed; after all, SE division and the Office of Medical Services were watching him.

CIA Director William Casey had more on his mind that summer than Edward Howard, however. Having just survived a major clash with the Senate over the mining of Nicaragua's harbors, he had decided on a major reshuffle at the agency. Clair George, Casey's point man in the mining controversy, would have to be pulled back from the Hill. Casey named George the DDO, replacing John Stein, the official who had made the decision to fire Howard. Stein became inspector general. At the same time Charles A. Briggs, the CIA's executive director, replaced George on the Hill, and James H. Taylor, the inspector general, succeeded Briggs. It was a game of

---

[1] A former CIA official said Howard had filed a claim with the Occupational Safety and Health Administration (OSHA), a division of the Labor Department, seeking to show that his problems were job-related and due to the stress of his CIA training. However, OSHA insisted it had no record of any claim by Howard.

musical chairs in which four top officials changed places at once at the end of June.

Around the same time David Forden, the chief of the Soviet division and the man who had originally approved Howard's selection for SE and Moscow, was quietly moved out of his job. As the chief of SE division Forden had been Mills's superior and Howard's ultimate boss. It was Forden who had fought to keep Howard on the payroll, parked in an innocuous job. He had been overruled.

Since he was a popular division chief, his departure caused gloom on the fifth floor. There was a going-away party in the division when Forden left, and he made a sentimental speech saying how much he would miss everyone. His replacement was Burt Gerber, the official who, with Gus Hathaway, later was responsible for debriefing Vitaly Yurchenko.

While these changes were taking place behind the scenes in Langley, Howard went about his work in Santa Fe and, by all accounts, performed well. He was traveling a lot for the state these days. In June Howard went to Los Angeles to attend another conference sponsored by DRI, the economic consulting firm. In July he traveled to El Paso, to visit the headquarters of El Paso Natural Gas, a pipeline company that was a major source of revenue for the state.

Outwardly Howard appeared to have put the night of February 26 behind him. By the summer of 1984, however, the evidence suggests that Howard had reached some sort of personal Rubicon and was getting ready to cross.

He could not get what had happened to him in the CIA out of his mind. It kept gnawing at him. He had almost gone over the edge the previous fall, when he lingered near the consulate on Phelps Place, flirting with danger, with revenge, with the possibility of taking money from the Soviets. He had, at some point, gone inside the consulate and left the letter.

He had taken another step in New Orleans in March, when he had proposed to Bill Bosch that they go together to the Soviet embassy in Mexico City. They could team up, do a job on the agency. That would fuck the fuckers in Langley.

His rage and frustration had reached the boiling point the night of the Peter Hughes shoot-out. It was dumb, it was stupid, it never should have happened, but it had. It was the drinking that did it, but it was hard to stop drinking. He really should, but God knows, he had reason to drink.

The firing by CIA, he could conceal that, hell, they *wanted* him to conceal it, he wasn't supposed to say he had even worked there. But the arrest, the shooting couldn't be concealed. It hadn't gotten much publicity, thanks to Morton Simon, but people knew. His friends and family knew, his neighbors, his co-workers. They knew. He had the probation hanging over his head, five years of that to look forward to. He had to keep seeing Neil Berman, the alcohol counselor; that was part of his sentence.

And it had been humiliating. True, he had been drunk and outnumbered, it was three against one; but he was supposed to be a trained agent of the CIA, and he had let three punk kids take his gun away from him. Bottle washers in pizza joints.

Then there were his in-laws. They were decent enough, but they always seemed to be visiting, protecting Mary, getting in his hair. Within the family there had been intimations that Mary's parents did not consider him a good enough provider for their daughter. So it was doubly humiliating to have to borrow most of the money from them to pay Peter Hughes.

For therapy! The kid had admitted at the court hearing that he had only a scratched finger, but now Howard had to fork over seventy-five hundred dollars, and the damn judge wanted to know if that would be enough. Enough! Christ, the kid could hire an army of shrinks at that price.

It was time to act, to stop being a wimp, to take arms against his sea of troubles. He could, with the right move, wreak revenge upon the CIA, solve his financial problems, and restore his self-esteem. He had already offered his services to the Soviets; perhaps it was time to contact them again.

By July Howard may have made up his mind, or very possibly the Soviets, by then, had responded to his letter, for that month he cashed in his Crown Life insurance policy. It was a whole life policy; he kept his term insurance to protect Mary and Lee. With the insurance proceeds, he informed Mary, they were going to take a trip to Europe.

15

Contact

They would stay with the Ferroni-Strattners near Bern, Howard told his wife. It would be wonderful to see Marco and Ann again, and it would save on hotel costs. They would also go to Milan for a DRI conference. After visiting their friends in Switzerland, they would drive through Austria to Munich, winding up at the Oktoberfest before flying home. It would be a whirlwind week, a little extravagant, but they deserved some fun.

Howard purchased round-trip tickets to Frankfurt on Delta Air Lines. After a year on the job he had some vacation time coming, and he arranged to take nine days by sandwiching two weekends around a workweek.

But first he had to take care of an important detail. Howard called on his boss, Curtis Porter. "He came in to my office and said there was a DRI conference in Milan," Porter said. DRI, the worldwide economic consulting firm, held a contract with the state. "He showed me the DRI brochure on it. There were a series of international economic forums around the world. One was in Japan, and it [the brochure] had Milan. He didn't want the staff to know; he just wanted my approval. He didn't want to be paid for it. He wanted me to say he could represent the LFC [Legislative Finance Committee]. He explained he could write the trip off and get the tax benefit and some vacation out of it." Porter agreed.

For eight days in September 1984, the Howards visited Europe, taking their eighteen-month-old baby with them. It was during this week, American counterintelligence of-

ficials believe, that Howard first met with officers of the
KGB, gave them classified information, and was paid. Vitaly Yurchenko reported that Howard had met with "senior officials" of the KGB "in Austria in the fall of 1984."
The formal complaint against Howard lists the trip to Austria as an overt act in a conspiracy to commit espionage.
Howard's movements during the week are, therefore, of
more than passing interest.

On Saturday, September 15, 1984, the Howards flew to
Frankfurt. They rented a car and, by Howard's account,
drove on September 16 to Zurich, where they spent the
night at the Mövenpick Hotel.

At this point both Howard and his wife give varying
and somewhat confused accounts of the sequence of events
in what was to become a crucial week in their life.

I asked Mary Howard about the trip. "We visited friends
in Switzerland," she said. "We visited Zurich and Lu-
cerne and then decided to go to Austria and then Milan."
In Austria, she said, they spent the night in the town of
St. Anton. Later I went over the trip again, this time with
the aid of a detailed map of Central Europe spread out
between us. Mary Howard said she was confused about
the sequence of the trip. "We'd never been to Austria, so
since we were so close, we decided to go there," she said.
"But maybe Milan was before St. Anton."

Howard, during the interview in Budapest, said that they
had visited Milan before going to Austria. After spending
the night in Zurich, he said, he contacted his friends Marco
Ferroni and Ann Strattner. "The next morning I called
Marco," Howard said.

Howard said that he and Mary drove from Zurich and
stayed with their friends near Bern. "From Bern we drove
to Milan." To his surprise, Howard said, when he and his
wife got to Milan, they discovered that the DRI conference
had been canceled.

"We drove back to Bern," Edward Howard said, "and
stayed three or four days at the Ferroni-Strattners' house."
The Ferroni-Strattners lived in Sariswil, a suburb about
seven miles northwest of the Swiss capital. Marco Ferroni
worked for the Swiss foreign aid agency; his wife, an ag-

ricultural economist, was American. Howard had met them
when they all were stationed in Lima several years earlier.
Ann Strattner, then single, had come to know the Howards
fairly well; Ed liked to prepare gourmet meals, and she
sometimes dined at their house on Sunday evenings.

The Ferroni-Strattners remembered the Howards arriving in Sariswil in their rental car, a green Opel Record,
with Lee asleep in the back seat. They told their Swiss
friends they had come from Milan. "They stayed two
nights as far as we can remember, and they did talk about
going to the Oktoberfest," Marco Ferroni recalled.

"We didn't know he had worked for the CIA," he said.
Howard Strattner took them sightseeing, to Aarberg and
Murten, two picturesque old towns nearby. The Ferroni-
Strattners had no recollection "that Ed did anything alone
during those two days, like going to Bern alone."

In fact, Ferroni said, there was only one unusual incident during the visit. Ann had prepared *Gschwellti*, a Swiss
dish of boiled potatoes in the skin, served with cheeses,
dips, and salad. "He didn't show up for dinner; he stayed
downstairs in their room," Ferroni recalled. "Mary sort
of insinuated he was feeling ill. Only after they had left,
I found out that the problem had been alcohol." Ferroni
discovered that Howard had consumed half a bottle of gin
or rum that he had taken from the liquor cabinet. "The
bottle was practically empty."

Marco Ferroni had a clear memory of the Howards'
visit; he had been interviewed about it by the Swiss
Federal Police at the request of the FBI. And he was sure
the Howards said they had come from Milan. "They said
he had been to Milan on business—a conference, I believe."

The Howards left Bern, and their friends' house, on
Thursday, September 20, and drove across the Swiss border into Austria. The FBI has established, presumably
from hotel records, that they stayed overnight in St. Anton, an Alpine resort in the Arlberg about thirty miles east
of the border.

"The day before the Oktoberfest started," Howard said,

"we drove from Bern to Munich through western Austria. We stopped in St. Anton."[1]

Mary Howard remembered the town. "We were only in St. Anton. I'm not aware of any goings-on in St. Anton. We were just driving around, and it was getting toward dusk, and it looked like a pretty little town. We were only there one night." She repeated that they had chosen the town randomly. "There was no rhyme or reason to go there."

They stayed at an inn. "We had a disagreement," she said. "Our fights were usually over his drinking. He took off in the car. I could see him drive away from the window. He drove around in the car." Could Howard have met the Soviets then? "He was only gone a short time," she said, "perhaps ten or fifteen minutes."

Was this the only place they stayed overnight in Austria? "I think so," she said.

And was Howard's absence, when he stormed out of the hotel in St. Anton, the only time they were separated on the trip? "I don't remember if he was away any other time," she replied.

Edward Howard gave a similar account of that night. "In St. Anton I had an argument with Mary. I wanted to go to a disco, and she wanted to have a quiet night. I had a beer and a cognac at the hotel. After the argument with Mary I drove around for half an hour. I found a restaurant and had one more beer. I drove back to the hotel. We had dinner, and I went to the disco with Mary."

The FBI affidavit that later formed the basis of the criminal complaint against Howard reports Yurchenko's statements that Howard met with the KGB in Austria in the fall of 1984 and adds: "Investigation has determined that

---

[1] After the Budapest interview I contacted Howard again and asked him a number of additional questions. I requested that he fill in more details about his movements during the September 1984 trip to Europe. In a handwritten reply, Howard provided the most detailed account yet. The letter differed from his recollection in Budapest in two respects; Howard now said he went directly to Milan from Zurich on September 17, without first visiting his friends in Bern, and he said he stayed in Bern with the Ferroni-Strattners only two days, not three or four.

Howard was in St. Anton, Austria on September 20, 1984.''[2]

But the government has not charged that Howard engaged in any espionage activities in St. Anton. That town is cited solely to demonstrate that Howard was in Austria that fall and because it was apparently the only place where the FBI was able to document his presence in that country. In fact, it is highly unlikely that the Soviets would have met with a former CIA man in St. Anton, a tiny village where the presence of Russians might attract attention and be remembered. For meetings with agents, the Soviets much prefer Vienna.

And the FBI did secretly charge that Howard, according to Yurchenko, met the Soviets in Vienna in 1984. An unpublished FBI affidavit, still under seal in the Howard case but obtained by the author, reveals that Yurchenko said that Howard ''met with the KGB in 1984 *in Vienna,* Austria and furnished classified information [italics added].''[3]

''We never went to Vienna or even Innsbruck,'' Howard insisted. After leaving Switzerland, Howard said, ''we drove through Austria and turned north before Innsbruck.'' They crossed the border into Germany, he said, and spent the night at a Best Western hotel north of Munich.

Mary Howard agreed with her husband. ''We were never in Vienna,'' she said.

Since the Howards, albeit with some contradictions and confusion, have accounted for their time during the eight days in Europe, telling of stops in Zurich, Milan, Bern, St. Anton, and Munich, when could Howard, as the FBI claims, have met the KGB in Vienna? It is possible, of course, that he drove the three hundred miles to Vienna after leaving St. Anton.

---

[2]The affidavit does not name Yurchenko but identified him as ''a confidential source with intimate knowledge of Soviet intelligence matters.''

[3]The affidavit, dated September 27, 1985, and signed by Special Agent Gerald B. Brown, was the basis for search warrants that allowed the FBI to search the Howards' home at 108 Verano Loop, their two cars, and a safe-deposit box.

But the key to Vienna may lie in Milan. The "Milan conference" is crucial to the Howard case because it provided a two-day period when Howard could have slipped into Vienna, or elsewhere, to meet with the Soviets.

The Howards assert that they went to Milan. Mary Howard, like her husband, said that the conference in Milan had been canceled. "We just stayed in Milan a day and continued on with the trip," she said. Mary Howard said she had seen a brochure announcing the conference; as she recalled, it gave a date of late September.[4]

Edward Howard was able to provide the name of virtually every hotel they stayed at, except for Milan. But he insisted he did go to Milan. He said he had called the DRI office in Boston and got an application for the conference and sent it in, to get the tax write-off and to avoid violating the terms of his probation, which permitted travel only on business. "There was a conference scheduled," he said. "Advanced Econometrics was the title. I was told two weeks later it was held."

There is only one difficulty with this story: officials of DRI's London office, which handles the firm's European conferences, searched their records extensively at my request and said they could find "no trace" of any DRI conference in Milan in September 1984 or of any conference that had been scheduled for that month and subsequently canceled or rescheduled.

I met with Alan G. Bright in DRI's London office early in July 1987. After checking his files, he said that the only conference held in Milan that fall took place on November 15 and 16, which would be almost two months after Howard's trip. It was entitled International Economic Outlook Conference.

Maria Tavolacci, the administrator of DRI's Milan office since early 1983, said flatly, "There was no conference in September of 1984. It's out of the question. We never had

---

[4]Curtis Porter could not recall whether the brochure he saw gave any date for the conference in Milan or whether he paid any particular attention to the date. Howard told him the conference was in September, Porter said, and he had no reason to question it.

a conference canceled. We didn't plan anything for September.''

Howard, it is clear, persuaded Curtis Porter that the ''Milan conference'' was to take place in September. He may have even told Mary the same story. He may indeed, aside from any other purposes, have hoped to write the trip off on his income taxes.

But in that case why bother to drive to Milan? If Howard *knew* that there was no conference in Milan, he could have deducted the trip in any event, later claiming, if audited, that the meeting had been canceled.

Yet Howard claims that he drove to Milan to attend a phantom conference that, according to all the objective evidence, was nonexistent, notional from the start. It seems much more likely that the alleged Milan trip provided cover for Howard to slip into Austria and meet with the Soviets in Vienna.

On Saturday, September 22, Howard said, they visited the Oktoberfest in Munich, and on Sunday they flew home from Frankfurt.

Curtis Porter recalled Howard's coming into his office soon after he returned to Santa Fe. ''I remember him describing Milan when he came back,'' Porter said. ''He told me where they stayed, where they ate, what a great bargain it was. How they went with a big group of people, and it was like twelve dollars a person for dinner, something ridiculous like that. He talked about the hotel and the traffic in Milan.''

According to Porter, Howard had also been enthusiastic about the meeting he had attended in Milan. Porter remembered clearly that Howard had enjoyed the DRI conference and thought it had been extremely productive.

''He said he got some good information about the world economy.''

16

The Confession

On Monday morning, September 24, the day after his return from Europe, Howard left his home in the desert early. He swung onto Interstate 25 heading west and took the first turnoff for Santa Fe.

He pulled up at a motel, parked, and got out. Two senior CIA officials were waiting for him. They were Tom Mills, Howard's old boss, the chief of the Soviet desk in SE division, and Dr. Barney Malloy.

They had not seen Howard since May, shortly after his drunken encounter with Mills in the driveway of the SE official's home. The two men had come to Santa Fe to meet Howard for breakfast.

They were there to check discreetly on his frame of mind and stability in the wake of the Peter Hughes episode and his confrontation with Mills. In view of Mills's position, and Malloy's, it was clear that the CIA was still extremely worried about what Howard might do. The head of the Soviet desk and the CIA's senior psychiatrist do not, as an everyday occurrence, fly to New Mexico for breakfast meetings with former employees who have been fired by the agency.

It is not likely that the two CIA officials realized that some twelve hours earlier Howard had arrived back from a trip that included a visit to Austria. Howard did not see fit to mention it.

"Right away they plopped an envelope on the table with two hundred dollars," Howard said. "They said, 'We want to reimburse you for the psychiatric testing you had during the Peter Hughes incident.' '' Under the terms of the plea bargain and sentence, Howard had to pay for his psychological evaluation by Sonny Rapoport. Howard had told the CIA about that.

"I said thank you and took the envelope," Howard related.

Malloy and Mills again urged Howard to see a psychiatrist.

"You guys are such assholes," Howard said. "You treat agents better than case officers."

How do you mean? Malloy asked in his soft southern accent.

"You have a responsibility to your officers," Howard argued. "When I left the agency, I was in a state of shock. I worked my butt off, twelve to twenty-four hours a day. Sometimes I started at eight and ended at midnight. Whatever they wanted, I did. I gave them my heart."

The two CIA men nodded sympathetically. Howard talked on about his feelings a year earlier, during the summer after he had been cast out by the agency. "I had some problems," he said. He described in detail the anger and resentment that had built up that summer.

Mills and Malloy were listening intently.

He had been so upset, Howard said, that on a trip to Washington in October 1983 he walked to the park near the Soviet consulate and sat there debating with himself whether to go inside, to sell the CIA's secrets. He told how he hesitated, sure that the Soviets would think he was a crank or a plant.

Besides, Howard confided to the two CIA officials, he felt the Soviets were cheap. "Kampiles only got three thousand dollars for the KH-eleven manual," he told them.[1] That was like selling a Cadillac for five bucks. He

---

[1] Williams P. Kampiles, twenty-two, went to work for the CIA in 1977 and was assigned to the watch center, where he had access to the manual for the KH-11, the nation's most sophisticated reconnaissance satellite. On a trip to Greece he sold the manual to the KGB for three thousand dollars. He was convicted of espionage on November 17, 1978,

told the two CIA men how he had figured if he went inside, they would give him five hundred dollars and kick his butt out the door and, finally, how he had decided he could not bring himself to do it.

The CIA officials were relieved to hear that Howard had not gone inside the embassy, or said he hadn't.

"But the fact I went and sat on the park bench," Howard went on, "means you guys should take better care of your officers. I was taught when you cut the relationship with an agent, make sure they're happy. Show them a letter from Casey if you have to." They hadn't done that for him, Howard said.

Mills and Malloy asked Howard what he thought they should have done in his case.

"Maybe a probationary period," Howard said. "Tell the person, 'We think you are concealing a crime.' Tell him he has to stay in Washington one year in a nonsensitive job."

"We want to help you if you're still having anxiety," Malloy said. "Find yourself a good psychiatrist, and when you find one you're comfortable with, let us know his name, birth date, and Social Security number. We'll clear him, and you just send us the bills."

Seen in retrospect, the whole breakfast meeting was surreal. Howard, the repository of the CIA's entire Moscow operation, had just confessed to two senior officials of the CIA that he was a colossal security risk. He had lingered outside the Soviet consulate for a long time, teetering on the edge of going in and revealing those secrets for money.

The CIA's response was to offer to pay for a psychiatrist.

It is entirely possible that the CIA already knew of Howard's presence outside the Soviet consulate the previous October. William Bosch claimed that he believed he had warned Peter Ringland about the episode. If so, and if

---

and sentenced to forty years. Howard had learned about the Kampiles case in his security lecture at CIA. The low payment was cited in an effort to impress the career trainees with the poor rewards and high risks of dealing in agency secrets.

Ringland had passed Bosch's forebodings along to the agency, the CIA would have known for six months that Howard, in October 1983, had almost sold secrets to the Russians. Howard's revelations at breakfast, in that case, would have been no surprise to Mills.

That may well be what really happened. Bureaucracies are not noted for spontaneity. It is extremely unusual, if not unprecedented, for the CIA to pay medical bills for a former employee, especially one who has been dismissed as a suspected thief. The fact that Mills and Malloy offered on the spot to pay for Howard's psychiatrist suggests that the decision had already been taken at headquarters.

In retrospect, the breakfast meeting is even more bizarre in the light of what Howard had been doing a few days before. At the time that Howard confessed to the two CIA officials that he had almost sold the agency's most vital secrets to the opposition, he had in fact already done so a week earlier, the government says. Mills and Malloy, the evidence suggests, were too late.

If Howard had just returned from Austria with Soviet money in his pocket, why did he confess the lesser sin of having merely contemplated espionage? American counterintelligence officials have grappled with that problem, and they have some tentative theories. One is that Howard, although he believed the FBI had no surveillance on the Soviet consulate, might have worried that he was wrong, that he had been spotted or photographed in the vicinity of Phelps Place. Better, then, to confess and reassure the agency that nothing happened. Another answer may be that Howard felt that by confessing the consulate episode, he would divert attention from his actions in Austria. Or he might have felt that if he were caught and charged with espionage, it might somehow mitigate the crime if he could point to the fact that he had tried to warn the CIA of his state of mind.

Whatever Howard's reasons, he had now confessed to the CIA that he was a man on the brink of committing treason. He had come tantalizingly close to confirming SE's worst fears about him.

Howard dropped Mills and Malloy at the airport and

drove to his office in the capitol. On the way he thought back over the past hour. He was pleased with the way things had gone at breakfast. There had been an nice touch at the end. He had insisted, and they let him pay the check.

It was the least he could do.

17

"No Paper Trail"

When Thomas Mills got back to Langley, he immediately reported the extraordinary conversation with Howard to his superiors in SE division. He told Gus Hathaway, the second highest official in the division.

Hathaway, who in six months was to be promoted to chief of counterintelligence, had made the decision: the agency would handle Ed Howard by paying for his psychiatrist. Malloy and Mills were acting now, and probably all along, with Hathaway's approval. But on a case of this magnitude Burt Gerber, the division chief, would also have been aware of the decision.

The CIA was now sitting on a time bomb. For months it had concealed the Howard case from the FBI. The agency had not notified the bureau when Howard was fired, nor had it told the FBI about this phone calls to Moscow on the special circuit or his driveway confrontation with Tom Mills. Containment was the watchword.

Howard's confession about the Soviet consulate, however, created a new situation entirely. It escalated the level of the threat. The possibility that Howard might be dealing with the Russians had now been directly raised by the best possible source—Howard himself.

By the fall of 1984 the cover-up of the Howard case had become so entrenched and accepted within the CIA that— shockingly—his confession was concealed from the FBI. Whether the original decision to stonewall the bureau was simply allowed to stand or was reaffirmed after the Santa

Fe breakfast is not known. But Howard's confession never saw the light of day.

Once Mills had reported on the Santa Fe meeting, Gerber and Hathaway had an additional problem. Even within the CIA what other officials and divisions should be told about Howard's startling confession? Aside from SE division, the counterintelligence staff, then headed by David Blee, and the Office of Security, under William Kotapish, would normally be expected to take an interest in a case officer who had been fully briefed on the agency's Moscow operation and was spending his time outside a Soviet embassy building.

Did SE share its knowledge with the CI staff and OS? Here the record is conflicting. As might be expected, the CIA is not anxious to air the details of its cover-up of the Howard case. A former high-ranking official of the CIA insisted that Howard's confession never got out of SE division. "That's where it was stuck," he said. The report, he added, never reached the level of Casey or McMahon.

"There was no paper trail," said another former CIA official who had access to the Howard files. "It [the consulate episode] never got out of SE as a report." By this time Clair George had replaced Stein as the DDO.[1] "Whether Clair was told at a meeting, I don't know," he added. "But there was no audit trail left to follow. No records."

Much later, after Howard escaped to Moscow, the CIA inspector general's office did a secret internal study of the case. A CIA source familiar with the document said, "The inspector general did not report any evidence that knowledge of the embassy episode went any higher than SE division."

In sum, a variety of CIA sources point to SE as the culprit. In any bureaucracy it is standard strategy, once improprieties or errors come to light, to maintain that the circle of officials responsible is as narrow as possible. Thus, within the confines of Langley, the finger of blame

---

[1]George resigned from the CIA at the end of 1987 after becoming entangled in the Iran-contra scandal.

was pointed at SE. But that is not what the agency secretly told the counterintelligence branch of the FBI a year later, when the case could no longer be concealed from the bureau.

The FBI was informed by the CIA that all three branches—the Soviet division, counterintelligence, and security—had signed off on the decision to conceal the consulate episode from the FBI. Not only were Gerber and Hathaway in SE division aware of Howard's vigil outside a Soviet embassy building, the FBI was told, but David Blee, the chief of the CI staff, also knew of the confession, as did William Kotapish, the chief of OS. Here an exactly opposite set of bureaucratic dynamics was at work. In explaining to the FBI why the Howard confession had been concealed, it was to the agency's advantage to maintain that a broader circle of officials was involved. There is safety in numbers.

While these Byzantine developments were unfolding in Langley, in Santa Fe Howard decided to take up the CIA on its offer to pay for a psychiatrist. "Frankly, I didn't think I needed help," Howard said, "but I thought, *Why not?* Make them pay a little, and maybe it can do you some good."

Howard was already seeing Neil Berman, his alcoholism counselor, once a week, and he asked Berman for the name of a psychiatrist.

"I found the guy in October. He was very strange at first when I asked him for his birth date and Social Security number. I started seeing him twice a month. I would send the bills to an address in Chantilly, Virginia."

The psychiatrist was Dr. Michael Dudelczyk, a bearded thirty-six-year-old therapist from Paterson, New Jersey, well established in Santa Fe, where he had practiced for almost a decade.

"Ed contacted me," Dr. Dudelczyk said, "and asked to see me. He said because of an alcohol problem."

Dr. Dudelczyk was aware that the CIA would be paying for the ninety-dollar-an-hour visits, that Howard would send the bills to the agency and be reimbursed. "What they did," Dr. Dudelczyk said, "was they ran a security check and said it was OK, and that took months. I didn't hear for quite a long time.''

To be precise, it took the CIA almost three months to decide that Dr. Dudelcyzk was sufficiently trustworthy to listen to what Howard might tell him. The clearance process dragged on until the end of the year—this at a time when Howard had already confessed that he almost went into the Soviet consulate to sell the agency's secrets.

In the meantime, Howard was still acting like a man under a great deal of stress. At the end of October he flew to Boston with Curtis Porter to attend a conference of the National Association of Tax Administrators. Some very odd things happened in Boston.

Two officials of DRI invited Howard and his friend David Abbey, who worked for the New Mexico Finance Department, to visit their offices in Lexington, Massachusets, for the afternoon. The New Mexico officials were staying in Boston at the Copley Square Marriott. Around noon, when the DRI representatives came looking for Howard to drive him to their offices, he could not be found at his hotel. The two DRI staffers and Abbey drove out to Lexington without him.

Curtis Porter, too, had noticed that Howard was missing. Around 4:00 P.M. he went up to the room they were sharing. "Ed was there," Porter said. "He was lying on the bed with a bandage on his head. His story was that he banged his head into a glass door. The lower level of the hotel is all glass. He said he'd been to Mass General. Two weeks later he came in with the emergency room bill and complained how expensive it was. He told how he had to wait in the emergency room with all the derelicts and shooting victims.

''There was a banquet that evening. They had given him some kind of painkillers at the hospital. He had a couple of drinks, and I noticed by the time he sat down he was slurring his words.''

At dinner Howard was seated next to an attractive woman. David Abbey decided that his friend was getting loud and boisterous and told him to cool it. Howard erupted in anger.

JON WISE

"He came walking toward me.... He was the Central Intelligence Agency's first defector.... He had been granted asylum by the Russians, but he was still a wanted man in every country of the Western World.... He extended his hand.

"'I'm Edward Lee Howard.'"

At the University of Texas at Austin in 1970, Howard (*circled*) joined the Taekwon Do Karate Club.

Howard joined the Central Intelligence Agency in January 1981. Within a year, he was being trained to operate as a spy in Moscow.

Howard learned basic espionage tradecraft at the Farm, a secret CIA installation near Williamsburg, Virginia, where he excelled at breaking and entering. Howard later used the skills he had learned in his training to escape from the FBI.

"We screwed up." CIA Director William J. Casey, who approved Howard's dismissal, later admitted that the intelligence agency had bungled its handling of the case.

The CIA planned to send Howard to Moscow under diplomatic cover as an embassy officer. His commission as a member of the United States Foreign Service was signed by President Reagan and Secretary of State George Shultz.

William G. Bosch, Howard's closest friend in the CIA, provided key evidence in the case to the FBI. Bosch is shown here in a 1966 photo.

After Howard was dismissed by the CIA, he telephoned the U.S. Embassy in Moscow and may have contacted "Raya," a female KGB colonel on the embassy staff. The tall, **blond** Soviet spy, known around the embassy as "Big Raya," is the woman on the far right. The photograph was taken at the marine ball at Spaso House, the ambassador's residence, in 1985. The man with his arm around Raya and another Soviet woman employee of the embassy is Master Sergeant Joey E. Wingate, the commander of the marine detachment. At left, in bow tie, is an embassy security officer with "Svetlana," a Soviet librarian at the embassy.

Howard and his wife, Mary, moved to **Santa Fe**, New Mexico, after his dismissal from the CIA and bought this house in the desert, from which he escaped, eluding FBI surveillance, in September 1985.

NEIL JACOBS

Howard confessed to CIA officials that he had lingered for hours in a park near the Soviet consulate at 1825 Phelps Place NW, in downtown Washington, thinking about going inside and selling agency secrets to the Soviets. The CIA concealed Howard's startling confession from the FBI for almost a year.

Howard was a federally licensed gun dealer. This document records that he sold a Smith and Wesson revolver in February 1983 while still employed as a CIA agent.

R. M. LUCERO

Howard fired a shot during a fight with Peter Hughes (*above*) in Santa Fe. Howard was arrested, convicted of a felony and ordered to pay Hughes $7,500 in compensation.

After Howard was dismissed by the Central Intelligence Agency, he had his federal license as a gun dealer transferred to his new home in Santa Fe, New Mexico.

Soviet defector Vitaly Yurchenko revealed the existence of a CIA mole, who was identified as Edward Lee Howard. Yurchenko, in a move that stunned the CIA, later redefected to Moscow.

Safe house at Coventry, near Fredericksburg, Virginia, where KGB defector Yurchenko was interrogated by CIA debriefers.

Yurchenko also fingered Ronald W. Pelton (*right*) with FBI agent. Pelton, a former employee of the National Security Agency, sold highly sensitive communications intelligence secrets to the Soviets. He was convicted of espionage and sentenced to life imprisonment.

The Howard case landed on the desk of James H. Geer, the assistant director of the FBI in charge of intelligence, during Geer's first day on the job.

These surveillance photos of Howard were taken by the FBI after Yurchenko's information led the bureau to the former CIA man. The FBI also tapped Howard's home telephone, hoping to gather the evidence that would permit his arrest.

Phillip A. Parker, the FBI counterintelligence official in charge of the Howard case, had the former CIA man almost within his grasp when a young FBI agent's incredible error permitted Howard to vanish into the New Mexico desert.

NEIL JACOBS

Mary Howard, trained by the CIA to work as a spy in Moscow with her husband, drove the getaway car on the night of September 21, 1985. The Howards used a makeshift dummy, similar to the one they had learned to use in the CIA, to fool the FBI.

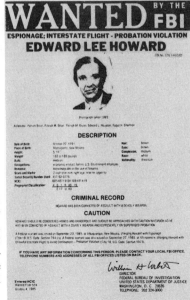

While the FBI conducted a worldwide search for Howard, the fugitive CIA man claimed he traveled in Europe, Latin America, and Canada on a false U.S. passport purchased in West Germany.

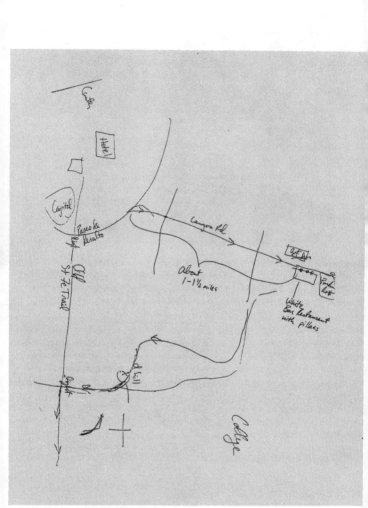

Sketch Howard drew for the author in Budapest showing spot, marked with a circled X, where he jumped from a moving car in Santa Fe to elude FBI agents. Building at far right is Alfonso's Restaurant, where Howard and his wife, Mary, had their last dinner together moments before he jumped. Handwriting on the map is Howard's.

Edward Lee Howard (*left*) interviewed by the author, David Wise, in Budapest in June 1987. Howard said the KGB had instructed him to meet the author in public places in case the interviews were part of a CIA trap.

Howard on Margaret Island in the middle of the Danube, where many of the secret meetings with the author took place, including their first contact.

Howard gave the author this photograph of the interior of his dacha outside Moscow. Pictures of his son, Lee, and wife, Mary, can be seen framed on the bookcase. The stairway leads to an upstairs study that serves as Howard's "office."

My house outside of Moscow
— the living room.
Ed Howard
6/27/87

Howard's inscription on the back of the photograph of his dacha.

In Moscow, Howard's patron is Vladimir Aleksandrovich Kryuchkov, the number-two official of the KGB and the man in charge of all Soviet foreign espionage.

Howard plays tennis and volleyball on KGB intramural teams in Moscow. At upper left he serves the ball at the Kozlekedesi tennis club in Budapest. Howard, who is closely supervised by the KGB, says he misses pizza, peanut butter, and the PTA. The FBI obtained evidence that Howard was paid at least $160,000 by the KGB and hid most of it in a numbered bank account in Switzerland.

Map on which Howard circled the Roman Catholic Church of St. Louis behind KGB headquarters that he attends in Moscow. Howard wrote on the map: "Area of the Catholic Church I attend. I don't know the name. It's the only one in Moscow that is active. EH"

Edward Lee Howard in Moscow, standing in front of St. Basil's Cathedral in Red Square. Howard, who had shaved the mustache he wore in Budapest six months earlier, provided this photograph to the author early in 1988.

"There was an exchange between him and Abbey that was short and abrupt," Porter recalled. "I asked him what happened, and he mumbled something about 'Abbey pissed me off.' Around appetizer time he got up and left."

"We finished dinner, and I went up to the room, and he had grabbed all the clothes out of the closet and thrown them into a suitcase. The suitcase was closed, but there were clothes hanging out of it. He was on the phone to the concierge making flight reservations to Vienna. He got kind of caught in the act.

"And he said, 'Sorry, I got crazy with the painkillers and booze. Don't worry, Mary knows every time I get drunk, I go to Vienna. Mary's the only one who can handle me when I get drunk.' " Then, Porter said, Howard said he realized he couldn't go to Vienna. "He said, 'I don't have my passport.'

"That's when he told me he had lied to me about working for the State Department. He said he had worked for the CIA. He told me that they fired him and it had to do with a lie detector test. He said it was the CIA that had gotten his shooting incident totally hushed up and that the CIA was paying for him to go to a psychiatrist in Santa Fe."

The news bewildered Curtis Porter. His roommate a CIA agent? A man who fired a gun when angered, walked into glass doors, and zipped off to Vienna when he got drunk? And the agency was paying for his shrink? It all seemed a bit too preposterous to be entirely believable.[2]

Howard did not return directly to Santa Fe from Boston. He flew to New York, instead, and spent three days visiting Bill Bosch at his mother's home on Long Island. A month later, in November, Howard found Bosch a job in

---

[2]Asked how he had cut his head in Boston, Howard said, "I hurried down an escalator. I wanted to grab a bag of potato chips between meetings. I was going to run across the street, and I ran into a glass door. There were no lines or markings on it; it was just clear. I went to the hospital. I wasn't drinking during the day. That night I had too many drinks. I can't explain the Vienna remark that Curt Porter reported. I don't recall making that statement."

Brownsville, Texas, as an assistant to a businessman who was involved in real estate and construction deals.

On December 28, three days after Christmas, Howard finally had his first session with Michael Dudelcyzk. "Ed said, 'You've been approved,' and we started," the psychiatrist related. For almost nine months Howard saw Dr. Dudelczyk in his office in downtown Santa Fe on the average of twice a month.

Dr. Dudelczyk knew that Howard had worked for the CIA, of course, since he was aware that Langley was paying the bills. But Howard did not tell the psychiatrist that he had met with the KGB in Europe, or that he had loitered near the Soviet consulate in Washington, or that he had proposed to another former CIA officer that they go into the Soviet embassy in Mexico City.

That he told the psychiatrist none of these things is apparent from Dr. Dudelczyk's stunned reaction when Howard later fled the country and was accused of espionage. "What happened with Ed was a total surprise to me, a total shock," Dr. Dudelczyk said.

The requirements of confidentiality between doctor and patient would not permit him to discuss what Howard did reveal in their meetings, he said. "Alcohol was the focus with me," he added. "I can't really say any more than that."

Howard himself talked about his sessions with the psychiatrist, however. "I told him I had worked for the CIA and why I was fired," he said. "I told him I worked for them and gave them my heart and one of their electronic machines had a glitch and they dropped me like a cold fish."

Although the CIA has its own psychiatrists, who serve under the Office of Medical Services, their numbers are too few to do very much treatment. Rather, the agency psychiatrists generally confine themselves to diagnosis and referrals.

Unlike employees of, say, the Agriculture Department, CIA workers who feel in need of psychiatric care are not free, under the agency's rules, simply to go out and find therapists on their own. They are required to see the agency's in-house psychiatrists, who may then refer them to outside psychiatrists on an approved CIA roster. The psychiatrists on the roster all have agreed to treat CIA patients and have been cleared after security checks by the agency. Typically the cleared psychiatrists treat nonagency patients as well.

The doctors on the approved roster have offices for the most part in northern Virginia, Washington, and suburban Maryland, the areas where the bulk of the CIA's employees live. Since Dr. Dudelczyk lived in Santa Fe, where the agency would not normally need an approved psychiatrist, he required a special clearance.

"If you work for CIA, you are expected to go to an approved shrink, someone on the roster," a former DDO man said. "You could go to see a psychiatrist who wasn't on the roster, but the polygraph would find you out."

Even so, some employees risk it, rather than reveal to the Office of Medical Services that they are having problems that need treatment. The fear is, of course, that such a disclosure might damage an employee's career.

The CIA maintains a roster of cleared psychiatrists for obvious reasons. If an employee talks about secrets, the agency wants to be as certain as it can that the psychiatrist is both a loyal citizen and discreet, so that the information will not be transmitted to a foreign power, either wittingly or otherwise.[3]

From a counterintelligence and security viewpoint, the CIA would have an interest not merely in having cleared psychiatrists to treat employees but in being alerted by the psychiatrists to any potential or actual security risk. If an employee dealing with sensitive materials tells his psychiatrist that he is meeting a Czech diplomat on his lunch

---

[3]Some psychiatrists refuse to participate in the agency's program. One doctor, who practices in Washington, said he turned down the CIA's request that he join the roster because there was "too much paperwork, a million forms to fill out." Others may not care to subject themselves to the CIA security check, which presumably includes questioning of friends, neighbors, and colleagues about the physician's loyalty and reliability.

hour and passing secrets to him, the agency would undoubtedly like to know about it.

That, of course, gets into an extremely delicate area, in which the requirements of doctor-patient confidentiality and the individual's expectation of privacy clash with the demands of national security. The CIA, as far as can be determined, does not contract with its approved outside psychiatrists to report back on security risks; many doctors, although not all, would refuse to do so.

One psychiatrist who had been cleared by the CIA and treated an agency patient said he was never contacted by Langley or asked to report back on any security risks that the patient might reveal.[4] That does not mean that the psychiatrist could not do so voluntarily, of course.

There are puzzling aspects to the CIA's handling of Howard's psychiatric treatment, however. This was no routine case of a CIA worker under stress who felt the need to talk to someone. In the first place, Howard was an ex-employee, and the agency does not normally pay for mental health care for its former workers.

Secondly, Howard had access at CIA to its most sensitive secrets, the Moscow operation. He had worked at the heart of SE division and was privy to its most guarded information. Finally, he had confessed that he had come within a hairbreadth of transmitting those secrets to the Soviet Union.

Given this set of circumstances, one might expect that the pressures would have been enormous within CIA to try to find out what Howard was telling Dr. Dudelczyk. But that does not appear to have been the case. "No one from the agency came out to see me," Dr. Dudelczyk said. "They asked me to send in a report, which I did."

But the psychiatrist said that the report he sent to Lang-

---

[4]The psychiatrist said he had participated in discussions, unrelated to his agency clearance, about whether a therapist loyal to his country could treat a patient who revealed he was disloyal. He concluded that their political differences would interfere with the treatment. "I would try to persuade a traitor to give himself up," the physician said. Other clinicians insisted that such action was not the proper duty or responsibility of the psychiatrist.

ley was "an evaluation of how Ed was doing." He added, "There was never any request for any information regarding a breach of security or that I report such information if it arose."

Dr. Dudelczyk remembers being surprised that the agency did *not* ask to be alerted if Howard said anything about espionage. "I was surprised at how loose they were about it," he said.

Suppose the CIA had asked Dr. Dudelczyk to alert it to any security problem that Howard might reveal, would he have done so? "If they had asked, that's something everybody decides for himself. If I knew Ed was involved in something threatening national security, I would have felt obligated to report it."

When I asked Howard if he was aware that his psychiatrist had reported back to the agency, Howard looked startled. "I wasn't aware he reported to the agency," he said. "I don't think he did."

Howard's psychiatrist said he did not sign any contract with the CIA. "At one point I received a psychiatric report from the agency that had been done just prior to his dismissal by one of their staff psychiatrists."

The CIA's psychiatric report on Howard dealt mostly with his alcoholism. It did not suggest he was mentally unstable.

The CIA does not pay for psychiatric treatment for a former employee in SE division solely for humanitarian reasons. When Gus Hathaway approved the payments, he and his colleagues in the Soviet division must have felt it would give the agency a string on Howard. For one thing, it would place him under some degree of obligation to remain in touch with the CIA since it was footing the bill.

The agency could hope that the Santa Fe psychiatrist, since he had been cleared, would in fact alert the CIA if Howard said anything of counterintelligence interest. To ask Dr. Dudelczyk to report any security matters might alienate him. He might be reluctant to play the role of a cop if invited to do so. Far better to get him to volunteer as a patriot.

Still, the CIA seemed remarkably unconcerned about

discovering what Howard might reveal to Dr. Dudelczyk. Perhaps the CIA had a genuine respect for Howard's privacy. Or there could be another reason. The CIA has been known to go to considerable lengths to protect its "sources and methods." There is no evidence, however, that the CIA went so far as to bug Howard's sessions with his psychiatrist, although it certainly had the technical capability to do so.

In March 1985, three months after he had started seeing Dr. Dudelczyk, Howard's doorbell rang.

The visitor explained that he was a neighbor who lived just two houses down, on the same side of the street, at 112 Verano Loop.

"My name is Bill Gillespie," he said. "I'd like to talk to you." He smiled at Howard. "I'm with the FBI."

18

Trouble in Moscow

The FBI agent took his time. He didn't work around to questioning Howard right away. Finally, Gillespie revealed what was on his mind.

"It's about Phil Troutman," he said.

Howard breathed easier. They weren't after him.

At the time Phillip E. Troutman, a state investment officer, had been indicted on charges of trying to extort two thousand dollars for the state Democratic party from a New York bank and was awaiting trial.[1] In his legislative work Howard had occasionally dealt with Troutman.

Under the Reagan Justice Department, William L. Lutz, the federal prosecutor in Albuquerque and a Republican, had been exceptionally diligent in rooting out corruption in the Democratic administration of Governor Toney Anaya. Thomas "Bill" Gillespie, as an FBI agent assigned to the state capital, was deeply involved in that effort.[2]

---

[1]Troutman was convicted in May by a federal jury of attempting to extort the two thousand dollars from the Irving Trust Company, which was seeking a contract to manage New Mexico's securities in New York. He was sentenced to two years in prison and fined five thousand dollars.
[2]Gillespie belonged to a group that got together every Sunday to drink and watch the Dallas Cowboys' football games on television. Governor Anaya's secretary, Pat Powell, a member of the group, swore that at one Sunday soiree in her home Gillespie tried but failed to enlist her as an informant against the governor. Asked whether he had told Ms. Powell that he wanted "to nail the governor," Gillespie replied, "I would think that probably we were all having a lot to drink and I can't remember if that was said. I doubt that Pat could either."

Howard answered the FBI agent's questions, and Gillespie thanked him cordially for his cooperation. He had enjoyed the opportunity to meet his neighbor. It was always a pleasure to interview a citizen who was ready and willing to help the FBI.

The same month the Howards celebrated their son's second birthday. An unusual gift arrived for Lee from Moscow. Barbara Mozur, whom Howard had met in Lima, was living in the Soviet capital with her husband, Michael, a career Foreign Service officer who was the first secretary of the American embassy. Mrs. Mozur had picked out a *shapka*, a tiny Russian fur hat, for Lee.

Howard liked the present so well that he wanted a Russian hat for himself. He wrote to Barbara Mozur with his size and asked if she would buy one for him. Howard also asked his friends Kate and Bob Gallegos whether they would like to order hats for Bob and their son, Jason, but they declined the offer.

The Gallegoses lived in El Dorado, a little more than a mile away from the Howards, who considered them their best friends in Santa Fe. The two couples often visited each other or had dinner together. Kate sometimes gave Mary clothes that Jason, who was three years older than Lee, had outgrown.

After Howard fled, the Gallegoses talked freely about him. "They weren't a very happy couple," Robert Gallegos said. "As we got to know Ed more, he was having several affairs with women in the office.[3] He described

[3]Gallegos made these remarks to me during an interview with him and his wife, Kate, at their home, on September 11, 1986. I included his comments in an article I wrote about Howard that was published in *The New York Times Magazine* of November 2, 1986. Since only four women then employed on the staff of the Legislative Finance Committee had worked there when Howard did, they were understandably up in arms at Gallegos's remark. Gallegos subsequently wrote to me denying that he made this statement, but he did. Howard said that "probably the basis for that was one night Bob, Kate, a secretary, and I went dancing after a reception. My wife knows about that. The secretary had to drive me back to my car. Bob kidded me afterward about that a lot of times. What was going on with the secretary when she drove me to my car?"

himself as a ladies' man. Every time he went out of town he'd describe his latest conquests. Mary was aware he played around. One night we were having dinner, and he said, 'I'd like to bring some of my lady friends over.' And Mary said, 'Well, tell us about it, Ed.' And he dropped it. He was four sheets to the wind.''

In fact, Howard's reputation as a womanizer appears to have been vastly exaggerated, part of the myth that accompanied the revelations that he was a spy who had escaped to Moscow. Not only Howard but a whole generation has been raised on James Bond, and the stories of Howard as a seducer of beautiful women may owe more to Sean Connery than to reality.

Howard did, on occasion, talk to David Abbey about going to Juárez to see the donkey show, a live entertainment that features women copulating with donkeys. Howard, in fact, visited El Paso with Abbey in April 1985. But the most he did is walk across the bridge to Juárez to buy souvenirs; there was no visit to the donkey show. Howard also told Abbey of watching X-rated videos with his wife, but if so, he was doing no more than millions of other Americans.

Howard did have an affair when he lived in Barrington and, according to two knowledgeable sources, one other "sporadic" liaison thereafter. Statistically Howard's record of fidelity was not far off the average for married American males.

Mary Howard said she was not aware that her husband had any affairs. "There are sides of a person one doesn't know anything about," she said. "The unhappiness in our marriage was the drinking. He drank too much." She said she did not remember Howard's remark about "lady friends" or the response attributed to her by Gallegos. Had she even heard rumors about other women? "No. Ed was a joker. He joked about a lot of things."

Although the Howards had been to Europe only six months before, that spring they told a few friends that they were planning another trip aboard. "He invited us to go to Germany in April of 1985," Gallegos said. "He also invited our neighbors, Dennis Hazlett and DoAnn Jasper.''

Hazlett, a co-worker and friend of Howard's, confirmed the invitation. Hazlett remembers strolling downtown with Howard on their lunch hour one day shortly before the trip. "Howard went into Shaya's jewelry store with me and picked up a brochure on Rolex watches.''

The Howards did go to Europe, but not to Germany. They went to Vienna. Although Mary Howard talked with me about many aspects of her own life and Howard's, she declined several times to discuss their second trip to Europe in the spring of 1985 or even to acknowledge that it had taken place. Howard confirmed, however, that he and his wife had made the trip in April.

"We went to Zurich and Vienna and flew home. Mary was with me. Her mother doesn't want her to admit she was with me. She feels the less she [Mary] is involved, the better.'' In Zurich, Howard said, "I bought a six-hundred-dollar Rolex.''[4]

In Vienna, Howard said, "we stayed at a small, cheap hotel. I don't recall the name.''

Howard was probably in Zurich and Vienna between April 28 and 30. He had asked for two days off: Monday, April 29, and Tuesday, April 30. By combining his leave with the weekend, he would have had four days. Since it takes a day to get to Europe and a day to return, Howard would have had only two days in Europe.

The trip would seem improvident, even extravagant—considering the brief time available in Switzerland and Austria—for a young couple with a small child living on a modest dual income.[5] Unless, of course, Howard went to Vienna to meet with the Russians.

---

[4]In Switzerland, in 1985, Rolex watches ranged in price from $200 to $21,500, with the most popular models selling for about $5,000. When Howard returned to Santa Fe from Europe, he told very few people he had been abroad. One of those in whom he did confide was Dennis Hazlett, who had accompanied him to the jeweler to get the Rolex brochure and who knew that Howard was planning the trip since he and his wife had been invited along.

[5]Howard was hired by the LFC in June 1983 at a salary of $30,000. He

There is at least some indication that Howard did not acquire the watch until he got to Vienna. Howard showed Hazlett the Rolex. "He told me he'd been to Vienna. He said a friend had helped him get it at a terrific discount." Hazlett formed the impression that Howard had bought the watch in Vienna. Howard did not mention Zurich to him.

Four days after the Howards returned from Vienna, they appeared at a conference at St. John's College in Santa Fe. The topic was "The Enigma of the Soviet People."

In Langley, Virginia, there was another personnel shift. Gus Hathaway moved over from SE division and succeeded David Blee as chief of counterintelligence. It was now Hathaway's responsibility to protect the CIA from Soviet penetrations.

Howard was buying Krugerrands. In May he purchased one of the South African gold coins through an ad in the *Wall Street Journal*. "Ed showed me some Krugerrands at the office and asked me if I had any," Robert Gallegos recalled. "I'm a coin collector. It was a stack of maybe six to eight coins. Each one is an ounce, so they were worth maybe twenty-four hundred dollars."

According to Gallegos, Howard visited the bank a lot. "Every morning around nine o'clock I used to drive from the capitol to the main post office to check my mail," Gallegos said. "Ed would quite a few times ask me to drop him off at the First Interstate Bank. He had a safe-deposit box at the bank. Sometimes he'd say he needed to check some house papers." Since Gallegos did not go inside the bank with Howard, he had no way of knowing whether Howard was putting Krugerrands in his safe-deposit box.

"Mary and I had about eight gold coins altogether,"

would normally have received a 5 percent raise after each year; that meant he was earning $31,500 at the time of his second trip to Europe in April 1985. His salary at the time he fled the country was $33,012. Mary Howard earned about $11,000, according to her husband.

Howard said. "I think three of these were gifts from parents, and the rest I acquired between AID and Santa Fe."

Howard, who was more conservative politically than many of his colleagues realized, not only collected Krugerrands but was opposed to a pull out by U.S. firms from South Africa. Phil Baca, who worked with Howard and had helped select him for the committee staff, remembered how surprised he was to hear Howard's vehement opposition to the divestiture policy recommended by New Mexico's Democratic governor. Howard did not defend South Africa's apartheid racial policies, but he considered it folly for U.S. companies to leave that country.

"Several times he commented how crazy we were," Baca said. "If everyone divested, it could lead to economic downfall in South Africa, and we had no guarantee that a new government would be friendly to the West. A Communist-bloc government might result. He was really uptight about that." Baca paused and shook his head, remembering Howard's defection to the Soviet Union. "It doesn't fit."

In June Curtis Porter left as staff director of the committee and went off to Las Cruces to work on his Ph.D. at New Mexico State University. Baca succeeded him, becoming Howard's new boss.

Baca, then approaching fifty, liked the young staff economist from Washington and his quiet wife. "He wasn't a clock watcher," he said of Howard. "What there was to do, he did."

To Baca, Howard was a pleasant, typical young staff member. As for reports of office romances, Baca said, "That was news to me. If he had marital problems, he never brought them to the office. He was always talking about his little boy. We'd talk about where to go camping."

Although Howard worked hard, he liked practical jokes, Baca recalled. "I remember one incident where he said, 'Watch me shake up the boys upstairs.' He wrote a fake AP bulletin on his computer: 'The bottom dropped out of the oil market today.' He said he would take it upstairs to Abbey."

But Baca was astonished when Porter took him aside during the handover and said, "There's something you need to know. His résumé says State Department. He told me he actually worked for the CIA."[6]

If Howard seemed normal enough to his co-workers, friends occasionally glimpsed other aspects of his personality. Robert Gallegos in a television interview said, "He used to love to bring in catalogs, for example, *Soldier of Fortune* magazine, with different weapons and protective techniques. 'Look at this, isn't this great?' 'Oh, yeah, Ed, that's wonderful.' One day he came in and showed me that he was a registered gun dealer. He had some very unusual weapons, things that you see in the movies that have very long barrels."

Once Howard poured a glass of water for Gallegos and dropped a piece of paper into it. The paper disappeared instantly. Howard told Gallegos that a friend of his in the State Department had sent him the dissolving paper.

And there were the hats from Moscow. Around the same time that Baca succeeded Curtis Porter, the fur hat that Howard had asked Barbara Mozur to send to him arrived in the mail from the Soviet Union. It was a type of headgear not often seen in Santa Fe.

On June 13 Howard was in Washington for the National Conference of State Legislators. His colleague Dennis Hazlett was there and remembers Howard's taking him around Washington the next day to the Smithsonian Institution and a string of bars. Howard, he said, "was a terrific tour guide."

By then Hazlett had heard that his friend was a former CIA man; after the shooting incident rumors had circulated that Howard got off because he had worked for the agency. "One of the places we went to was a CIA hangout in northern Virginia," Hazlett said. "It was called the Vienna Inn. There were pictures on the walls of guys wad-

---

[6]There were other parts of Howard's past that remained hidden. Baca, who comes from a Hispanic family that traces its roots back three hundred years, was amazed when I told him that Howard's mother was also Hispanic, also from New Mexico. "Ed never mentioned it," he said.

ing through the swamps with rifles over their heads. There were autographed pictures of CIA agents on the walls.'' He remembered ''a lot of strange characters hanging around, and there must have been ten calls that came in on the pay phone.'' Hazlett, bug-eyed, regarded the Vienna Inn as the high point of his trip. He had actually been in a CIA bar.[7]

The same day in Moscow the KGB caught Skip Stombaugh.

Paul M. Stombaugh, Jr., was a CIA officer assigned to the Moscow station. He was a street agent who had taken over some of the assets that Edward Howard would have handled had he been sent to the Soviet Union.

Stombaugh, then thirty-three, had grown up in St. Louis and Washington, where his father was a forensic expert for the FBI. A dark-haired, athletic youth, he went to Clemson on a football scholarship but later transferred to the University of Maryland in his hometown of College Park. He joined the FBI laboratory, then became a special agent. In 1977, when the bureau proposed to transfer him back to the lab, he resigned and joined the CIA.

At the agency Stombaugh vanished into the Clandestine Services. In August 1984 he was sent to Moscow by SE division, his first overseas assignment. He was under diplomatic cover as second secretary of the embassy.

Burt Gerber, the division chief, must have felt the Howard slot was jinxed because in January Stombaugh did something that was, many months later, to cause a great deal of difficulty for reporter Nicholas Daniloff and the Reagan administration. The CIA man's inexplicable action

---

[7]Hazlett was in Washington in October 1986 and visited the bar again. He was surprised to find all the pictures gone. ''The proprietor said the CIA had asked him to take them down. But it was ridiculous, because people could still look at them; he had them all in a scrapbook.'' Mike Abraham, owner of the Vienna Inn, a venerable saloon favored by the CIA for decades, said he had asked if he couldn't just take down the covert pictures, but the agency said no; it was best if he did not know which of the individuals in the photos were covert operatives. Abraham complied. ''We still have a lot of them coming in here,'' he said. ''We don't even ask where they work anymore.''

may have helped to bring about the Daniloff affair, the incident that nearly derailed the Reykjavik summit meeting between President Reagan and Soviet leader Mikhail Gorbachev in October 1986.

In January 1985 Daniloff, a Moscow correspondent for the magazine *U.S. News & World Report,* found a letter in his mailbox from a Soviet acquaintance whom he knew as Father Roman, supposedly a dissident Russian Orthodox priest. When he opened it, he found inside another envelope addressed to the U.S. ambassador. Daniloff gave the envelope to the American embassy. It contained yet another letter, addressed to CIA Director William Casey. Later, in the secure bubble inside the embassy, Daniloff gave the CIA the priest's phone number.

Incredibly Stombaugh both telephoned and wrote to "Father Roman," informing him that the "journalist" to whom he had passed the letters had given them to the embassy. Although he avoided mentioning the correspondent by name, it was enough to put Daniloff in the soup. More than a year and a half later, in August 1986, Daniloff was arrested by the KGB and charged with espionage, in a move clearly designed to counter the FBI's arrest for espionage in New York of Gennadi F. Zakharov, a Soviet intelligence agent working as a United Nations scientific officer.

"Father Roman" turned out to be a KGB plant, so Skip Stombaugh's error in tradecraft—mentioning a "journalist"—had compromised Daniloff. President Reagan and the CIA knew that if Daniloff was placed on trial, Stombaugh's actions would make it look as though somehow the reporter had been involved with the CIA, lending some credence, however slight, to the trumphed-up spy charges against the correspondent. The United States would lose face in the battle for world opinion.

Very little was said publicly about Stombaugh's handling of the "Father Roman" letter, but it was there in the wings, just offstage, as the superpowers maneuvered over the Daniloff-Zakharov cases and the coming summit meeting. Finally, on September 29, Daniloff was freed, and the next day Zakharov, after pleading no contest, was sent home in a trade that Reagan denied was a trade.[8]

On June 14, 1985, six months after Daniloff had passed the letters to the American embassy, TASS, the Soviet news agency, announced that Stombaugh had been detained in Moscow. The Russians later indicated he had been meeting an asset. The story appeared in the Washington *Post* the next day, when Howard was in Washington. It quoted the brief TASS announcement saying that Stombaugh had been caught ''in the act of committing an espionage action.'' He had been declared persona non grata and was being expelled from the Soviet Union.

Howard must have read the news account with more than passing interest. One of his successors in the Moscow station had been nabbed.

In their announcement the Soviets carefully avoided any reference to the person Stombaugh might have been meeting at the time of his detention. But the KGB had arrested a Soviet citizen at the scene. He was charged with espionage for attempting to pass materials to the CIA man.

It was three months before Moscow disclosed the name of the Soviet citizen, in another brief announcement. He was a defense researcher, a leading expert on stealth aircraft technology.

His name was Adolf G. Tolkachev.

Ed Howard's asset.

---

[8]Dissident Yuri Orlov and his wife, Irina, were allowed to leave the Soviet Union as part of the deal.

19

"I Did It"

South Padre Island is a beach resort in the Gulf of Mexico at the southernmost tip of Texas, part of a chain of barrier islands in an arc that runs from Galveston three hundred miles southwest to the Mexican border.

A thirty-four-mile strip at the end of the chain, South Padre is a place of high-rise hotels and condominiums that prides itself as the Miami Beach of the Southwest. By the summer of 1985 Bill Bosch was living there and working on the mainland in the job that Howard had arranged with the businessman in nearby Brownsville, Texas.

On the July Fourth weekend, Mary Howard had cousins coming to Santa Fe from California. Howard decided to bail out; it would be a good weekend to visit his friend Bill Bosch. They could drink a little beer, lie on the beach, and watch the girls go by.

Howard flew to Harlingen, Texas, where Bosch met him at the airport. Howard stayed with Bosch for the holiday weekend at his condo on the beach. Bosch had clearly prospered since the previous October, when he had been drawing unemployment and living with his mother in Westbury. He had his own place on South Padre Island and was tooling around in a black 911 Porsche.

Bosch complained a lot to Howard about his job, but Howard urged him to stick with it. They talked as well about the CIA. The agency, Bosch grumbled, still had his retirement funds frozen.

Although South Padre Island is only ten miles from the Mexican border, Howard said there was no more discussion that weekend of going to the Soviet embassy in Mexico City.[1] But Howard's proposal in New Orleans had not been forgotten by either man.

The first night of Howard's visit the two friends had drinks together at the condo. It was clear to Bosch from the way Howard was talking that he still harbored a deep anger toward the agency. Howard was drinking heavily.

Then he said something that made Bosch's blood run cold.

"Ed shook me by the shoulders and said, 'I did it. You think you're playing hardball. I'm *really* playing hardball. What do you want—five, ten, fifteen thousand dollars?' "

Bosch was aghast.

"I said, 'Ed, what the fuck are you telling me?' I was scared. I was white as a sheet. I asked him, 'What are you talking about, Ed?' He said, 'Nothing.' He dropped the subject, said he was joking around."

The next day Bosch brought the matter up again, trying to draw Howard out, but all he would say was "Forget it."

In New Orleans Howard had confessed to hanging around the Soviet consulate, wanting to go in and sell secrets to the Russians. He had proposed they visit the Soviets in Mexico City. Against that background Bosch feared that Howard's statement—"I did it"—and his offer of substantial sums of money meant that Howard had crossed the line from fantasy to action and was a spy for Moscow. With dismay Bosch must have remembered all the information he had exchanged with Howard on the long drive from New Orleans to Santa Fe the year before.

In an affidavit filed in federal court in Albuquerque on October 2, 1985, ten days after Edward Lee Howard fled the country, the FBI said that Bosch, who is identified as a "confidential source," informed the bureau that in July 1985 Howard told him he "had met in Europe with the

---

[1]As it turned out, Howard and Bosch did go to Mexico, however briefly, that weekend. "On July Fourth weekend," Howard said, "Bill and I went to dinner in Matamoros, across the border from Brownsville, with a couple of his sister's friends."

Soviets, gave them information, and had received cash"
and that "the Soviets have paid for his trip to Europe in
1984 and Howard met his KGB contact while in Europe."[2]

Bosch now denies that he made these statements to the
FBI. According to Bosch, Howard offered no specifics
about any espionage activities. Bosch said Howard did not,
for example, talk about his travels in Austria in September
of 1984 or his trip to Vienna in April.

Howard, he said, "did not tell me and did not say he
gave the Soviets secrets." Nor did Howard admit, Bosch
said, that he was paid money, or that the Soviets paid for
his trip to Europe, or that he met with his Soviet case
officer in Europe. Bosch claims that Howard never said
anything about a Soviet case officer. "And that's what I
told the FBI," Bosch said.

Bosch agreed, however, that the FBI could have concluded from Howard's "I did it" statement, and offer of
money, that Howard had met with the Soviets and been
paid for CIA secrets. It would be a "fair inference," Bosch
said. But he insisted he had not provided the FBI with the
specifics about Howard's meeting with the Soviets in Europe.[3]

In Budapest Howard gave a different version of his conversation with Bosch. "On South Padre Island," Howard
said, "I got three bottles of expensive wine, and he
[Bosch] was giving me a hard time about how I could
afford the wine. He said, 'Where did you get this money?'
I got very sarcastic. 'My Soviet case officer gives it to
me.' It was a joke. He's all over me; he takes it seriously.
He says who, what, where, when? I looked at him like
he's an asshole. And I forgot about it. I never tried to
recruit the man."

---

[2]There is absolutely no question that Bosch is the "confidential source"
cited in the affidavit, which is signed by Martin R. Schwarz, an FBI
agent assigned to the Albuquerque division. The affidavit is based upon
extensive FBI interrogation of Bosch on South Padre Island in the days
just before Howard escaped.
[3]The FBI said its affidavit is accurate. It is, therefore, not possible to
resolve the conflict between the FBI account of what Bosch admitted,
as given in the FBI affidavit, and his later statements to the author.

However, Bosch told the FBI that at some point during their conversation on South Padre Island, Howard asked him, "Do you want to work for me?"

"I never said anything to Bill Bosch about a meeting in Austria," Howard said. "I never received any money from the Soviets before I left the country."

Although Bosch and Howard do not agree on precisely what was said on South Padre Island on the July Fourth weekend, the 209th anniversary of American independence, Bosch came away from their encounter a frightened man.

Bosch claimed he had warned the CIA through Peter Ringland after the New Orleans meeting, but he kept his silence after South Padre Island. He must have been worried about his own position. Espionage can mean a life sentence. The thing with Ed Howard was getting too hairy.

Asked why he said nothing to anyone about Howard's statements on South Padre Island, Bosch replied that he felt he had already done all he could; the agency must be on top of it by now.

Howard returned to Santa Fe. On Saturday, July 27, Kate and Bob Gallegos went to the Howards' home for dinner. "He had two fur hats, one for him and one for Lee," Robert Gallegos said. "They were in a box with Russian writing. He said he had asked a friend in the State Department to send them to him."

It was late in the afternoon, Gallegos said, and Howard and his young son modeled the fur hats for their guests. Gallegos said he had an indelible memory of Howard standing inside the house, "wearing gym shorts and a fur hat, smoking a cigar, and drinking a St. Pauli Girl."

Howard did not know it, but time was running out for him. Five days later Vitaly Yurchenko vanished in Rome.

Flown to Andrews by the CIA, whisked to the safe house in Virginia, and debriefed over the weekend, he named "Robert" as the CIA mole who had met with senior KGB officials in Austria in September 1984.

The volcano was erupting. The Howard scandal could no longer be contained within the quiet corridors of power at Langley. Gus Hathaway had done his best, but it was too late. The CIA had no choice.

Four FBI agents were sitting right there in the safe house, listening to Yurchenko, when he revealed the existence of the CIA mole. The game was over.

Now the FBI knew.

20

Parker's Case

The case could not have come at a worse time for James H. Geer. Monday, August 5, 1985, was his first day on the job as assistant director of the FBI in charge of the intelligence division.

A six-foot, solidly built man with reddish hair and fair skin, Geer had the weathered face of the good sheriff in a movie western. He spoke with the measured drawl of his native Tennessee. On this morning he was two weeks short of his forty-sixth birthday.

After twenty-one years in the bureau he had finally risen to assistant director of one of the two most prestigious divisions in the bureau. As head of Division 5, the intelligence division, it was Geer's job to catch spies.

Ed O'Malley had retired on Friday as head of the intelligence division—they had given him the luncheon out at CIA the day before, on Thursday, August 1—and Geer had moved from director of the FBI lab to the spy catcher job.

He knew he was stepping into a very different world, a maze of deception. On the wall of his large office, room 4012, on the fourth floor of the J. Edgar Hoover Building, was a framed quotation from Eric Ambler: "I think if I were asked to single out one specific group of men, one category, as being the most suspicious, unbelieving, unreasonable, petty, inhuman, sadistic double-crossing set of bastards in any language, I would say without hesitation: 'the people who run counter-espionage departments.' "[1]

Geer hardly had time to enjoy his spacious new surroundings when his deputy, Phil Parker, asked to see him. The two men had adjacent offices, separated by a reception area that housed their secretaries. In a few moments Parker breezed in. A tall, handsome man, with thinning blond hair and a bushy, handlebar mustache that gave him a somewhat Victorian look, Parker did not fit the stereotype of an FBI agent. He dressed elegantly, spoke Russian and Spanish, and kept a thirty-foot cabin cruiser, the *Alexandra,* at his home in Norfolk, Virginia.

The mustache, in particular, was the source of much comment among his colleagues. It made him look rather like a villainous landlord or perhaps a bartender in New York's Tenderloin district at the turn of the century. FBI agents are not supposed to have flamboyant mustaches that twirl at the ends. Moreover, Parker had not learned to keep his head down in the bureaucracy. He was outspoken, and not always tactful, in dealing with FBI director William Webster, perhaps one reason why Geer had the division now and Parker did not.

But Parker had spent most of his twenty years with the FBI in counterintelligence. He knew the spy-catching game, from street agent to the executive suite. Parker was accompanied into Geer's office by Rodney Leffler, the acting chief of the Soviet section, a taciturn man with slick black hair who was born on a farm in Hayes County, Nebraska, and Lane Crocker, a red-haired, square-jawed all-American type who was the unit chief in the Soviet section.

"The agency has a problem," Parker said. "His name is Robert."

Quickly Parker filled Geer in on the sketchy details then available. Vitaly Yurchenko, his debriefing begun by the CIA over the weekend, had identified two penetrations of American intelligence, the ex-NSA man and "Robert," a former CIA employee who had been slated to go to Mos-

---

[1]The quotation is from Ambler's book *The Light of Day.*

cow and then was pulled off the assignment. The KGB, Yurchenko said, had met "Robert" in Austria in the fall of 1984.

Two Russian-speaking FBI agents from WFO, the bureau's Washington field office, were out at CIA headquarters now, trying to help the agency narrow down the field of suspects who might be "Robert."

Geer, although it was his first day as director of the division, was not a complete stranger to counterintelligence. He had been an administrator in the division in years past, and in the jargon of the bureau, he had "worked the Yugos" as a street agent in WFO.[2]

Those days were over. As head of intelligence Geer had the task of administering the division, not of running cases. That job belonged to Parker as the deputy assistant director for operations (DAD).

Once the agency had identified "Robert," Parker's task would be to locate the former CIA man and follow up on Yurchenko's lead. If enough evidence was developed, the FBI would catch a Russian spy.

Geer knew that Parker would, if anyone could. Now that Ed O'Malley was gone, he was the most experienced counterespionage agent in the FBI. Even before Geer had been promoted above him, Parker had decided to retire when he turned fifty the next spring. The business of hunting spies was fun, but there was tremendous pressure and long hours. It was not a nine-to-five job, and his family had sacrificed enough. He wanted to spend more time with them. And there were bluefish waiting for him in the Chesapeake.

All that was off in the spring, however. In the meantime, he must uncover the NSA mole, and above all, nail "Robert." If there was a CIA man selling out the Moscow operation to the Soviets, Parker wanted him.

He could imagine how much Gus Hathaway wanted him,

---

[2]FBI agents in the Washington field office, rather than in headquarters, are assigned the task of keeping Soviet and other Communist-bloc intelligence officers under surveillance in the capital. Geer had specialized in Yugoslavians.

too. The agency's counterintelligence chief had always worked closely and amicably with the bureau on CI cases. Gus must be frantic at this very moment, Parker thought, trying desperately to figure out who Robert was.

Soon the man's identity would be established by the CIA, and the bureau would get him. Parker had the credentials and the experience. He had been born in Chesapeake, Virginia, across the Elizabeth River from the house in Norfolk that he had just bought two months earlier, in June, in anticipation of his retirement. His father had been a radio operator on merchant ships, and his mother worked as a printer. Parker enrolled in the Virginia Polytechnic Institute as an engineering student but ran out of money and flunked freshman chemistry at about the same time. He decided to join the Air Force as an enlisted man in 1955 and was sent to Syracuse to study Russian.

The Air Force then sent Parker in an intelligence job to England, where he met his future wife, Gillian, an Englishwoman from Bedford. After returning to the States, Parker got married and went back to college. He earned a bachelor's degree in secondary education and Spanish at Old Dominion University and a master's degree in Russian at Indiana University. He also traveled to the Soviet Union, visiting Moscow, Baku, Tbilisi, Sochi, Sukhumi, Kiev, and Leningrad.

Parker came home and taught Spanish and Russian at Virginia Beach High School. His contract also required him to coach junior varsity football. At age twenty-nine, Parker liked teaching, but he was trying to support his now-growing family on fifty-five hundred dollars a year. "It wasn't too great," he said, "so I applied for a job at the bureau."

The year was 1965. The FBI sent him to language school in Monterey to learn Bulgarian. In 1967 he was assigned to the Washington field office, where he acquired the basics of counterintelligence and trailed Bulgarians around the capital. Then Parker was moved into a special squad, now known as CI-3, which tracked Soviet GRU (military intelligence) agents and handled Polish and East German cases as well.

By 1973 Parker was head of the squad, and three years later he transferred into the intelligence division at headquarters. Six years after that he was promoted to unit chief in charge of surveillance of all Soviet installations throughout the United States. By 1982 Parker was chief of the Soviet section, and the following year he was named number two man in the division under O'Malley. In sum, by the time Vitaly Yurchenko warned of "Robert," Parker had been matching wits with Soviet intelligence for eighteen years.

He could do nothing, however, until the CIA identified "Robert." And all day Monday, August 5, no word came from the agency. They were checking their files. As soon as they knew anything, Parker would hear.

Yet Yurchenko, on Friday, had already provided the essential clues to "Robert."

"Vitaly told us he was a former agency type," Parker said. "He knew that 'Robert' was being prepared for Moscow but never went."

Gus Hathaway, chief of the CI staff, and Burt Gerber, chief of SE division at the CIA, must, with a sinking feeling, have known instantly whom Yurchenko had fingered. Dr. Dudelczyk could not help them now. The game was up.

In retrospect, the FBI wondered why there had been a delay. The CIA could have immediately identified "Robert" to the bureau.

The answer is that some sort of charade was going on at Langley. To admit to the FBI that it knew exactly and instantly whom Yurchenko was talking about would put the agency in a most awkward position. It would be tantamount to admitting that the CIA had known all along that the ex-CIA officer in question was a serious security risk. But in that case how could the CIA explain to the FBI why it had never said anything about the case?

Like most FBI men, Parker was reluctant to criticize his colleagues in the agency. But the truth was obvious.

"I daresay the moment the news came in [from Yurchenko] they knew exactly who it was," Parker said.

Norman A. Zigrossi was head of the FBI's Washington

field office at the time. He later retired and became inspector general of the TVA in Knoxville. It was his Russian-speaking agents who were out at CIA headquarters attempting to assist the agency in identifying "Robert." The FBI agents were unwitting props in the CIA's charade. Asked about the delay by the CIA in identifying "Robert," Zigrossi replied, "They should have known right away, yes."

As it turned out, the delay was crucial.

In Santa Fe Howard told his boss, Phil Baca, that his grandmother was seriously ill. "He was going to visit her," Baca said. "Then he told me that she had died and he needed to go two days earlier."[3]

On Tuesday, August 6, while Parker was still waiting for the CIA to identify the mole, Howard, alone, flew to Zurich and then to Vienna.

In Vienna he checked into the im Palais Schwarzenberg, an elegant hotel in a beautiful baroque palace, with a garden, just off the Ringstrasse.

It was Wednesday, as Parker remembers it, before the CIA finally told him it had, through painstaking analysis of its files, identified "Robert."

The officer, the CIA said solemnly, was undoubtedly one Edward Lee Howard.

By that time, Parker later concluded, Howard was on his way to meet with his Soviet control in Vienna. The FBI did not realize until months later that Howard had slipped off to Vienna the day after the bureau got the case and at the very moment it was waiting for the CIA to identify the mole.

Why had it taken the CIA five days to come up with Howard's name? "Maybe it took that long to figure out how the hell they were going to tell us," Parker said.[4]

---

[3] Howard's maternal grandmother had died in November 1982 in Reserve, New Mexico. His other grandmother, although elderly, was alive and well and living in Michigan.

[4] There is no indication that any male SE officer but Howard had been prepared for Moscow and then did not go. In fairness to the CIA, could

Once the FBI had a name, it ran a file check and discovered that Edward Lee Howard had been interviewed by
the FBI only five months before in a white-collar crime
investigation. Bill Gillespie, Parker learned, had called on
Howard at his home in Santa Fe in connection with the
Phil Troutman case.

Parker assigned Rod Leffler, the assistant chief of the
Soviet section, and Lane Crocker, the Soviet unit chief,
to try to gather the evidence against Howard that would
stand up in court; below them, a supervising agent at
headquarters would coordinate with the field. Headquarters alerted William D. Branon, head of the FBI's Albuquerque division, that a major counterintelligence case was
brewing on his turf.

As it happened, like Jim Geer, Branon, a tall, sandy-
haired Irishman partial to suspenders and shirtsleeves, had
just taken over in Albuquerque. He had worked in Norfolk, Richmond, and in an executive post at headquarters
before he got the division. From the two-story sand-
colored FBI building on Grand Avenue, in the downtown
section, Branon was responsible for the entire state. It
wasn't like his native Vermont; New Mexico is flat and
huge, and Branon did not like to fly. As a result, he spent
a lot of time driving to cover the territory.[5]

Branon was concerned about manpower to handle the
case. He had fifty-three agents in New Mexico, including
four in Santa Fe, but there were other, ongoing cases to
handle. Headquarters assured him that additional forces
would be deployed in New Mexico to help draw the net
tight around Edward Howard.

While these arrangements were being made, FBI agents

---

it really have been using the five days to eliminate other possibilities?
"If they had other guys who fit the description," Parker said, "that's
scary."

[5]In FBI parlance, the territory covered within a state is known as a
division. In addition, there are resident agencies, smaller offices around
the state. In New Mexico, for example, the FBI has half a dozen resident agencies, including one in Santa Fe, where Howard lived. In more
populous states, such as Texas, the territory is split, and there is more
than one division within the state.

checked to make sure that Howard still lived in El Dorado and worked in the state capitol. They learned that Howard did, but was out of town that week. Perhaps in San Antonio, his office thought.

Much later Parker learned that Howard had not been in San Antonio that first week in August but had left the country. Initially, when this was learned, the FBI believed Howard had skipped to Mexico. No one yet knew that he had gone to Vienna. When Parker learned the truth, he said, "I thought he had been given some sort of a signal for a meeting. It looked like an emergency meeting with his handlers."

Parker and other counterintelligence officials reasoned that when Yurchenko disappeared on August 1, the KGB had to assume the worst: that he had defected. Howard may then have been given an immediate signal to come to Vienna, where he would have been warned he was in danger.

Howard's haste in leaving for Vienna, and his false excuse for taking the week off, would fit this scenario. Originally Howard told Phil Baca that he would have to visit his ailing grandmother on Thursday, August 8. Then he informed Baca that because of her untimely death, he would have to leave two days earlier, on Tuesday, August 6. Baca, a humane and gentle man, said he, of course, understood and gave Howard permission to leave.

Espionage is an invisible crime. Unless the criminal is caught in the act of meeting with agents of a foreign power, or chooses to confess, espionage is extremely difficult to prove. There are seldom any witnesses and rarely any evidence lying around.

Parker and Geer knew they could not arrest Howard on the basis of Yurchenko's statements alone. "Yurchenko never saw him," Geer said. "He had no physical description. He didn't know him by name. It was a circumstantial case. You have to have much more than one man's word."

Parker needed corroboration in order to meet the legal standard of "probable cause" necessary to obtain a warrant for Howard's arrest. In the jargon of the bureau, he did not have his PC.

"Some editorials later suggested we should have just scooped him up," Parker said. "We couldn't do that. Until we have a warrant in hand from a duly authorized magistrate or judge, we aren't going to yank anyone off the street."

Howard would have to be watched discreetly, and his telephone tapped. By placing Howard under both physical and technical surveillance, Parker and his team in Division 5 hoped that he might make an incriminating move, allowing the FBI to close in and arrest him. The hope, in short, was that Howard himself might provide the probable cause.

The five days that went by before the CIA identified "Robert" to the FBI as Edward Lee Howard were extremely costly. If Howard met the Russians in Vienna and had been under surveillance, the government would have had the evidence it needed to move in and make an arrest. As it was, he left New Mexico before the FBI knew his name. The lapse may have cost the government its one chance to catch him.

Even when the FBI had Howard's name, however, it did not move as swiftly and efficiently as it might have to find out precisely where he was. The FBI simply did not know he was in Vienna or even that he was out of the country. On the other hand, at this early stage, the bureau did not want to make a lot of obvious inquiries about Howard in Santa Fe; the last thing it wanted the ex-CIA man to know was that the FBI was going around asking questions about him.

Within a week the bureau had begun quietly moving extra agents into New Mexico from other offices around the country. In time Parker deployed two dozen agents to supplement the more than fifty already in place under Branon. Even in a major spy case the wheels of bureaucracy grind slowly; Division 5 had to work with Division 3, the FBI's administrative arm, to wangle a bloc sum for travel and hotel costs.

As soon as Parker got Howard's name from the CIA, he set in motion procedures to wiretap the Howards' home telephone at 108 Verano Loop. The FBI does not like to speak of "taps" and "bugs"; it prefers to call a tap a "tesur," bureau argot for a telephone surveillance, and a bug a "misur," or a microphone surveillance.[6]

The days of J. Edgar Hoover, when the FBI could drop in bugs or tap telephone wires at will, are past. Since 1978, under the Foreign Intelligence Surveillance Act (FISA), wiretaps or bugs for national security purposes must be approved by a seven-member wiretap court.

The court itself is so shadowy that it is not listed in the telephone book or government directories. It has no regular courtroom but meets on the guarded sixth floor of the Justice Department in a room periodically swept for electronic bugs.

Parker ordered the FISA package, the paperwork for the wiretap request, typed up and sent across the street to Mary C. Lawton, the Justice Department attorney who handles electronic eavesdropping requests to the secret court. Lawton, in turn, submitted the papers to the wiretap judges.

In Santa Fe William Branon assigned his deputy, Rodney K. McHargue, to ride herd on the Howard case. McHargue, lean, six feet two, intense, with flecks of gray in his brown hair, was the ASAC,[7] the assistant special agent in charge of the Albuquerque division. Branon already had four men regularly assigned to Santa Fe, including Don Jochem, the resident agent, Howard's neighbor Bill Gillespie, and David T. Bibb.

Branon also decided he would need the services of Gerald B. Brown and assigned him as the case agent. Jerry Brown was a sound man. An inconspicuous electronics expert of medium build, with graying dark hair and rimless glasses, he had the reputation of being one of the bureau's most tenacious wiretappers. Brown would supervise the technical details of tapping the Howards' telephone in their desert home.

While the FBI sound man was studying the niceties of getting the tap into Verano Loop, Howard was making his

---

[6]The words are pronounced "teshur" and "myshur."
[7]Pronounced "a-sack."

third trip to Europe in less than a year. He did not, he said, go directly to Vienna, but spent two days first in Zurich, on August 7 and 8.

Since Howard's grandmother was neither dead nor in Switzerland, why was he in Zurich? "To sell huacos," he said. "Huacos are antiques buried in the ground, bowls and pots from the eleventh and twelfth centuries that the Incas used for food. In Peru I collected a lot of huacos. You buy them for a hundred dollars and sell them for two thousand dollars. There is some scandal connected with them because diplomats sneak them out in the pouch. You're not supposed to take them out. We had ten or twelve. We shipped them with our household goods when we left Peru."

We were sitting on a park bench under a shade tree on the Margit-sziget when Howard spun his tale about the Peruvian pots. "The Germans and Swiss," Howard went on, "are nuts about huacos. I saw a store in Zurich when we were there in April that had huacos, and I said, 'I'm gonna go back there.' I hadn't considered selling them, but after the trip in April I saw the prices. I sold six huacos for ten thousand Swiss francs [$4,363 at the exchange rate in August 1985]. I was trying to avoid IRS, having to pay taxes on the money."[8]

On Friday, August 9, Howard said he flew to Vienna and checked into the im Palais Schwarzenberg. "We fell in love with the town in April," he said. "That [August] weekend in Vienna, I went to a carnival, a museum, just kinda goofed off."

I told Howard that I was frankly skeptical of his huaco

---

[8]He was not sure of the name of the antique shop in Zurich, Howard said, but it was located in the old town near the water. He thought it might have been called Mermos. The 1985 Zurich telephone directory lists no such dealer. At the time, as far as could be determined, only one firm in Zurich dealt in pre-Columbian antiquities, the Merrin Gallery. It was on the Todistrasse, not far from the Zürichsee. However, Edward Merrin, whose New York gallery had operated the branch in Zurich, said, "I never heard of Howard. He did not sell anything to me."

story and regarded the timing of the trip to Vienna as significant. We had this exchange:

> Q. Yurchenko had come out only about a week earlier. Didn't you go to Vienna to get your escape plan from the Soviets?
> A. No, there was no escape plan. I didn't know Yurchenko had come out. I was never told that by the Soviets.

Howard again insisted, as he did throughout our conversations, that he had not been in contact with the Russians before escaping from Santa Fe a month later. After spending the weekend in Vienna, he said, he flew back to the United States, arriving home on Monday, August 12, with the ten thousand Swiss francs in cash.

Why did he return? If, as Phillip Parker believes, Howard was meeting with his Soviet control in Vienna and was warned that he was in serious danger because of Yurchenko's defection, why did he come back?

A former CIA man who has detailed knowledge of the Howard affair offered one explanation. "When he went to Vienna, the Soviets told him he was in trouble and set up his escape route. Then he returns to the U.S. To arrange his insurance, take care of his family. He came back for their sake."

The former spy offered an even more Byzantine motive: "If you're a Yurchenko conspiracy theorist, that's another reason for Howard to have come back, so as not to blow Yurchenko's cover as a plant. Because if Howard ran, it would mean the Soviets *knew* he would reveal his identity, and how could they know that?"[9]

---

[9]The theory that Howard came back to protect Yurchenko is unconvincing. If Yurchenko was a real defector, the Soviets would have to assume that as the KGB official in charge of operations in North America he would know about "Robert" and would reveal him to the CIA. James Geer, the chief of FBI counterintelligence, and Phillip Parker, his former deputy, as well as most CIA counterintelligence experts, believe, on balance, that Vitaly Yurchenko was a genuine defector. No one is entirely sure, however.

Even after Howard's return his phone had not yet been tapped. "Howard was in Vienna while the FISA request was languishing in the Department of Justice," the former CIA man said. "Mary Lawton didn't push it, and neither did the FBI. No one knew how serious this was."

Mary Lawton, the Justice Department attorney who handles wiretap requests, said, "There was a legal reason for the delay, but I can't go into it."[10]

Howard took a day off after his return from Vienna but was back in his office in the state capitol on Wednesday. Phil Baca remembers asking him solicitously about the last rites for his grandmother. Although a sad occasion, had the trip gone all right?

Howard said it had. Howard indicated that he had been in Michigan, which is where his father's mother had lived. "He told me he drove back to Dallas with his father," Baca said, "from wherever the funeral was."

---

[10]Lawton, the Justice Department's counsel for intelligence policy, said that for any FISA request, "the head of the agency requesting the tap and the attorney general must sign, and then you can go to the court. In the nature of bureaucracy you're talking time." It can be done in twenty-four hours, if necessary, she said, "but that would be an emergency, very rare. The norm from initial proposal to court approval is probably three weeks." That is about the length of time it took to get the wiretap in place on Verano Loop.

21

The Debriefing

In Erice, Sicily, on August 20, the fifth international symposium on nuclear war opened without the participation of the Soviet delegation. The twelve invited scientists from Moscow did not show up.

A Reuters dispatch quoted Italian Foreign Minister Giulio Andreotti as saying their absence might be linked to the disappearance in Rome, three weeks earlier, of a Soviet diplomat, Vitaly Yurchenko, whose whereabouts were still unknown.

Renato Scrimaglio, a member of the organizing committee of the symposium, said the disappearance in Madrid the previous spring of Soviet scientist Vladimir Alexandrov, who had attended the Sicily meeting the previous year, might also be a factor in the absence of the Soviet delegation.

Several U.S. scientists, including physicist Robert Budwine of the Lawrence Livermore National Laboratory, who was working on "Star Wars," expressed disappointment at the Soviet absence. "The atmosphere certainly would have been different, and the give-and-take would have been interesting if they had come," he said.

Edward Teller, the father of the hydrogen bomb and a delegate to the conference, also issued a statement. He said that a nuclear war would not mean the end of mankind.

At the safe house in Coventry, near Fredericksburg, Virginia, Yurchenko was providing enough information to keep the CIA's counterintelligence staff and the Soviet division working overtime.

Burt Gerber's debriefers, Hathaway's CI staff, and the FBI intelligence division had more than the NSA mole, who was still unidentified, and Edward Lee Howard to deal with.

Yurchenko also warned the CIA that Oleg A. Gordievski, the KGB resident in London, was in mortal danger. He had quite recently come under suspicion by the KGB and was at the moment back in Moscow. If you are working Gordievski, Yurchenko warned, get him out.

In fact, the KGB's suspicions were well founded. Gordievski had been an agent in place for the West for almost twenty years, beginning in 1966, when he was posted to Copenhagen with the title of press attaché. Gordievski began working with MI6, the British secret service, and the Danes as well.

In 1982 he was sent to London as embassy counselor, and MI6 took over the exclusive handling of what may have been the British service's most important Soviet asset. To the delight of MI6, Gordievski was promoted to chief of the KGB residency in London in 1985.

That spring he went to Moscow briefly, then returned to London. Later in the summer, however, he was called back to Moscow. After Yurchenko's warning had been relayed to London by the CIA, MI6 agents in Moscow were able to make contact with Gordievski and rescue him in a "clandestine exfiltration," according to U.S. intelligence sources.

Yurchenko's information about Gordievski "allowed the British to perform the miracle of getting him out," a former SE officer said. "Unfortunately he left his wife and family back there."

According to a version of Gordievski's rescue published in the British press, the KGB man, while jogging, met his MI6 contact, who smuggled him into the British embassy as guests were arriving for a party for the new ambassador, Sir Bryan Cartledge. MI6 then spirited Gordievski out

of the Soviet Union in a false compartment in a white van
that was carrying diplomatic mail to Finland.[1]

On September 12 the British government announced the
defection of Oleg Gordievski, but said nothing about the
KGB man's having been brought out of Moscow. Rather,
the announcement implied he had sought refuge in London. Later stories hinted he was being held in a safe house
in the south of England. In the wake of the defection London expelled thirty-one Soviet diplomats as spies, and
Moscow kicked out out an equal number of Britons.

Yurchenko also warned the CIA that the KGB was using
"spy dust" to track the movements and contacts of the
agency's case officers in Moscow. There was consternation
inside U.S. intelligence at Yurchenko's disclosure because
it was feared at first that the tracking chemical being used
by the Soviets might be harmful, that it might cause ge-
netic damage and cancer.

The KGB was dusting steering wheels, doorknobs, and
other objects that would leave minute traces of the chemical on anything that the CIA officers might touch. The
traces would also be left on the skin and clothing of Soviet
citizens whom they met, presumably allowing the KGB to
identify the agency's Soviet assets. The State Department
strongly protested the practice. A team of U.S. scientists
studied the chemical, and the State Department concluded
it "does not pose a health hazard."[2]

Yurchenko also provided new details of a ten-year-old
mystery, the disappearance in Vienna of Nicholas G.
Shadrin, an American double agent for the CIA. According to Yurchenko, Shadrin was accidentally chloroformed
and killed while struggling in the back seat of a car in
which Soviet agents were trying to abduct him. Shadrin,

[1]This account of Gordievski's exfiltration appeared in the London *Daily Mail* on July 27, 1986.
[2]Spy dust proved to be nitrophenylpentadienal (NPDD), a synthetic chemical virtually unknown in the United States and apparently developed specifically by the KGB to track CIA agents. The Soviets were also using other chemicals, principally luminol, which is used in an alkaline solution for analytical testing in chemistry. The U.S. statement said that luminol did not appear to be dangerous to humans.

whose real name was Nikolai F. Artamonov, was the youngest destroyer commander in the Soviet Navy when he defected with his Polish fiancée by sailing across the Baltic Sea to Sweden in a motor launch. The couple moved to the United States, where Shadrin was contacted by the KGB. He agreed to become a double agent for U.S. intelligence. In 1975 he was sent to meet with the KGB in Vienna, where he was abducted.

In addition to all these leads, Yurchenko told his CIA debriefers that the KGB considered the Navy spy ring headed by John A. Walker, Jr., the "most important" operation in its history, according to the sworn affidavit of Admiral William O. Studeman, the director of naval intelligence.[3]

After the excitement of his initial interrogations and disclosures, however, Yurchenko appeared gradually to become increasingly unhappy with his circumstances. What had prompted him to defect in the first place? Assuming he was a genuine defector, and most, although not all, U.S. experts believe he that he was, Yurchenko appeared to have mixed motives for breaking with the KGB.

He had risen to a high position in the KGB and had all the comforts and perquisites of that office, including the right to shop in special stores and other privileges reserved for the KGB, the military, and the Communist party elite.

But Yurchenko, according to one U.S. intelligence officer who participated in his debriefing, complained that the KGB was an unfair system. "He said there wasn't much room for independent action. The number one thing everyone does is CYA—cover your ass. He said the system had worn him down."

Yurchenko, the official said, also explained that advancement in the KGB depended less on merit and ability than on having a protector, or mentor, a higher-level officer who looked out for his protégé. In addition to his stated disillusion with the KGB, Yurchenko was escaping an unhappy domestic situation.

---

[3]The Studeman affidavit was filed in federal court and made public on November 6, 1986, the day that Walker was sentenced to life in prison.

Every defector feels isolated, cut off from the society in which he was nurtured. Especially at first, these feelings of loss can be overwhelming. Often, as in Yurchenko's case, the defector has left behind his family. His friends, his roots, his people are thousands of miles away. He is alone in an alien culture. Even the strongest personalities find the adjustment extremely difficult.

Yurchenko was susceptible to these feelings. An emotional, volatile man, he missed his teenage son. The boy was sixteen, and he had problems with his schoolwork and his behavior. It was hard being so far away from him.

Early on, while Yurchenko was still in the safe house in northern Virginia near CIA headquarters and before he was moved south to Coventry, Phil Parker went to see him. Was there anything he needed? No. Was everything all right? Yes. If there is anything you need or want, Parker told him, don't hesitate to ask. "Yurchenko was a little nervous, I thought, but he seemed happy. There was no fear. There was no indication of his later discontent."

Anxious to please their prize defector, and to keep him working for U.S. intelligence, the CIA offered Yurchenko enormous sums of money and material rewards. The Russian later claimed he had been offered $1 million tax-free, beginning on November 1, and a lifetime annual salary of $62,500 a year that would triple with cost-of-living adjustments. The CIA, he claimed, also offered him all the furniture in the safe house in Coventry, valued, he said, at $48,000.

There was independent evidence, aside from Yurchenko's later statements, tending to confirm, in part, the claim about the safe house furniture. On August 19 a well-tailored gray-haired woman who identified herself as Katherine Shannon visited Powell's furniture store near Fredericksburg. She came alone and returned two days later with Yurchenko and two other men.

Dave Richardson, a bespectacled young salesman in the store, was flabbergasted when the foursome proceeded to buy a dining-room suite, three bedroom suites, a living-room suite, a color television set, and other items, adding up to $18,835. It was not every day that Powell's had that kind of sale. Shannon and her friends seemed to be willing to buy whatever the mustached man with the foreign accent wanted. According to Richardson, the woman selected most of the furniture, but Yurchenko chose his own bed, the TV set, and a writing desk.

"She told us it was for a place they would go for retreats," Richardson said. "I really didn't care. When someone is spending that much money, you don't ask a whole lot of questions." The furniture was delivered to the safe house five days later. It was paid for with a certified check, and the bill of sale was made out to an Arlington lawyer, Earl E. Shaffer.[4]

But the promise of riches beyond the dreams of most people and bedroom suites from Powell's did not, it appeared, make Yurchenko happy. He considered his CIA handlers insensitive and his guards goons.

Most of all, Yurchenko pined for Valentina Yereskovsky, an attractive woman with whom he had had an affair when they both were stationed in Washington in the late 1970's. At the time Yurchenko was in charge of security for the Soviet colony in Washington, and Yereskovsky was married to a Soviet diplomat in Washington, Alexander S. Yereskovsky. The couple was now stationed in Montreal.

Yurchenko pleaded for a chance to meet with Valentina. Perhaps he could persuade her to defect as well, and they would build a life together in the United States. The CIA could do it; surely it had the ability to slip him over the border into Canada to see her in a safe location.

Burt Gerber said he would think about it. It was an unusual request, and the Canadians would take some persuading. But nothing was impossible. Perhaps a rendezvous could be arranged.

---

[4] I reached Earl Shaffer at his home in northern Virginia on September 14, 1987. The conversation went this way: Q. "It's about Mr. Yurchenko. Can you comment on why you were buying his furniture?" A. (in voice with a slight southern accent) "I have nothing to say." Q. "Are you employed by the CIA?" A. "It's none of your business." Q. "Well, information in books has to come from somewhere. Can you confirm you bought his furniture?" A. "I have no comment. I'm not confirming nothin', period."

22

Closing In

With Howard back in Santa Fe, Parker was ready to make his first move.

"On Wednesday night after my return from Vienna, I drove to Farmington, New Mexico, on a business trip," Howard said, "an LFC hearing on oil and gas. Thursday night the FBI calls me at my hotel. It's Bill Gillespie, the FBI man who had interviewed me early in the year about my dealings with Phil Troutman.

"He wants to talk to me again about the Troutman case. I thought it was funny. Why couldn't he wait two days until I got back?

"Looking back on it now, I think he just wanted to find out where I was. That call was the first funny thing. The Troutman trial had been over for three months."

By now Parker had moved the Gs into place in Santa Fe. The FBI's Special Support Group, or Gs, as they are often known within the bureau, are a special team of surveillance experts, trained to look like a variety of ordinary citizens. Little old ladies with shopping bags, bearded and beaded hippies, beer-belly good ol' boys in pickup trucks, street repair crews in yellow hard hats, young lovers kissing in the park—all may, in reality, be Gs on the job.[1]

---

[1] The Gs are civil servants, not FBI agents, and earn lower pay than the agents. But all are trained in surveillance, photography, and communications. They are selected precisely because they don't resemble typical FBI agents. The Gs were in place, looking like New York subway riders, when Soviet agent Gennadi Zakharov was arrested on a Queens subway platform on August 23, 1986.

Even with the special team, however, the bureau had a problem in placing Howard under surveillance. The houses in El Dorado sit widely spaced in the desert, and any stranger approaching is immediately spotted by the residents and dogs. It was hardly the type of urban environment where the Gs operate best.

"The Gs were there," Parker confirmed. "They do dress up as repairmen or joggers, and we did some of that, but there are problems with it. You can't work on the same pothole for three days."

Bill Gillespie's house, only two houses down from Howard's, would have been an ideal observation post, of course, but unfortunately he had just sold it.[2]

By late August Howard had detected the first signs of surveillance. It was not surprising; one of the FBI's problems was that its target was a man it had trained to detect surveillance.

"I saw guys in baseball caps circling the house," Howard said. "They had no business there. I jumped in my Jeep and followed them. I drove out on a dirt road and stopped. I just stood still for fifteen minutes. It was at night, and a little plane was circling overhead. I assume he had an infrared device.

"I told Mary, 'I think I have surveillance.' She thought I was whacko. After that incident they were very discreet for three or four days, then more visible in September. I was beginning to question myself. Was it real, or was I only imagining the surveillance?"

Since Howard does not admit that he had passed secrets to the Soviets at that point, why did he think he was under surveillance? "I considered it had something to do with the agency. Maybe ten officers in the Soviet division were all under surveillance for some reason."

Howard assumed it was the FBI that had him under surveillance. "I bought a three-hundred-dollar scanner at

---

[2]David Lovro, who bought Gillespie's house, said he moved in on August 4, which was the day before the case landed on Jim Geer's desk. "The FBI did not use my property for surveillance," Lovro said. "They did not ask to use the house."

Radio Shack in late August after the dirt road thing,'' he said, ''to try to listen to the broadcasts and see who was after me. The Radio Shack guy gave me the frequencies for the New Mexico State Police. I thought, *Maybe their undercover unit thinks I'm dealing.*''

But Howard was never able to pick up the FBI. ''They don't use those frequencies,'' he said ruefully. Disappointed, Howard returned the scanner to Radio Shack and got his money back.

On August 24 Howard paid his last visit to Dr. Dudelczyk and sent the bill, as usual, to the CIA accommodation address in Chantilly. The agency had financed a total of fifteen visits to the psychiatrist, over a period of eight months.

Around the time Howard had begun to suspect someone was following him, Phil Parker, too, got some disturbing news. He learned, for the first time, of Howard's September 1984 confession to the CIA that he had lingered near a Soviet embassy building in October 1983 and contemplated passing secrets to the Russians. The word came to him through the two agents from the Washington field office who had been working with the agency on the Howard case. Parker realized that the CIA had sat on the explosive confession for almost a year.

Parker is an even-tempered man, given to understatement. FBI counterintelligence agents are extremely reluctant to criticize the CIA, with which they must cooperate on myriad investigations. Moreover, Parker respected Gus Hathaway and had worked well with the agency's counterintelligence chief on other cases. Even so, he did not conceal his chagrin at the disclosure.

''It was not a pleasant discovery,'' he recalled. ''I was disappointed. I was very upset that—for whatever reason—it fell through the cracks.''

Gradually Parker learned the truth: how, first, the agency had kept silent when Howard was fired; how it said nothing about Howard's alarming calls to the Moscow embassy or the drunken confrontation with his ex-boss in the driveway of his home; and finally, most damning of all, how it had maintained silence over Howard's presence near a Soviet embassy building and his confession.

Asked why in particular Howard's admission to the CIA of the embassy incident had not been passed on to the FBI, Parker replied: "I think it's fair to say they thought they could handle it in-house and that they had a psychiatric string on Howard as well."

Historically CIA-FBI relations, in the words of the final report of the Senate Select Committee on Intelligence, have been "marked by turbulence." The lowest point came in 1970, when FBI Director Hoover actually ordered an end to "direct liaison" with the CIA. He did so over the bizarre case of Professor Thomas Riha, a Czech-born professor whose disappearance in 1969 from the University of Colorado has never been solved. Hoover clashed with CIA Director Richard M. Helms over the case and simply broke off all relations with the agency. Liaison was not restored until after Hoover's death in 1972.[3]

By the end of August Parker finally had his wiretap order from the Foreign Intelligence Surveillance Court. He did not get the FISA package out of the Justice Department as rapidly as he had hoped.

Even if it had come sooner, Jerry Brown, the case agent, would have had to move with caution in arranging the installation. The court order required the telephone company to facilitate the wiretap for the FBI. "Santa Fe is small," Parker said. "There was some question about who Howard's friends and acquaintances were. We couldn't take a chance that some phone company people might turn out to be friends or neighbors of Howard's."[4]

---

[3]The CIA's chief of base in Denver, Michael M. Todorovich, was told by an FBI man that Riha was alive and well, an assurance that the CIA man passed on to the university's president, who promptly made a public statement that the missing professor was safe. Hoover went off like a rocket and demanded that Helms yield up the name of the talkative FBI agent. Todorovich refused to tell, and Hoover, like a head of state, broke off relations with Langley and recalled his ambassador, Sam J. Papich, who found his job eliminated after seventeen years as liaison man with the CIA.

[4]As it happened, both parents of Gina Jackson, a teenager who was the

By about September 1 the wiretap was in place in Howard's home. The FBI wiretappers were not set up at the telephone company headquarters but at another location. There is some evidence they were working out of a mobile van.

The FBI was not simply tape-recording Howard's conversations; because of the importance of the case, agents with headphones were listening. The wiretap law requires "minimization" of intrusion into privacy. In theory the FBI tappers were to record only those conversations that seemed relevant. But the agents would also note whether Howard was placing a call from home, a fact that would help confirm his location at that moment.

A telephone wiretap permits the government to eavesdrop on phone conversations but does not pick up room conversations within a house; that requires physical entry and the planting of a tiny transmitter, or bug. According to Parker, "there were too many problems getting in to place a microphone." Mary Howard and Lee were usually at home, or a baby-sitter was there.

Asked why Howard's office telephone was not tapped, Parker said there were technical and other problems. "There was some question about what we could do and limit it to Howard," he said. "With some rotor systems you can't limit a tap to one person. It was additionally sensitive because it was a state agency." Howard was frequently seen using a pay phone near his office in the lobby of the state capitol, but that telephone was not wiretapped by the FBI.

The "take" from the wiretap on Howard's home was in the form of written summaries, not verbatim transcripts. But Howard said nothing on the telephone that gave the listening agents any leads, let alone probable cause to arrest him.

"The target was a trained intelligence officer," Parker

Howards' regular baby-sitter, worked for Mountain Bell and were neighbors at 43 Verano Loop. Larry Jackson was a systems technician, and Cherry Jackson, who knew Mary Howard, was a service representative.

said. "I don't think anyone expected a smoking gun from the technical coverage, whether a mike or a telephone."

Even so, Parker considered the tesur not without value. "It was a matter of time before we were going to have to approach Howard," he said. "What we were doing with the tesur was to try to get as much information as possible, so when we sat down, we would have overwhelming knowledge of his activities, his personality, his strengths and weaknesses. So we would have the interview to our best advantage."

With the wiretap in place, Jerry Brown's crew listening in, the Gs working on the potholes, and the FBI maintaining ground and aerial surveillance of Howard, Parker was still frustrated. They were into September now, the division had had the case for almost a month, and the bureau was no closer to springing the trap on Howard.

That's when Parker learned about Bill Bosch.

The CIA did not volunteer Bosch's name to the FBI. Shockingly the agency was still stonewalling on the Howard case, weeks *after* Yurchenko's information had finally forced the agency's hand, leaving it no choice but to reveal Howard's identity to the bureau.

Even the most cursory internal inquiries by the CIA would have revealed that Bosch was Howard's closest friend in the agency. The CIA was well aware that the FBI would have had more than a passing interest in questioning Bosch.

Moreover, Bosch said that in March 1984 he had alerted Peter Ringland, his ex-father-in-law, about Howard. If that information was passed on, the CIA may well have known that Howard and Bosch met in New Orleans and that Howard had proposed that the two former CIA officers go together to the Soviet embassy in Mexico City.

It was not as though Bosch had never come to Langley's attention. Far from it. Because of Bosch's currency problems in Bolivia, the defaulted CIA car loan, and his frozen retirement funds, the agency had ample reason to know who Bill Bosch was. Yet the CIA remained silent.

Nor had Bosch himself come forward to report Howard's alarming conversation on South Padre Island. It was only two months earlier that Howard, according to Bosch, had shaken him by the shoulders, said, "I did it," and asked Bosch whether he wanted "five, ten, or fifteen thousand dollars."

The FBI found Bosch by going through Howard's long-distance toll calls. The bureau obtained Howard's telephone records, going as far back as possible. It went over the long-distance toll slips one by one to identify each person with whom Howard had spoken. The names were then checked against the FBI's own files.

Bosch's name, according to Parker, was probably in the FBI files because of an applicant investigation; at the time that Bosch had applied to the CIA in 1973, the agency would have asked the FBI for a name check. When Leffler and Crocker in the Soviet section under Parker discovered that William George Bosch had been an employee of the CIA, alarm bells went off at FBI headquarters.

"There was consternation that we hadn't been told about Bosch," Parker recalled.

The FBI tracked Bosch down to South Padre Island, but for the moment they did not dare approach him. Now that Parker had uncovered Bosch, he had a new dilemma. The former CIA officer obviously might be a very important witness in the case, but if Bosch was interviewed, Parker worried that he might tip off Howard. The Bosch interview was put on hold.

About September 14, Howard said, he got a call from Bosch. "Bill called, really down, and said he was two or three months behind in the rent. I said I don't have much but offered him five hundred dollars. He didn't accept it." The FBI agents listened to the call.

That same weekend Howard and his wife flew to Los Angeles and Seattle, en route to an oil and gas conference in San Francisco on Monday. The tension was running high inside the FBI, because it was Howard's first out-of-town trip since Gillespie had reached him in Farmington a month earlier. The FBI had the Howards under close surveillance throughout the trip.

In Seattle Howard rented a car for the weekend. The day after arriving in Seattle, Howard said, "we decided to go to a wilderness park. First we took a ferry across the sound." The Howards probably visited Point Defiance Zoo, a large wildlife park across Puget Sound. "In King County," Howard said, "the last seventeen miles, a plane started buzzing us. The plane was circling me all the way. I was always told the FBI used high-altitude surveillance, maybe five thousand feet. This guy was two hundred feet. He was so obvious it wasn't funny."

The Howards flew to San Francisco, and Howard, representing his legislative committee, attended the two-day conference. Then they flew back home.

Soon afterward Howard was in his car, driving in Santa Fe, when he looked in the rearview mirror and thought he saw someone familiar behind him. "He pulled over right beside me," Howard said.

There had not been much doubt after the airplane circling low overhead in Seattle. But now there could no longer be any question. Howard knew that face. "He was the same man I had seen on the plane to L.A."

In Brownsville, Texas, on Wednesday, September 18, Bosch was in the office of an apartment complex where he had formerly lived when he heard two men approach the front desk, asking questions about him. The men identified themselves as special agents of the FBI.

Bosch approached them and asked what they wanted. The agents asked how he spelled his name, Bosch said. "Then they said, 'Oh, the man we are looking for spells it differently.' " At the time Bosch was planning to return to South America to try to put together some real estate investments. "I thought the agency was using FBI credentials and wanted to stop me from leaving the country," Bosch said. "Wednesday night I called Ed and said, 'Goddamn, the agency is up to its old tricks.' "

In Washington that day Parker had already made up his mind. Howard was too shrewd to make a move. He must, by now, have assumed his telephone was tapped, and he had probably detected the surveillance. He knew from Bosch's telephone call, which the FBI had overhead, that agents were closing in on Bosch on South Padre Island.

The time had come to approach Howard, to confront him as a spy.

There was a risk, of course. He might run. But by now Parker had an army of FBI agents deployed in Santa Fe. It would be almost impossible for Howard to slip through the net. The risk was minimal. And it would have to be taken because they weren't getting anywhere by waiting.

From Parker's fourth-floor office in the intelligence division at FBI headquarters in Washington, the order went out to the Albuquerque division: Howard was to be approached.

Tomorrow.

23

Confrontation

Parker decided they would need "Wags."

For the crucial confrontation with Howard he wanted the FBI's best interrogator. By universal agreement that was Michael J. Waguespack, a dark-haired, muscular man who had the reputation of being the bureau's most artful interviewer, an agent who could be friendly or tough as the situation demanded.

Waguespack had persuaded suspects to talk in a number of sensitive foreign counterintelligence cases.[1] He had already been flown in from San Diego and was waiting in the wings in Santa Fe. The other FBI agent selected for the approach to Howard was Jerry Brown. As the case agent he knew what was going on inside the Howard household and, presumably, would be best attuned to Howard's frame of mind.

It was now Thursday, September 19. The FBI booked a room at the Hilton of Santa Fe. They waited until Howard had returned to his office from lunch. Then Brown placed the call, got Howard, and identified himself as a special agent of the FBI.

"Jerry Brown called at one-thirty P.M., right after lunch," Howard recounted, "and he said, 'We have some-

[1] He had, for example, interviewed Richard Craig Smith, a former army intelligence officer, who was accused of taking eleven thousand dollars from the Soviets to reveal Royal Miter, an army double-agent operation mounted against the KGB, and five other double-agent operations. Smith, who claimed that he was acting for the CIA, was acquitted by a federal grand jury in Alexandria in April 1986.

thing important to talk to you about.' I said OK. It was a ten-minute walk to the Hilton. I went up to the room. There were maps of Vienna on the table.

"Waguespack is sitting in a chair by the bed. Jerry Brown is by the window. I'm in the middle chair."

There was someone else waiting in the hotel room at the start of the meeting. Tom Mills had flown in from Langley. Howard had not seen him since the scene in Mills's driveway more than a year before. "Mills said, 'Ed, it's okay to tell these guys everything you know.' Then he left and came back in toward the end.

"Waguespack grabs the Washington *Post*. He shows me a story about Gordievski's defection." As Howard reconstructed the interview, it went like this, with Waguespack pointing to the *Post* story:

"Does this concern you?'

"No, why should it?"

"Because this man has fingered you as a Soviet agent. He has identified you as a CIA informant."[2]

"It's not true."

"Why don't you tell us everything and you can relax? We know you went to Austria last year, in September."

Howard was silent.

"We want you to take a polygraph."

"No way. The polygraph fucked me once before. I want to see a lawyer."

"We're going to talk to everybody," Howard claims the FBI agents then warned him. "Your employer, your friends, even your little boy."

"I said, 'He's only two and a half.' "

A shouting match ensued, according to Howard.

"We know what you did."

---

[2]Word of Yurchenko's defection to the CIA had not yet leaked to the American press on September 19, as the FBI questioned Howard for the first time. But Gordievski's defection had been announced in London one week earlier on September 12, and several stories about him had appeared in the Washington *Post*. Thus, it is entirely possible that the FBI chose to tell Howard that he had been fingered by Gordievski, rather than by Yurchenko.

"No!"

"You're lying!"

"You guys screwed up. Something serious happened someplace."

Howard stood up and started to leave. "They blocked my way. I said, 'What? Are you going to arrest me?' They said, 'No, but we'll talk to your boss. You have one day to get a lawyer and give us an answer about the polygraph.' "

Howard ran back to his office and called Mary. "I said, 'Babe, the most incredible thing has happened. The FBI says I'm a Soviet agent.' " Howard said he drove home, with FBI cars ahead of and behind him. Now that Howard had been approached, there was no longer any need for the FBI to try to conceal its presence. The agents switched to what the FBI calls "nondiscreet" surveillance.

As Howard arrived at his house on Verano Loop, he said, two FBI agents, a man and a woman, got out of a car and began questioning Mary, who was in the road, a short distance from the house. "I go in the house and call Morty Simon. He says break it off, don't talk to anyone." Howard jumped in his Jeep, drove to where Mary was talking to the agents, and told her the attorney had advised them to break off.

An hour later Dr. Dudelczyk called to say he had been visited by the FBI. "I said, 'They think I committed a crime. Can you prescribe a tranquilizer for me?' He did, and said not to worry. Mary and I drove to the pharmacy, picked up the tranquilizer, and drove home."

Meanwhile, FBI agents had gone to the state capitol and asked to see Phil Baca, Howard's boss. Baca was at a public hearing and reluctant to leave; but his aides said the FBI men were insistent, so he went back downstairs to meet with them.

"They said it was national security," Baca said. He remembered what Curtis Porter had told him, that Howard had been in the CIA. "They requested all his per diem travel records and all dates of sick leave and annual leave. They told me not to discuss it with him."

That evening Howard called Bill Bosch in Texas. "Don't

worry," he told him. "They're not investigating you;
they're after me."

Restless, Howard left his house at midnight to go for a
walk. "Parked near Moya Road was a camper trailer I'd
never seen before," he said. "When I waited there, I heard
some movement from that trailer."

Howard had apparently stumbled on the FBI surveillance post. Although the bureau declined to discuss any
aspect of its surveillance arrangements at the Howard
home, it was learned that a trailer, equipped with television monitors, was indeed used to watch 108 Verano Loop.
Hidden video cameras were trained on the house.

Howard, even more nervous now, walked home. With
the help of the tranquilizer he fell asleep.

At 6:00 A.M. on Friday, September 20, Bill Bosch awoke
to pounding on the door of his condo on the beach on
South Padre Island. Special Agent William H. Koopman
of the Albuquerque division and an FBI agent from San
Antonio were at the door.

This time the agents did not pretend to be looking for
anyone else. They asked to question Bosch, who invited
them in. The two FBI men interviewed Bosch for about
an hour and a half, asking general questions about his
relationship with Ed Howard.

"They asked if I would take a polygraph," Bosch related. "I said yes. They set it up for Saturday, the next
day."

When the FBI agents had left, Bosch drove to work in
Brownsville. It was his last day on the job; he planned to
leave for South America in ten days.

The same morning in Santa Fe Howard was up early to
keep a breakfast date with two economists. As it happened, it was at the Hilton. Howard had to walk past several FBI agents in the lobby.

At the state capitol Phil Baca was getting edgy. The
8:30 A.M. staff briefing, to prepare the legislators for a
9:00 A.M. public hearing was about to begin, and Howard
was uncharacteristically late. "It was almost eight-thirty,

and Ed wasn't here yet,'' Baca said. ''Ed was always on time. He finally came in at twenty-five after. He did a beautiful briefing on what a consultant would be telling the committee on the eighteen-month economic outlook. He had graphs. During the hearing some questions came up on the price of oil. He answered them and was completely calm.''

In retrospect, Baca was amazed at how cool Howard was during the hearing. ''It was sort of uncomfortable,'' Baca said, ''because we were sitting elbow to elbow and I knew he was in trouble.''

Around noon, while a vice-president of Citicorp was droning away, Howard tapped Baca on the arm and said he wanted to talk to him. They stepped into a nearby office. ''Some federal officials may be asking you about a trip I took,'' Howard said. ''Curt approved the trip, and it was sponsored by the DRI in Boston.''

''I said, 'No problem,' '' Baca recalled. ''I didn't want to let on I knew anything.''

Around 2:00 P.M. the hearing broke up, and Howard asked Baca for the afternoon off. Howard was due in Austin on Monday for a business meeting, and he briefly discussed his upcoming trip with Baca. He planned to leave Sunday and return on Tuesday, Howard told him.

Howard went to the bank and said he withdrew three hundred dollars in cash. He then walked a few blocks to Morton Simon's office. Simon told Howard he was not an expert on federal criminal law and gave him the name of Nancy Hollander, a lawyer in Albuquerque.

Howard drove back to El Dorado, picked up Mary, and at 4:00 P.M. they went together to the Safeway in Santa Fe. An FBI agent was trailing the Howards as they made their way past the vegetables and the frozen foods. Howard recognized the agent and went up to him.

''I want to see Jerry Brown,'' he said. Howard suggested they meet back at his house.

The agent, embarrassed, asked Howard how he had spotted him. Howard said he had seen him around. The FBI man then went to a telephone and came back in a few moments. ''Mr. Brown wants to see you, but not at your house," the agent said. "Why don't you go over to the hotel right now?"

Howard agreed and had a second meeting with Brown and Waguespack at the Hilton. "I told him I would talk to the woman lawyer in Albuquerque," Howard said. "I said I would talk to her on Monday. And I said I would cancel my business trip."

The FBI agent was pleased. Howard seemed much more conciliatory than he had the day before. And Howard was willing to remain in Santa Fe; the bureau would not have to follow him to Austin.

That same afternoon in Moscow the KGB had an announcement. In June the Soviets had disclosed the detention and expulsion of Paul M. Stombaugh, Jr., one of Howard's successors in the CIA's Moscow station. But it had not revealed the name of his asset, Adolf G. Tolkachev. The TASS announcement read:

The USSR State Security Committee has uncovered and arrested an agent of the U.S. secret service—A. G. Tolkachev, a staff member of one of Moscow's research institutes. The spy was caught in the act during an attempt to pass on secret materials of defense nature to Paul M. Stombaugh, an officer of the U.S. CIA, who acted under the cover of the second secretary of the U.S. embassy in Moscow.

It has been established that the U.S. secret service provided Tolkachev with miniature cameras of a special design, by means of which he photographed secret documents, as well as with means of cryptography, codes and ciphers, quick-acting two-way communication radio apparatus, and other equipment for espionage work. Potent poisons which had been given to the spy by Americans were also seized from him.

The contents for the instructions of the U.S. Central Intelligence Agency, discovered at Tolkachev's place, indicate that the use of him as a spy was linked with the CIA's plans to conduct large-scale subversive activities against the Soviet Union. The investigation is going on.

In Washington Parker received word of Jerry Brown's late-afternoon meeting with Howard and of Howard's apparent willingness now to cooperate with the FBI. Satisfied that things were moving well in Santa Fe, he drove to Norfolk to spend the weekend with his family. Lane Crocker would have the duty on Saturday.

In Santa Fe Howard drove home after the meeting with the FBI and talked with his wife some more. Thursday's approach to Howard by the FBI, Mary Howard said, "was the first I knew of any trouble." She added, "We did a lot of talking that weekend." She paused, thought a moment, and said, "In saying we did a lot of talking, I don't mean to imply that he told me he had committed espionage. We were talking about the FBI meetings with him."

Howard knew he would have to act. "I hadn't decided what to do," he said. "I walked around Verano Loop." It was dark by now, almost pitch-black in El Dorado. The Sangre de Cristo Mountains—the words in Spanish mean "blood of Christ"—loomed to the north, a dark and brooding presence in the desert.

"Friday night I couldn't sleep," Howard said. But a plan was beginning to take shape in his mind. He went back to the house to await the dawn.

24

Escape

Early on Saturday morning, September 21, Howard began making plans to escape. At that hour, he said, he had not yet made his final decision. But he thought it prudent to prepare a plan "just in case."

In the CIA's Denied Areas Operations Course Howard had learned to jump from a slowly moving car with Mary at the wheel. The maneuver had to be carried out at night, preferably with a dummy, and the jump point had to be selected with care. Right after a sharp turn was best.

At 9:00 A.M. the Howards drove into Santa Fe. "Saturday morning Mary and I drove around, looking for places to jump. We looked for escape points from nine to eleven-thirty A.M." Aware of FBI surveillance, the Howards stopped occasionally to make it appear that they were running normal Saturday morning errands. Howard found several jump spots that looked promising.

That same morning Kate Gallegos gathered up a bundle of clothes that her son, Jason, then four, had outgrown, put them in a shopping bag, and drove over to the Howards' house to leave them for Lee. "No one was home," Mrs. Gallegos said, "so I just set it inside the screen door." It was about 11:00 A.M.

The Howards returned to their house just before noon. Howard got out a map of Santa Fe and studied it, marking down all the jump points. The one that he finally selected was a spot almost a mile south of the capitol where Garcia Street curved sharply into Camino Corrales, just before the Old Santa Fe Trail. There was a house with some bushes right after the sharp turn.

By midday Howard had made up his mind. He asked Mary to come outside. "We walked outside to talk because I didn't know if they had a device. Lee was getting a fever that day. Mary said, 'Why don't you stay and fight this thing?'

"But they had a full deck. I was under probation in Santa Fe. I knew that they had the goods on me for that. I thought, *It's best to split*. All three trips to Europe were a violation of probation. They could put me in for nine years for that. I won't even survive one year in jail. I saw what it was like for one night. Terrible. Homosexuals, you're confined to one place. I knew I was probably going to jail anyway. I didn't want to spend one day in jail. Mary was against my going, but she didn't understand the whole thing.

"I told her I had to go. She was sad but said, 'It's you they're after; it's your decision.' So I prepared the dummy."

Howard had not been permitted to keep the jib, the jack-in-the-box dummy he had used at CIA, so he had to manufacture a makeshift dummy.

"Mary had a white Styrofoam head she used to put wigs on. I got a broomstick and cut it to a meter and took a coat hanger and wired it to the pole. For the hair I used a brown wig I had from my agency training. I had used the wig for disguise training and makeup."

The dummy would require some clothes as well. "I put a Calvin Klein field jacket on the dummy," Howard said, "a beige army-style field jacket I had bought in Tysons Corner."

Next, Howard put a blank cassette in a tape recorder, pushed the record button, and taped a message for Dr. Dudelczyk. He gave Mary detailed instructions on how and when to play the tape over the telephone. "I had talked to him Thursday about the tranquilizers. And I said on the tape I was still nervous and wanted to see him that week."

After selecting the jump site on the map, preparing the dummy, and making the tape recording, Howard gave

Mary a final briefing. It was Edward Howard's last operation. Everything was ready.

Mary Howard was distraught. Her husband was leaving
her, and she did not know when, if ever, she would see
him again.

"Mary talked about the future," Howard said. "She
tried to rest. She was very nervous."

Howard said he gathered together the three hundred dollars he had withdrawn from the bank, seven hundred
dollars "that I had in a box in the house," and the ten
thousand Swiss francs, which he said he also had in the
house. In addition, he took his American Express card and
his passport. With a smile he put one more item in his
wallet: his TWA Getaway card.

It was midafternoon now, and there wasn't much time
left.

At 3:00 P.M. Rosa Carlson got a telephone call from her
friend and neighbor Mary Howard. The Carlsons lived
only a block away, and the two women normally walked
together at 7:00 A.M. each day, before Mrs. Carlson left
for work at the travel agency she managed in Santa Fe.

The friendship had begun over a bottle of pisco. Ed
Howard had heard that Mrs. Carlson was visiting her native Peru, where the Howards had lived, and he asked her
to bring back a bottle of pisco, the national liqueur. Howard invited the Carlsons over and made everyone pisco
sours. That was during the summer of 1984.

Now Mary was calling about a minor problem. As they
had the same baby-sitter that day, would it be all right if
the sitter walked over with Lee to the Carlsons and combined the two jobs? Mrs. Carlson said that would be fine.

Sometime during the afternoon Robert Gallegos picked
up a message from Ed Howard on his answering machine,
thanking his friends for the clothes that Kate had left.
Howard said there was no need to call back; he would see
Kate at the office on Monday. The message struck Gallegos as odd; he thought that Howard was supposed to be
in Austin on Monday.

On South Padre Island late that afternoon two FBI agents
came for William Bosch. One was William Koopman; the

other, R. Dion Rankin, was a polygraph operator who had been flown in from headquarters. They took Bosch to the Bahia Mar Hotel. The interview began. After two hours of questioning, Bosch would be wired to the "box."

At 4:00 P.M. sixteen-year-old Gina Jackson arrived at the Howards' house in Santa Fe. A junior at St. Michael's High School, Gina Jackson was five feet six and brown-haired, with freckles on her nose and braces on her teeth. She was the Howards' regular baby-sitter.

"As I went through the house," Gina Jackson said, "I thought I heard two people talking. Out of the corner of my eye I saw a completely bald-headed person standing in the entranceway between the den and the living room."

Later, Gina said, "the FBI told me it wasn't two men talking; it was Ed Howard with a tape recorder and a dummy."

Mary Howard did not stop to chat with the sitter in her usual friendly manner. Instead, she led Gina and Lee directly out back to the patio. Mary seemed distracted. She did not provide the sitter with a phone number but told her the name of the restaurant, Alfonso's, where they were going to dinner.

Howard recounted the last moments in his house. "I remember holding Lee, and I said, 'Good-bye, be a good boy.' It was in front of Gina, so I couldn't show a lot of emotion. Lee started crying as I handed him to Gina. He was only two and a half, but he knew something was going on."

Mary slid shut the patio door, Gina said, leaving her and Lee outside. That struck her as unusual because normally they would have been left in the house. The Howards may have needed that moment to carry the dummy into the garage and hide it inside the car.

"We had to walk out and act normal in front of Gina," Howard said. "I was holding back tears. As soon as I got in the car in the garage, I knew I could let myself go a little bit. We got in the car, and my eyes were moist. I wiped my eyes with a handkerchief."

Mary Howard started up the engine. In a moment Gina Jackson heard the car pull out of the garage.

What happened next is baffling, an incredible human error combined with a failure in communication. Only one FBI surveillance agent was on duty, inside the trailer that was parked several hundred feet from the Howards' house. Other FBI agents were spread out in cars a few miles away, linked to the trailer by radio. Although it was 4:30 P.M. and broad daylight, the Howards drove away in their dark red 1979 Oldsmobile undetected.

How could it have happened?

The hapless FBI man was a "first office agent," a fairly new man for whom Albuquerque was his first field assignment. An FBI source tried to explain the error: "The surveillance agents were in cars down the road. A single look-out man was the key. I guess he may have had the phone tap, too. Obviously he missed him. Apparently he was looking on a monitor. There were problems with reflection and glare. The sun is very strong in the desert."

Edward Lee Howard, a major Soviet spy suspect, slipped away unseen by the FBI agent because of glare on a TV monitor? "More likely he never paid attention to the screen," the FBI man said. "He was close enough to look out at the house, so I'm not sure why he didn't look directly, visually, why he even relied on the screen."

Later agents of the FBI's inspection division investigated what may be the most embarrassing episode in the history of the bureau's counterespionage operations. They found that the trailer's log had no entry showing the Howards' departure. They never got a satisfactory explanation from the agent of why he had failed to see the Howards leave.

Ed and Mary Howard left El Dorado, turned left onto Route 285 for a short distance, and swung onto Interstate 25, heading northwest for Santa Fe. Other FBI agents were waiting in their cars at intervals along the way, out of sight of the highway. They were awaiting word by radio from the trailer to move out and follow the Howards.

The signal never came.

The Howards were blissfully unaware that through an incredible error, they had eluded the FBI's surveillance. As far as the FBI knew, they were still in their house on

Verano Loop. They left the highway at the Old Santa Fe Trail and drove out past the art galleries on Canyon Road to Alfonso's, a white-pillared restaurant.[1]

"We ordered sandwiches and mushroom entrées," Howard said. "The conversation was trite and tense. I regret that now. I should have said more, but I was concentrating on the escape plan. I was operational."

Howard does remember assuring Mary that he would not be gone long. "At dinner I said, 'Everything will be OK. I'll be gone a few weeks, months, maybe a even a year, babe. I've been confronted as a Soviet spy. But maybe things will change.'" She had nothing to worry about as far as the FBI was concerned, Howard told her. "They're after me."

Somewhere along the line during dinner, Howard claimed, he became aware that they had no visible surveillance. "It makes you more nervous when you don't know where they are," he said. "I've had old case officers tell me that."

Howard went to a phone. "I made a call home to Gina. Lee had a temperature. I was checking on him but also to let the FBI know where I was." Howard told the sitter he was calling from Alfonso's.

Gina reported that Lee was upset. "He cried the whole time," she recalled. "He'd never been like that before. He didn't stop crying for anything, screaming the whole time until we got to the Carlsons."

The FBI agent monitoring the tap, apparently the same agent in the trailer, heard the call from the restaurant. Now the FBI had a chance to recoup its error and reinstitute the surveillance.

"About ten minutes later a car pulls up and a guy comes into the bar," Howard said. "Mary said, 'I think that's our man.'"

Mary Howard was wrong. The FBI had not acted after Howard's phone call, compounding its earlier mistake. "That contributed to the problem," an FBI man agreed.

---

[1] Alfonso's is gone. In 1986 the name of the restaurant was changed to the Carriage Trade.

"There was a misinterpretation about what was said by Howard in the call.[2] He would not elaborate, but perhaps the listening FBI agent, believing Howard to be at home, thought he was placing an *outgoing* call.

The Howards lingered over dinner, waiting for dark.

Around 6:00 P.M. Gina Jackson walked a block to the Carlsons with Lee. Rosa Carlson had already left for a party at her partner's house for twenty clients who had come back from trekking in the Andes; the party was to celebrate their return from Peru. Her husband, Gary Carlson, was still there with two houseguests when Gina arrived but left after ten minutes.

Gina watched while Lee and the two young Carlson boys, Zac and Jonathan, played with water and plastic toys in the bathtub. The three children were a handful.

At the restaurant Howard used his American Express card to pay the check. About 7:00 P.M. he and his wife left the restaurant. Howard disconnected the brake lights; he had learned that, too, in his CIA training.

"We got in the car. Mary kissed me. She said she loved me. I said I loved her. She was almost in tears. We drove away, south and west toward the Old Santa Fe Trail."

Mary Howard was at the wheel. She turned off Canyon Road onto Acequia Madre, then south on Garcia Street. They were getting closer to the jump point that Howard had marked on the map.

"The dummy was hidden on the front floor of the passenger seat, covered with my raincoat," Howard said. "I got the dummy in between us. Mary said, 'OK, we're here.' "

She was turning sharply onto Camino Corrales.

"I looked at her. She looked at me, a kind of frozen half second. Nothing was said. I popped up the dummy, and I jumped from the car. She did it perfect. Just like she was trained."

---

[2]Phillip Parker confirmed that the FBI never caught up with the Howards at the restaurant or thereafter. "We didn't have him anytime that night," he said.

When Mary Howard arrived back home on Verano Loop around 7:20 P.M., the dummy was in the passenger seat in place of her husband.

The surveillance agent on duty in the trailer was surprised to see the Howards *returning* because they had not been seen leaving—surprised but immensely relieved, since they were together. Ed Howard seemed to be wearing a hat, but in the dark the FBI man could not be sure.

The automatic garage door opened, and Mary Howard drove inside. She drove out a few minutes later, alone. She arrived at the Carlsons' house at 7:30 P.M. to pick up Lee.

She came to the door, but by now Lee was having such a good time he didn't want to leave. ''Let's go say good-bye to Daddy,'' Mary said. Gina Jackson did not give the remark any thought; perhaps Howard was going on a trip.

With Lee in the car, Mary Howard drove back the short distance to her house and into the garage. The surveillance agent dutifully logged them in.

Howard hit hard when he landed. The jump had not gone as well as it had in training. ''I nearly broke my arm,'' Howard said. ''It was blue for a week.''

At the place Howard had chosen there was a house with bushes and a high fence. Howard barely had time to hide in the bushes when the people came out of the house. They passed very close to him as they walked by. It was after 7:00 P.M. and completely dark by now. ''They didn't see me. They got into their car and drove off.''

Howard, nursing his bruised arm, half jogged to his office in the capitol. It took him about ten minutes to get there. He knew there would be no one in the capitol at this hour on a Saturday night.

He let himself into his office, room 247, a modest-size room with a window, a desk, two chairs, and an IBM personal computer. Historic photos of New Mexico decorated the walls, and the bookcases were filled with red, leather-bound statutes of the state of New Mexico. Howard remained there briefly, then walked along the corridor that curves around the capitol to Phil Baca's office. He typed a short letter to the staff director, using the typewriter in Baca's outer office. He placed the letter, a handwritten note to Mary, and the keys to his office in an envelope, which he sealed and left on Baca's desk.

He hurried down the hill to the Inn at Loretto, where he caught the last Shuttlejack, the van to the Albuquerque airport. "The van stopped at the Hilton," Howard said. "I nearly panicked. The entire FBI surveillance team was staying at the Hilton. I knew there were ten to fifteen agents there."

Howard made it to the airport. He took the first flight out, which happened to be going to Tucson. He paid cash for his ticket, and by 9:10 P.M. he was aboard the plane. In a few moments he was winging his way southwest to Arizona, passing over the mountains near Reserve where he had learned to shoot rabbits as a boy.

He was no longer the hunter.

On Verano Loop Mary Howard, following her husband's instructions, took the tape recorder and held it to the mouthpiece of her telephone. She dialed Dr. Dudelcyzk's office. Because it was the weekend, she got his answering machine, just as Howard had planned.

At the wiretap location a listening FBI agent adjusted his earphones, alert to the call. There was activity on the Howard's line. He would listen in "live."

Mary waited until Dr. Dudelczyk's voice had finished explaining that he wasn't in right now, but the caller could leave a message after the tone. At the beep she pressed the play button on the tape recorder. Howard's voice began speaking, asking to see the psychiatrist next week.

The listening FBI agent was reassured. Their target was still in the house and would be staying in town.

On South Padre Island Bill Bosch was finally talking. During the two-hour interview at the Bahia Mar, even before he was wired to the polygraph, he began to open up with Agents Koopman and Rankin.

For the first time Bosch told the FBI agents about Howard's proposal that the two men go to the Soviet embassy in Mexico City to "really do a job on the agency."

The FBI interrogators pressed Bosch hard. As close friends Bosch and Howard had talked about their work to each other; how much had Bosch revealed to Howard about CIA operations in Latin America?

Bosch told the FBI how, on the drive from New Orleans to Dallas and Santa Fe, he and Howard had taken turns describing the secrets they knew that, if revealed, could harm the agency. Bosch had talked about Latin America during the drive.

A former CIA official said Bosch, perhaps inadvertently, had revealed a good deal. "Bosch had worked on the Latin American desk at headquarters before he was sent to Bolivia, so he knew a lot," the former CIA officer said. "He knew names of agents and technical ops. If there was a tap or a penetration, Bosch would know about it. Bosch admitted to the FBI that he told Howard all this."

In his interview with the author Bosch denied that he ever gave Howard any detailed information about operations in Latin America. "Ed knew what job I had in Bolivia," he said. "He knew because he probably had access to that information in his job.[3] He knew what countries I was working on. But I never gave him specific information." Howard's suggestion that the two men go to the Soviet embassy in Mexico, described as "joking" by both Howard and Bosch, was taken seriously by the CIA and the FBI. "This was a proposal [by Howard] for an espionage partnership," the former CIA officer said. "It was a classic attempt to recruit a subagent." Bosch insisted he had never agreed to Howard's suggestions.

---

[3] Although Bosch would not describe his work in Bolivia, his statement provided further evidence that his targets included Soviet intelligence officers stationed in La Paz under diplomatic cover; that would explain why Howard, in the Soviet division, would have had access to Bosch's operations.

But he provided more and more details to his interrogators.

It was early evening at the Bahia Mar now, and the story was tumbling out. The FBI agents turned to the events of the July Fourth weekend on South Padre Island. Bosch said he recounted Howard's "I did it" conversation, the reference to "hardball," and his friend's inquiry about whether Bosch would like five, ten, or fifteen thousand dollars. And he told the FBI of Howard's blunt question: "Do you want to work for me?"

The FBI asked Bosch whether he thought Howard's statements meant that Howard had met with the Soviets and given them information. "I told the FBI that's what he could have been referring to—the Soviets—but I'm not taking it seriously." Yet Bosch, by his own account, had been "scared" and "white as a sheet" at Howard's statements.

Bosch was shaken, as well, when the FBI informed him of an execution in the Soviet Union. "The FBI told me that within a day or two it would be announced that a Soviet helping the CIA was executed. It turned out to be Tolkachev. They didn't mention Tolkachev's name. But Ed told me in Washington, when we were in the agency together, Ed told me he had an agent who fit that description. It sounded like the guy Ed talked about. I knew it had to do with aircraft."

There was no secure phone line on South Padre Island, so even as Bosch was being questioned, the electrifying reports of his interrogation had to be driven three hundred miles to the FBI office in San Antonio, then teletyped to the intelligence division on the fourth floor of FBI headquarters.

Bosch was under pressure in the Bahia Mar. "They kept asking me about a case officer: Did Ed go to Vienna, did Ed meet with his Soviet case officer, did Ed receive money, did they pay for his trip? Ed did not tell me that, nor did I tell the FBI that."

Despite Bosch's denials, as previously noted, the FBI affidavit signed by Agent Martin Schwarz states that Bosch, identified as a confidential source, did say that Howard told him he "had met in Europe with the Soviets, gave them information, and had received cash. Howard told the confidential source the Soviets have paid for his trip to Europe in 1984 and Howard met his KGB contact while in Europe."

After two hours of interrogation, the agents wired Bosch to the polygraph machine. The questioning then went on for about another six hours.

With Bosch on the polygraph, the interview went over much of the same ground as before: what had Howard told him in New Orleans and on the July Fourth weekend. Then Bosch found the questions shifting toward him. "There were a lot of counterintelligence questions on the polygraph. The next thing I know there were a lot of questions about Bill Bosch committing espionage." The FBI had no evidence against Bosch, beyond his own statements to the bureau, and was never charged with spying or any other crime.

The eight hours of questioning was taking its toll. "I became hysterical during the interrogation," Bosch said. "I hyperventilated, and he had to stop the polygraph."

But Bosch had talked. During the long interrogation he had provided the information that the FBI needed to seek the arrest of his best friend.

It was a day that Bosch would remember for another reason: September 21 was his thirty-seventh birthday.

Seventeen hundred miles away at FBI headquarters Lane Crocker, the unit chief in the Soviet section, studied the communications from the Bahia Mar. To Crocker and the other agents on duty that Saturday night, it appeared they might finally be getting closer to the evidence they needed. The next few hours would tell.

As the teletype reports of Bosch's questioning clattered in to headquarters, Crocker read them with mounting excitement. This was it. He placed a call to Parker in Norfolk.

It was after midnight in Washington, two hours later than in Santa Fe, before the FBI decided it now, at last, had probable cause to seek a warrant for the arrest of Edward Howard. It could not be obtained at that hour, on a weekend, but there was no reason to worry.

The lights had gone out at 108 Verano Loop. The surveillance was still in place in the desert, and the Howards were safely tucked away for the night.

25

Vanished

Late on Sunday afternoon Phil Baca paid an unexpected
visit to his office in the state capitol; he had decided to go
in for a while to catch up on his work and prepare for the
Monday morning staff meeting.

On his desk he found an envelope and inside it, the brief
typewritten letter from Ed Howard, along with the keys to
the office and a smaller envelope addressed by hand to
Mary Howard, which Baca did not open. The first letter
said:

Dear Phil,
    For personal reasons I hereby tender my resignation
from my position with the committee effective immediately. Please process the appropriate paperwork and
see that all balances due me (travel reimbursements,
leave, salary, and my P.E.R.A. retirement) is given to
my wife, Mary C. Howard. I hope someday to be able
to explain this to you and the rest of the staff.

Sincerely,
Edward L. Howard.

In the darkened, empty capitol, a spooky place on a
Sunday toward nightfall, Baca began to worry and listen
for footsteps. "When I saw the letter, I figured he'd flown
the coop," Baca said. "I thought, *Hell, I'm alone in this
building.* He might be around somewhere, and I recalled
the altercation he had had the previous year, that he was
capable of using a weapon."

Baca decided to get out of the building. It was dusk, close to 7:00 P.M., when he left. He drove to his home nearby and called the FBI office in Santa Fe at 7:15 P.M. "I got an answering machine. It gave me the FBI number in Albuquerque." Dutifully Baca dialed Albuquerque and left a message saying Ed Howard had resigned.

The FBI was stunned at the news. A little after 8:00 P.M. Baca got a call from Agent David Bibb of the Santa Fe office, who asked if he could pick Baca up and return with him to Baca's office.

Other FBI agents rang the Howards' doorbell on Verano Loop and learned from Mary that Howard was gone.

Around 9:00 P.M., from his office, Baca reached Mary and told her he had a letter of resignation from her husband. "Her reaction was 'Ed had problems.' She did not indicate whether she was surprised. She was very noncommittal. I told her of the letter addressed to her, and we made arrangements for her to get the letter the next day. It's my understanding she made it available to the FBI."

The handwritten letter to Mary said, in part: "Well, I'm going and maybe I'll give them what they think I already gave them." The letter also instructed Mary to "sell the house, Jeep, etc., and move with one of our parents and be happy." Howard also told Mary to tell Lee that "I think of him and you each day until I die."

The letter added that "national security is like holding a royal flush in Santa Fe."

Since Mary Howard had helped her husband escape, driven the car when he jumped, arrived home with a dummy in the front seat, and played the tape recorder for the psychiatrist to fool the FBI, it was obvious that she was not learning the news of her husband's escape for the first time from the letter. It was also clear that there had been time for the Howards to discuss financial arrangements, such as selling the house and the Jeep, and where Mary might move.

It was plain, therefore, that Howard had written the letter to make it appear, if possible, that Mary had not participated in his escape. I asked Howard about that in Budapest. "Yes, the letter was to protect Mary," he said.

And the reference to national security and a royal flush, what did he mean by that? Howard indicated that he felt that if he were brought to trial in Santa Fe, he would not have much chance of being acquitted. There were a large number of defense-related and military installations in the area. The reference to a "royal flush," he said, meant that "people in Santa Fe jump up and salute if someone says national security."

Baca called Mary Howard a second time, around 9:30 P.M. on Sunday, to advise her that he needed her to sign a form in order to release the retirement pay. She agreed to meet with Baca in the morning. "It was a tough meeting," Baca said. "Mary was very emotional, and it affected me, too."

On Sunday night, as the FBI discovered that Howard had escaped, Parker was in his car, driving back from Norfolk to his apartment in the Maryland suburbs. He arrived around midnight after the four-hour trip, still unaware of what was happening in Santa Fe.

On Monday morning Parker walked into his office at FBI headquarters. An aide—Parker thinks it was Lane Crocker—told him that Howard had vanished.

"Oh, shit," Parker replied.

He immediately asked what was being done to find him. Steps had been taken on Sunday night to seal the borders, he was told, to the extent that could be done on a weekend. The airlines, international airports, and immigration and customs agents along the Canadian and Mexican borders had been alerted. All Soviet installations across the country—in Washington, New York, and San Francisco—were being watched. FBI attachés in embassies overseas were being notified to try to gain the cooperation of police in other countries. But so far no trace of Howard.[1]

---

[1] It is, of course, a lot easier to intercept someone entering the country than leaving it. Only incoming passengers must show their passports to the Immigration and Naturalization Service. Airline ticket agents normally ask departing international travelers to show their passports, to make sure the passport matches the name on the ticket. For that reason the FBI alerted the airlines to look for Howard. "But you have to con-

Parker was upset. He was sure that with a twenty-five-hour head start, Howard was already out of the country. They were too late. He knew it.

"It was a blow," he said, thinking back on that morning. He desperately wanted to get to Albuquerque to find out what had happened in the desert, but he was frustrated even in that. He had to leave for Boston in a few hours, to lecture the next morning at the Fletcher School of Law and Diplomacy at Tufts University. The topic was the espionage aspects of technology transfer. On Wednesday he was due in Las Vegas for an important FBI regional meeting on counterintelligence operations. It would be Thursday, Parker figured, before he could get to Albuquerque.

In Santa Fe United States Magistrate Sumner G. Buell issued a warrant for the arrest of Edward Lee Howard, charging him with violation of the espionage law.[2] The court papers were sealed.

The fact that Yurchenko was in the hands of the CIA, or that Edward Lee Howard, a former CIA officer, was suspected of espionage, had not yet leaked to the press. Nor was it known that Howard had been under surveillance in Santa Fe for more than a month and had slipped through the FBI's net and escaped.

On South Padre Island early Monday morning FBI agents were back at Bosch's condominium in a grim mood. "Monday the FBI comes screaming, and all of a sudden I'm being advised of my rights," Bosch said. "Ed couldn't be found. I was scared. There was a lot of pressure on me to cooperate or I'd be arrested.

"I gave them permission to search my apartment, and they did. They asked me if I would go to New Mexico. I volunteered to go and talk to Mary." The FBI arranged

---

sider the massive numbers of people leaving the country," Parker said. "By the time we had alerted all the airlines, he was gone."

[2]Howard was charged on September 23 with violating Title 18 of the United States Code, Section 794(c), which carries a maximum penalty of life imprisonment. On September 25, Judge Kaufman issued a bench warrant on a state charge of probation violation. A second federal warrant was issued on September 27, charging Howard with unlawful interstate flight in violation of the terms of his probation.

to fly Bosch to Albuquerque on Tuesday for further interrogation.

In Dallas Kenneth Howard was at work in his job at Texas Instruments when he got a call from Mary in New Mexico. The FBI was with her, she told him; they wanted to know if he knew where Ed was. He did not.

Kenneth Howard cooperated with the Dallas FBI office over many months thereafter, but he worried about his security clearance at Texas Instruments. Howard worked on classified projects for TI, including FLIR, an infrared radar system that allows jet fighter pilots to locate targets at night. As it turned out, he need not have worried; TI followed an enlightened policy and did not penalize Kenneth Howard because his son was an accused spy.

As soon as Howard fled, the FBI obtained search warrants for his home, two cars, and safe-deposit box. Armed with the search warrants, the FBI agents removed boxes of Howard's possessions and papers, even his baby pictures, Mary later complained to her father-in-law.

Mary Howard fairly quickly conceded to the FBI that she had helped her husband escape. To their chagrin, she explained how they had done it: the jump from the moving car; the dummy; the tape recorder. Only later did she learn that the FBI agent on surveillance duty had not seen them drive away from the house and that Howard's jump from the moving car was, as it turned out, unnecessary. No one was following them.[3]

In helping Howard escape, however, Mary Howard was completely in the clear because at the time Edward Howard was not yet a fugitive from justice. Howard jumped and vanished into the night on Saturday, September 21. It was not until Monday, September 23, more than thirty-six hours later, that a federal warrant was issued for his arrest as a spy.

The more serious question confronting the FBI was how much, if anything, Mary Howard knew about, or even

---

[3]The dummy ruse was successful, however, because it fooled the FBI when Mary Howard drove back home and gave Howard a crucial, twenty-five-hour head start.

participated in, any acts of espionage by her husband. The FBI began questioning her intensively for days, shuttling her back and forth between Santa Fe and Albuquerque.

On Tuesday, September 24, while Parker was lecturing at Tufts, Bill Bosch was flown to Albuquerque. Once there he was interrogated and polygraphed again by the FBI. He is said to have provided even more details of how Howard admitted he had met with the Soviets, who had paid perhaps seventy-five hundred dollars for his trip to Europe. Once more he broke down. "The interrogation stopped when I went into hysterics," Bosch said.

Bosch was allowed to return to South Padre Island, but the FBI questioning continued. During an interrogation in his apartment, Bosch said, he told the FBI that he had tried to warn the agency through Peter Ringland. To try to prove his point, Bosch said he attempted to telephone Peter Ringland while he was being questioned by the FBI.

"I got Tanya," he said. " 'What's it about?' she asked. 'I need to talk to Peter about a conversation we had about Ed. You remember when I was talking to you about Ed.' Tanya acknowledged I did have a conversation with Peter and with her." Bosch said the FBI had taped the call to Tanya Ringland.

On Wednesday Parker flew to Las Vegas for the FBI meeting. To his dismay he learned that word of Vitaly Yurchenko's defection to the CIA had leaked to the press. The report, by the conservative columnist Ralph de Toledano, had appeared in that morning's Washington *Times*. Headquarters informed him that there was still no trace of Edward Lee Howard; he had not been seen in the United States or anywhere else. At his hotel Parker sent a suit to the cleaners, and they immediately lost it. His week was not going very smoothly.

On Thursday Parker finally made it to Albuquerque. As he met with the field agents and tried to sort out what had gone wrong, his wife, Jill, distraught, called from Norfolk.

Hurricane Gloria had hit the Virginia coast during the night and the water was rising rapidly outside their new riverfront home. The waves and howling, high winds were battering the deck, and the water was threatening to crash through the glass picture windows and inundate the house. Jill was there alone with their young daughter.

"I talked to Jill several times as the water was rising," Parker recalled. "It was sort of a helpless feeling."

The Albuquerque division was in turmoil. The FBI was still trying to piece together how it had happened, how Edward Howard had managed to slip through a small army of agents and vanish, why the lone lookout had failed to see the Howards drive away on his TV monitor, and how the communications mix-up had occurred, with carloads of agents waiting for a radio signal from the trailer that never came.

At that point the FBI still did not have all the answers to what had gone wrong. The bureau was busy as well, trying to pick up Howard's trail. Where had he gone?

It was Saturday before Parker got back to Norfolk. Gloria had passed through by now. The water had subsided at the last possible moment, and his family and the house were safe. But trees and limbs were down all around, and the wind was still blowing briskly. The place looked like a disaster area.

"I spent a lot of time that weekend thinking," Parker said. "Not so much about what had happened as how we could get him."

Parker longed to board the *Alexandra* and go off by himself, to sort things out. It was too late for blues at the lower end of the Chesapeake, but the sea trout would be running.

He was out of luck. "I couldn't go," he said. "There were still small-craft advisories."

Landlocked, Parker spent the weekend cleaning up after the storm. The hurricane was over, but it had left a lot of debris.

26

Mary

"I didn't see him meet with people."

We had been talking for hours in a hotel suite at the Sheraton Midway in St. Paul. It was late in the afternoon, almost a year to the day since Howard had fled the country.

Mary Howard gave that answer when I asked what she knew about his spying for the Soviets.

In my interviews with her over a year's time I asked her point-blank many times whether she knew her husband had spied for Moscow. Her denials were always less than categorical.

"I don't have any knowledge he spied," she said. "I knew he was real dissatisfied." Perhaps by "no knowledge" she meant she had not observed any act of spying and had no *direct*, firsthand knowledge. Had he ever told her of his espionage activities?

"That's a tricky question," she said, and refused to elaborate. But did she think her husband had given secrets to the Soviets? "I don't want to say yes or no," she replied.

Then from what was she helping him escape? "The FBI had confronted him with the spy charges," she said, "and he felt he was in a no-win situation, that in a small community like Santa Fe, in an easily controlled environment, there was little chance that he would be acquitted."

I said it seemed to me that a wife would ask her husband, "Did you do it?" Mary Howard said she would not discuss that.

She did go so far as to say that sometime after lingering around the Soviet consulate in Washington, Howard told her about it and said that he had thought of going in and selling secrets to the Russians. "Ed mentioned the embassy contemplation," she said. "He did mention what he wanted to do."

Mary Howard, trained to work as a CIA spy in Moscow, had no difficulty living her cover, telling friends and neighbors that she was a State Department wife. At the same time, with her straight midwestern all-American background and strong religious roots, Mary Howard paradoxically came across as a woman uncomfortable with dissembling.

Mere knowledge of lawbreaking is not in itself a crime. Mary Howard, to the extent that she knew her husband had told secrets to the Soviets, broke no law by remaining silent.

On the other hand, when Howard vanished, the FBI was very interested in learning what he might have told his wife because it might provide valuable leads to finding and prosecuting him. And of course, the FBI had to try to determine whether Mary Howard herself had assisted her husband in his espionage activities.

"There was a lot of discussion of possible prosecution of Mary Howard," Parker said, "possibly for conspiracy. But I opposed it, and so did others. It would have made us look a little silly. Here goes Howard, so we go for the wife."

Aside from these tactical considerations, the FBI had no evidence that Mary Howard had ever engaged in espionage. James Geer seemed to say as much. Asked whether the FBI had considered prosecuting Mary Howard, he replied, "It was not a case that has much prosecutive merit."

Howard had confided in Bill Bosch and offered him money and even proposed a trip to the Soviet embassy in Mexico. The FBI assumed that Howard might have been at least as forthright with his wife. Mary Howard was questioned intensively about what she knew and about what Howard had told her of his activities.

The FBI was adroit in its handling of Mary Howard. At first she resisted the interrogation and was reluctant to cooperate, according to FBI sources. But the bureau befriended her. Her husband had left, and she was alone with a small child. The FBI brought in Wendy Woskoff, an agent from Los Angeles. A petite, athletic woman with frosted blond hair, Woskoff managed to become very close to Mary Howard.

Yet the agents who dealt with Mary Howard were not simply being manipulative. Several of those who questioned her came to like her, to regard her as a decent person, and even to sympathize with the difficult position in which she found herself. At the same time they were never sure they were getting the whole story.

"Mary hated them at first, and then they became friends," said Rosa Carlson, who had come to know Mary Howard well on their daily morning walks. "On her birthday, I think, an FBI agent took her out to dinner, and they went dancing. Apparently he got in trouble for that. There was one agent she used to walk with, a woman. It may have been Wendy. Mary had established friendships with them. She knew their names and hobbies."

Mary Howard was in an almost impossible position, caught between loyalty to her husband and her country. She helped him escape. But there must have been, at least initially, anger as well at the man who had abandoned her with their young son and no assurance of when, if ever, he would return.

Trapped by these conflicting emotions and loyalties, undoubtedly worried as well about whether her new friends in the FBI might be trying to gather evidence against her as well as her husband, Mary Howard gradually began to share more information with the FBI.

Most of the time Mary Howard was questioned by the FBI in motels in Santa Fe. Soon after the questioning had begun, she agreed to take a polygraph, and did so, during an FBI interview at the High Mesa Inn.

Yurchenko had said that Howard met the KGB in Vienna in September 1984. The first break in the questioning came when Mary Howard admitted to the FBI that the Soviet Union had paid for her husband's trip to Europe. "She said he got money, that his trip was paid for by the Soviets, that he was reimbursed or even perhaps advanced money for the trip," an intelligence source said.

"She gave us corroboration he was a Soviet agent after he made his escape," said a former FBI official who worked on the case. "Her original story was he made trips for work or job seeking. She eventually admitted he met with the Soviets in Europe, in Austria; he gave information to the Soviets and was paid. She eventually came around." Other FBI sources confirmed this account.

The agents pressed Mary on Howard's first contact with the Soviets? How had he approached them without being detected by the FBI?

It was his CIA training again. As he told me in Budapest, Howard knew that the FBI, at least in 1983, had no coverage of the Soviet consulate on Phelps Place. He must have also known that tourists and business people seeking visas often visit the consulate, to file their applications or pick up their completed visas. So walking in was easy, and the risk was low.

Howard left the note with the Russians, identifying himself as a disgruntled former CIA man. Mary knew; he had told her. At first the Soviets would have been extremely cautious, suspecting a provocation, a CIA trick. But eventually the Soviets took the risk; they got back in touch with Howard, or he recontacted them, probably before his trip to Europe in September 1984.

Where was the money? What Howard knew—the entire Moscow operation—was worth a great deal to the KGB. They must have paid many thousands of dollars. What did Howard do with it?

Reluctant at first to answer, Mary Howard could not

turn back now. In a motel room in Santa Fe, she told the FBI the truth: Howard had a numbered back account in Switzerland.

It was a joint account, she said. With Mary Howard.

He had set it up that way, he told her, so that she could get at it if anything happened to him. She provided the FBI with the account number and two signature cards that Howard had given to her to enable her to withdraw money from the account. But she had not done so.

She had not touched any of that stuff, Mary Howard told the FBI agents. "I didn't want anything to do with it," she said. "I didn't want to know about it. I didn't want to hear him; whenever he said anything, I would just turn it off."

She had not told anyone because she kept hoping he would change and stop. She said she had no bank statements showing how much money was in the Swiss account. She did not know.

The Swiss are extremely reluctant to lift the veil on numbered accounts, and Swiss banking secrecy laws are the strictest in the world.[1] A treaty with the United States does permit Washington to request information about persons under investigation or being tried for crimes. But the treaty does not apply to political offenses, and espionage falls into this category. Officially Washington could not approach the Swiss government to find out how much was in the account or even to verify that it still existed.

Armed with the account number, however, the FBI, probably through the CIA, made informal inquiries about the Howard numbered account. It was a very delicate matter since any disclosure about the bank account to the CIA would violate Swiss law.

Mary Howard had revealed the existence of the Swiss bank account about a week after her husband escaped. The FBI intelligence division got back word within two weeks

---

[1] Under Clause 47(b) of the Swiss Banking Act, any bank officer or employee who reveals confidential information may be fined up to twenty thousand francs or imprisoned for up to six months.

that there was, at that time in mid-October, about $150,000 in the account.

But FBI officials were unable to pin down the money amount officially, as far as is known. Nor was there any way that Washington could, under the treaty, request that the money in the account be frozen. Howard may well have cleaned out the account when he was on the run in Europe. Certainly he could have done so once he reached Moscow.

The FBI agents were stunned at Mary Howard's revelation about the existence of the Swiss bank account. Was that it? Or did Howard have more Soviet money somewhere?

Yes, she told the FBI. There was something more.

He had hidden some of the money in a box and buried it in the desert.

Mary Howard made this startling disclosure while being questioned in a Santa Fe motel. It was about a week after Howard had vanished.

The FBI did not know where Howard was; he might still be in the area, hoping to recover the contents. They would have to try to get there ahead of him.

Although it was late at night now, the agents insisted that Mary Howard lead them there immediately. Accompanied by four FBI agents, she did. One of the FBI men located a shovel, and the strange caravan headed out into the desert. They drove for about twenty minutes beyond the Howards' house on Verano Loop.

Then Mary told the agents to stop the car. They got out. Near a group of trees in a rocky area she pointed to a couple of rocks that marked the spot.

That agents began digging. They hit metal and pulled out an olive drab military-issue ammunition box. They unsnapped the latches. Mary Howard was sobbing.

It was almost midnight when they opened the box. The night was dark and moonless, and the desert air was chill under the stars as the group stared at what was inside the box.

Even by starlight, they could see the silver bars glinting,

and the gold. There was U.S. currency as well, the silver bars, and a few gold Krugerrands.

When they counted the contents, they realized that Edward Lee Howard had just over ten thousand dollars in KGB treasure buried in the New Mexico desert.

27

On the Run

Howard spent Saturday night at the airport motel in Tucson. In his room he tried to change his appearance. "I put dye on my hair. It looked like hell. Made it a dirty blond color. I rinsed it out and went to bed.

"In the morning I walked to the airport. I didn't know where to go, north, east, west, or south. Finally I used my TWA Getaway card to buy a ticket to Copenhagen."

For the first leg Howard boarded TWA Flight 388, which left Tucson at 7:55 A.M. for John F. Kennedy International Airport in New York, with one stop in St. Louis. Howard took his seat, trying to look as inconspicuous as possible and, at all costs, to avoid attracting attention.

Suddenly passengers were craning their necks to get a look at the big, rawboned man who sat down in the empty seat next to Howard.

It was actor Lee Marvin.

"I asked him for his autograph," Howard said. Deciding to make the best of things, Howard struck up a conversation with Marvin. "I was reading *The Hunt for Red October*," Howard recalled. "He had read it and said the author had a good source in the Navy." Howard said he agreed that Tom Clancy must have had a good source.

"At St. Louis Lee moved up into the first-class section," Howard said.[1]

---

[1] Lee Marvin, sixty-three, died of a heart attack in Tucson on August 29, 1987, after I had interviewed Howard in Budapest but before I had a chance to ask the actor whether he recalled his seatmate on Flight 388

Flight 388 landed in St. Louis at 12:30 P.M., eight minutes ahead of schedule, departed for New York an hour later, and arrived at Kennedy at 5:16 P.M. Howard changed planes and boarded TWA Flight 730, which left New York at 6:26 P.M. for London.

Since Phil Baca, after discovering the letters on his desk, placed his first call to the FBI answering machine in Albuquerque at 7:15 P.M. local time, it was already 9:15 P.M. in New York when the bureau received its first hint that he might have fled. By then Edward Lee Howard was almost three hours into his transatlantic flight. The Styrofoam dummy, the CIA wig, and the broomstick had done their job.

Howard was in London before dawn. After a one-hour stopover and another change of planes at Heathrow, the flight took off for Copenhagen, where it arrived at 9:33 A.M. on Monday, September 23.

"In Copenhagen I stayed in transit and didn't go through customs. Three hours later I flew to Helsinki." Since TWA does not fly from Copenhagen to Helsinki, Howard said he used traveler's checks to pay for that leg. He said he did not recall when he had purchased the checks but told himself, "Get rid of them right away."

"In Helsinki I took a taxi to a hotel. I walked around, deciding what to do. That's when I went under. I knew right away I had to get a new passport."

Howard had kept his CIA diplomatic passport after he was fired from the agency, but on the trip to Helsinki he used his regular United States passport. By Monday, he knew, both passports were useless.

"I flew to Frankfurt," he said, "and in Munich I met some people and got a new passport. I knew a section of town, Schwabing, from my student days where the radicals hang out.

on September 22, 1985. However, Jim Mahoney, of Mahoney/Wasserman & Associates, Marvin's publicists, said the actor, who had a ranch near Tucson and lived there full time, often flew to New York from that city. Mahoney said he had no record of the flight because the actor customarily made his own travel arrangements.

"I contacted some people in a disco, and they put me in touch with the people who sold me the passport. I paid almost two thousand dollars for it."

On October 2 *The New York Times* reported that federal agents were searching for Edward L. Howard, who had been identified as a Soviet spy as a result of information from a high-level KGB defector, Vitaly Yurchenko.[2] Later that day an amended criminal complaint, briefly outlining the charges against Howard, was filed in federal court in Albuquerque. The story became major news in the United States and abroad.

In Santa Fe Rosa Carlson was listening to the evening news on television. She picked up the phone and called her husband at his regular Tuesday night poker game. "Gary, you better listen to this," she said.

Lee Rosner, who had shared the house in Cali with Howard when they were both in the Peace Corps, was at Millie and Al's restaurant in Washington with some friends when he saw Howard's face flash on the television screen. His first thought was: *Ed won the Nobel Prize.*

In Washington Jim Lockwood picked up the Washington *Post* and saw the front-page story and the photograph of his jogging partner. "I was in a state of shock," he said. Lockwood had not even known his friend had worked for the CIA.

On Scotch Haven Drive John Matejko also stared at his morning paper in disbelief. Later, when he thought back on it, he was chagrined. He concluded that on some of those weekends away the Howards must have been at the Farm. "They were training to be spies, and I was taking care of their dog."

If Howard was still in the West, as he claims, and not yet in the Soviet Union, the news stories and photographs

---

[2]The story, by Washington correspondent Stephen Engelberg, was carried on page one and headlined EX-C.I.A. MAN REPORTEDLY SOUGHT IN SPY CASE.

of him increased the danger. There was now a chance he might be recognized, anywhere at any time.

The FBI did trace Howard as far as Helsinki. Within the bureau, opinion on where Howard went after that is divided. Phillip Parker was convinced that Howard went from Helsinki directly to the Soviet Union; nothing else was safe. James Geer believed Howard, because of his previous experience in Latin America, was hiding there.

Other FBI counterintelligence specialists tended to believe that Howard did not go immediately to the Soviet Union. "Howard had studied the Soviet Union," one expert said. "He knew what he faced in the Soviet Union and would not have decided so quickly. Maybe he flew to Helsinki to throw us off. He is smart enough. To make the FBI and the CIA *think* he went in. A way of buying time before making his decision to go in."

In the absence of any other evidence, there is Howard's account. With his fake United States passport, Howard said, he spent the next nine months traveling on two continents.

"After Helsinki," he said, "I was in Latin America and Canada under an assumed name. I was questioned by Canadian customs agents and almost arrested twice. Two women agents pulled me out of line in western Canada. No, I won't say where.

"I knew I could never go to anybody who knew me. I knew the FBI was searching for me. Back in the Peace Corps I had a Costa Rican girlfriend. I thought of going to her and then thought no. But I was in Costa Rica when I was on the run, and in Colombia. I went back to Buke and Cali for short periods.

"I taught English in Latin America," Howard said. "I got jobs in Europe. I was a man Friday to an executive—a combination chauffeur, butler. It was in northern Europe, that's all I want to say. On the run, I grew a beard."

If Howard had stashed $150,000 of the money he received from the Soviets in his numbered Swiss bank account, as the FBI believes, the picture of him acting as batman to an executive in northern Europe strains credulity. On the other hand, if he did bank that amount, he might not have had access to it while on the run. He could not be sure whether Mary had revealed the bank account to the FBI; if she had, it would be dangerous to go to the bank to withdraw the money.

"I called Mary in March of 1986 from Latin America. It was a bad connection. I asked her about her situation and said I was OK, and I was trying to find a country to live in. I called her in the morning, and by noon I was on my way out of the country, in case the call was traced."

Howard's mother, Mary J. Howard, said she remembered her son's call to his wife. "But they didn't know where he was calling from." In a telephone interview in July 1986, Howard's mother said she was sure that her phone was monitored. "The phone was ringing a lot, and there was no one there, and finally the man on the line said, 'I just want to make sure the trace is working. We have a trace on your phone.' "

Howard also said he gave a letter to a tourist addressed to his parents but meant for Mary as well. "This was around February of 1986. In June I sent a letter from Vienna, saying I was trying to find a place to live in peace."

Kenneth Howard remembered the letter from Vienna. It was addressed to Mary Howard, known as little Mary to avoid confusion with Howard's mother. "We called Mary, and she said to open it. He said in the letter he was OK, and he really hadn't done anything wrong and apologized for any hard feelings, and he loved us. He's still our son, and we love him very much. We sent the stamp and postmark to Mary because the FBI wants to know everything."

In June 1986, after nine months on the run, Edward Howard said, "I made my first contact with the Soviet government."

Nine months in hiding had taken its toll. "I was a nervous wreck. You don't know what it's like. Every time there's a knock on the door you wonder, *Is it the FBI? An Interpol officer?*"

Howard said he walked into a Soviet embassy; it was clear he meant in Budapest.[3]

"They smiled and said, 'We know who you are. We wondered how long it would take.' "

---

[3]Howard would say only that the embassy was in "an Eastern European country." But at other points in our conversations he mentioned more than once that Hungary was the easiest of the Communist countries to get into. "You can get visas at the airport, and from Finland and several other countries you don't need a visa." He also said he had never been in Poland and had been in Prague only once while a student in Munich. Partly by process of elimination, it became clear that the embassy he was talking about was the Soviet embassy in Budapest.

28

"Yes, Home!"

Late in September, about the time that Howard escaped, the CIA whisked Vitaly Yurchenko over the border into Canada to meet with his former lover, the wife of a Soviet diplomat in Montreal. The operation was closely coordinated with the Canadian Security and Intelligence Service (CSIS).

Yurchenko was flown in a lightplane to Burlington, Vermont, accompanied by two CIA agents, and from there driven over the border. The assignation was arranged at a safe location in either Montreal or Ottawa and guarded by both CIA agents and Canadian security forces.

Valentina Yereskovsky was the wife of the Soviet consul in Montreal, Alexander S. Yereskovsky. Her affair with Yurchenko had begun when the couple and Yurchenko were stationed in Washington in the late 1970's. The Yereskovskys had been transferred to Montreal late in 1979. She was a pediatrician with two children back in Moscow, an attractive ash blond woman of medium height, who wore designer sunglasses and stylish clothes.

The couple lived in a sixteenth-floor apartment on Drummond Street in an upscale neighborhood in Montreal. A neighbor, film producer Jean Boisvert, said the Yereskovskys seemed very close. "They take long walks arm in arm on weekends," he said. "They wear sporty, trendy clothes, leather jackets, and they are always together."

Mrs. Yereskovsky had traveled back to Moscow alone

in the spring of 1985 and presumably had seen Yurchenko then, above five months earlier.

But Vitaly Yurchenko, top KGB official in charge of operations in Canada and the United States, had apparently looked a lot more attractive to Mrs. Yereskovsky than Vitaly Yurchenko, defector. Yurchenko sought to persuade her to join him as a defector, under the protection of the CIA. She spurned his efforts to resume their relationship, and Yurchenko, bitterly disappointed, was spirited out of Canada.

American counterintelligence officials think that Mrs. Yereskovsky's rejection of Yurchenko played an important part in his ultimate decision to escape from his CIA handlers and return to Moscow.

But Yurchenko was also unhappy with the series of sensational leaks in the American press about the information he was providing to the CIA's SE division and to the CI staff. Congress suspected the CIA was tooting its own horn with what Senator Daniel P. Moynihan, the New York Democrat, called "self-promotion." Within the intelligence community there was suspicion that some of the leaks were coming from the White House, which was being provided by the CIA with running accounts of Yurchenko's data. There were reports circulating in the intelligence world that William Casey had even sent videotapes of Yurchenko's debriefing over to the White House.

"After the Nosenko affair," one former CIA man said, "Dick Helms issued classified instructions on the care and handling of defectors, to make sure there would be no more abuses. They have twenty-four-hour visual and audio monitoring. So if someone yells torture, the agency can present the evidence that it didn't happen."

The old agency hand went on: "In this town, if you were *really* on the inside, the measure of whether you were truly in was whether you saw the Yurchenko tapes the next day. If you were lower on the pole, you saw the transcripts three days later. That's why they debriefed him in English. Because the guys in the White House don't speak Russian."

Whatever the source of the leaks, they were rampant.

First the very fact that Yurchenko had defected and was in the hands of the CIA was leaked. Then came the story that he had named Edward Lee Howard as a KGB spy. Then, late in October, Yurchenko's statements about the Shadrin case were published. Yurchenko was allowed to watch television and read the newspapers. At each new disclosure in the press he became increasingly upset.

His stomach was bothering him as well. Yurchenko became convinced he was dying of cancer. The CIA, he later claimed, dressed him up in a white-haired wig, false eyebrows, and glasses and took him, posing as "Friedrich S. Hoffman," a Swiss millionaire, to see Dr. Samuel P. Harrington, a gastroenterologist with offices at 3301 New Mexico Avenue, in Northwest Washington. Yurchenko was diagnosed as having only an ulcer, nothing fatal.

Dr. Harrington said he did not recall treating Yurchenko-cum-Hoffman but added, "It is possible I did because I see a variety of patients from the State Department and the Defense Department."[1] He said he did not remember the CIA's contacting him to see a patient during the period that Yurchenko was in the United States.

Although Yurchenko may have worried less about his health after the visit to the doctor, his increasing discontent was not even assuaged by a private dinner with William Casey in the CIA director's office at Langley headquarters.

As Yurchenko later related the encounter, "I was told that I was going to meet with Mr. Casey, they spent two days preparing me for that meeting. . . . They were concerned that I was going to say more than I was supposed to, they were telling me that I must be polite, that I should be discussing political issues with him, that maybe I might not be happy about the circumstances I was in, but I was not supposed to show that I was protesting. . . .

---

[1] "I did not see anyone under his name, Yurchenko," Dr. Harrington said. After checking his medical records he called back and said, "I have never seen anyone named Friedrich Hoffman, under any variation of the spelling of the name." He also said that the published photographs of Yurchenko did not resemble anyone he had treated.

And they gave me drugs also several hours before that meeting with Mr. Casey, but a lesser amount of drugs than was usual. So I do remember that meeting, but everything seems to have happened as if in a fog.

"I remember that I was brought to the main building of the CIA headquarters in Langley and that I was taken by elevator to the seventh floor to Mr. Casey's office. There was in the office, Mr. Gerber, one of Casey's deputies, and Charley Thompson [identified by Yurchenko as another CIA official]. . . . I was in a condition, obviously that was the point of the strongest effect of the drug, that when Mr. Casey entered the office I at first did not recognize him. For that reason, Mr. Thompson gave me push and said, 'Please say hello to Mr. Casey, this is Mr. Casey.' I rose, greeted him, and later we went to Mr. Casey's dining room."

On Saturday, November 2, Yurchenko said, he was taken on a shopping trip to a department store in Manassas, Virginia by his young CIA guard, whom he identified as Tom Hannah. When the CIA man left him alone momentarily, he telephoned the Soviet embassy, or so he claimed, and said he would try to make his way there.

That evening, Yurchenko persuaded his CIA keeper to take him to Georgetown. Two Soviet films were playing at the Biograph, and Yurchenko told the CIA man he wanted to hear Russian spoken again.[2] They could have dinner and take in the films.

What is known is that Yurchenko, accompanied by only one young CIA officer went to dinner in Georgetown at Au Pied de Cochon, a restaurant at the corner of Wisconsin and Dumbarton. While not noted for haute cuisine, the restaurant does have the virtue of being open twenty-four hours a day. From Yurchenko's point of view, it also had the virtue of being only a little more than a mile from the Soviet compound on upper Wisconsin Avenue. According to Yurchenko, his CIA guard was again Tom Hannah.

---

[2]The Russian-language films playing at the Biograph that night were *Moscow Does Not Believe in Tears*, which won the Oscar in 1980 for best foreign film, and *The Cranes Are Flying*, a 1958 antiwar movie.

Au Pied de Cochon has a saloonlike atmosphere, with square white marble tables, banquettes in red leather, a brass rail, and an old, dark wooden bar running the length of the room. It was crowded on Saturday night.

According to published accounts attributed to "intelligence sources," Yurchenko asked his guard, "What would you do if I got up and walked out? Would you shoot me?"

"No, we don't treat defectors that way."

"I'll be back in fifteen or twenty minutes," Yurchenko replied. "If I'm not, it's not your fault."

And with that, Vitaly Yurchenko, probably the highest-ranking KGB official ever to fall into the hands of the CIA, left the restaurant and disappeared into the crowded Saturday night sidewalks of Georgetown.[3]

He hailed a taxi and within a few minutes was at the gates of the Soviet embassy compound. He identified himself and was let inside.

If Yurchenko's CIA guard had immediately telephoned the FBI, it is possible, although unlikely, that Yurchenko could have been intercepted. But the CIA man did not do so.

Norman Zigrossi, the head of the FBI's Washington field office at the time, said he got the news from his ASAC (assistant special agent in charge). Did the CIA call fast enough? "I don't recall the time frame," he said. "It was quickly, but not quick enough."

The FBI does not have regular surveillance of the Wisconsin Avenue compound, which houses a residential complex and a new, but unoccupied, Soviet embassy. As a result, it would have had to get agents in radio cars to the compound before Yurchenko's taxi arrived there.

---

[3]Yves Courbois, owner of Au Pied de Cochon, said business went up 25 percent after it became known that Yurchenko had dined there just before escaping from the CIA. Yurchenko's presence, he said, saved the restaurant from bankruptcy. In gratitude, he put up a brass plaque on the wall that reads: "Yurchenko Last Supper in the U.S.A. Saturday November 2, 1985." Bartender Dennis Walker said that the restaurant "also serves the Yurchenko Shooter in honor of Vitaly, consisting of equal parts Stolichnaya and Grand Marnier." The drink is four dollars a shot. "Tourists still buy them," Walker said.

"As soon as we heard that Yurchenko was gone," Zigrossi said, "we went to three Soviet installations in Washington, the embassy, the consulate, and the new building. We had forty to fifty people on the street. The ASAC ordered them out before he called me. But it was too late."

There was consternation at the CIA when word of Yurchenko's escape spread through headquarters. Now, not only Edward Lee Howard but the Soviet official who had fingered him had managed to escape, Howard from the FBI and Yurchenko from the CIA. Langley, which had hooted at the FBI when Howard vanished into the desert, was silent.

So far no one on the outside knew what had happened, but at 4:00 P.M. Monday, Boris Malakhov, the press counselor of the Soviet embassy, called the Associated Press' State Department correspondent to announce that there would be a news conference at the Soviet compound at 5:30 P.M. with Vitaly Yurchenko.

The press conference was a mob scene. A nervous, highly agitated Yurchenko, sipping water, sat at a table covered in green felt cloth, flanked by Viktor Isakov, minister-counselor of the Soviet embassy, and Vitaly Churkin, the smooth, bespectacled second secretary. Yurchenko, wearing a gray striped suit and a polka-dotted gray tie, spoke alternately in Russian and accented English. He told a wildly improbable story of having been kidnapped in Rome, brought unconscious to the United States, drugged by the CIA, and held against his will.[4]

Did he reveal secrets to the CIA? "When I was drugged . . . I don't know what I was saying," Yurchenko replied. He railed against his CIA keepers, especially Colin Thompson, known as Mr. Charley, whom he called "my main torturer."

---

[4]While the CIA has the capability of kidnapping and drugging a Soviet agent, to do so would set off a war in which both sides would end up snatching each other's officers off the streets. Neither the CIA nor the KGB would find that to its advantage. "If anyone starts kidnapping, boy, do you get it back in your face," said Harry Rositzke, a former CIA officer who ran operations against the Soviets for many years.

A reporter noted that Yurchenko was said to have provided the information that led to the identification of Edward Howard as a Soviet agent and that Howard had provided information that had led to the arrest of Tolkachev. "First time I recognize name Howard, Tolkahev, and so on and so on, from newspapers," Yurchenko said.

Yurchenko complained at great length about his guards at CIA. "Because twenty-four hours, I even went, excuse me, when I was sleeping, they prohibited to even to close the door. Door should be closed, and next room was sitting such a fat, quiet, stupid—excuse me, nonemotional person who is following the order. Only following the orders. Sometimes I thought I was among crazy persons. . . . And if I try to close the door, he opened the door and [was] sitting [watching] TV."

Yurchenko grumbled that he was completely isolated, unable to use the telephone, forced to speak English, allowed no communication from his family. His guards were gorillas who allowed him no privacy.

He railed against the newspaper leaks, particularly the story about Shadrin, "that allegedly he was killed, and I asked . . . Gerber, aren't you ashamed? I will be taken to court, to the American court, when they had a suit against CIA . . . because it seems that I am going to be the only witness for that, and he told me, don't worry, we'll settle everything, the main thing is to influence people."

He told of his dinner with Casey, of the alleged one-million-dollar offer to remain in the United States, and rambled on about the insensitivity of his CIA guards. Vitaly Yurchenko clearly appeared agitated, and he was either one of the best actors ever to walk the Russian stage or a man truly in emotional turmoil. Anyone watching his performance that afternoon would probably be forced to conclude that he was a real defector who for various reasons had changed his mind.

He had, of course, every reason to be nervous, to fear for his future in the Soviet Union, unless he was a plant sent to embarrass U.S. intelligence. But his whole demeanor that day was of a man distraught, not a clever

KGB plant dispatched to fool American counterintelligence.

The State Department said Yurchenko had defected to the American embassy in Rome voluntarily and had requested and been granted political asylum. Yurchenko could return to the Soviet Union if that action was "of his own choosing," the department added. "We will insist on a meeting with him in an environment free of Soviet coercion to satisfy ourselves about his real intentions."

At 6:07 P.M. the next day Yurchenko, at the center of a phalanx of Soviet officials, arrived at the State Department for the meeting. He emerged an hour later. A reporter shouted a question. Was he going back to the Soviet Union? Yurchenko clasped his hands over his head like a boxer and declared, "Yes, home!"

CIA officials quietly explained to reporters that in the wake of the mistreatment of defector Yuri Nosenko two decades before, the agency was bending over backward not to use improper methods in such cases. Yurchenko, they claimed, was guarded for his own protection but kept on a loose leash; he could not be restrained from redefecting to the Soviets.

Other intelligence specialists said that while this might be legally and technically true, the agency had seriously erred in allowing Yurchenko out with one inexperienced young guard and in taking him to Georgetown, so close to the Soviet compound.

On Wednesday, November 6, Yurchenko, carrying a bouquet of red roses, stepped from a Soviet embassy van at Dulles Airport. At 4:15 P.M. he boarded an Aeroflot Ilyushin jet for Moscow. On the steps of the plane ramp he turned and waved; the gesture was caught by television and still photographers and seen by millions of people. What the public did not know was that Yurchenko was waving to the two FBI agents from the Washington field office, both fluent in Russian, who had helped debrief him.

Was Yurchenko a true defector? U.S. counterintelligence experts are not unanimous in their assessment, but most think he was genuine.

James Geer, the head of FBI counterintelligence, said,

"On balance we got more than he did. Oh, he knows who some of our people are. But we never assume that a defector will be here forever, and we don't reveal too much to them."

American counterintelligence officers considered the possibility that Yurchenko had been sent to the United States, not merely to embarrass the CIA but to protect a current senior mole inside the agency by giving away Howard, who had already left the CIA. But the theory cannot be proved, one reason that the world of counterintelligence has been called "a wilderness of mirrors." Where the reflections end and reality begins, nobody knows.

Counterintelligence officials acknowledge that Yurchenko appeared to have become discontent with his handlers. A former FBI counterintelligence agent put it bluntly: "Yurchenko went back because he got pissed off because everything he gave he read in the newspaper. That was one of the conditions he had set: he didn't want leaks."

Norman Zigrossi, the FBI official whose agents worked with Yurchenko, gave this assessment: "Overall his needs were not being met. He's a high official, lives a good life. He gives it all up to come here. Everything he'd anticipate collapses: the woman in Canada, and no one is taking care of him. He's depressed. He sees leaks—the fact that he is being held, Pelton, Howard, Shadrin—and slowly realizes he is a pawn in a bigger game; he is being used. The agency fronted him before he was even resettled. All of a sudden he's a public figure. He reads the papers. What does he think is going on?"

If Yurchenko was real, why did he leave, risking imprisonment or execution in the Soviet Union? The answers are speculative. One possibility is that Yurchenko reasoned that he could, by charging he had been kidnapped, become a propaganda showpiece for the Soviets, which might help ensure his safety. He may have hoped that Moscow would treat him well to demonstrate the folly of defecting and to encourage others to believe they could safely come home.

Donald F. B. Jameson, an old SE hand and vice-president of the Jamestown Foundation, which helps re-settle defectors in the United States, said that in the past the KGB has sometimes sent out "phony defectors" to penetrate émigré groups or for other reasons. He cited one example, in which a fake defector was dispatched to test relations between two intelligence agencies. "A Soviet trade delegate defected in Manila in 1983 and was debriefed in Munich, where much of the regular debriefing went on, because the KGB said, 'Let's see how close Marcos is to Langley. Have him jump in the mouth in Manila and come out the ass in Munich.' "

But, Jameson said, there have been no phony defectors of top rank, which would appear to be further evidence that Yurchenko was real. "What was missing for Yurchenko was a case officer," Jameson said "For any Russian, there has to be a *khozyain,* a boss to whom he can take problems. With Yurchenko, word came down to do whatever he wants. We don't want anything to go wrong. So they gave him a nice house, probably had a nice cook, but no *khozyain,* no case officer, and that is the only real essential. He said, 'Hey, I'm real unhappy. My wife has left me, my son is going to be kicked out of school, the woman in Montreal doesn't love me.' When that happens, a case officer says, 'OK, let's go to Hawaii.' You get him out of Washington.

"I understand the fellow who took him to the restaurant was a young security man who knew nothing about the Soviet Union. They ended up in Georgetown, near the embassy, because Yurchenko said, 'Let's go to a French restaurant.' 'I don't know any,' the kid says. 'Let's go to Au Pied de Cochon,' Yurchenko says. If the security man had said, 'Let's go to Chez Andrée in Alexandria,' the whole story might have had a different ending. The point is that the immediate situation is very important; it influences the outcome."

Two days after Yurchenko returned to Moscow, the CIA took the unusual step of issuing a three-page biography of the man who had, until he walked away, been its prize catch. The biography confirmed that Yurchenko had been the KGB official in charge of operations in the United States and Canada from April to July 1985, and it revealed that his previous job, for five years before that, had been unusually interesting. Yurchenko, the CIA said, had been chief of the Fifth Department of Directorate K, the counterintelligence directorate. His department was responsible for rooting out suspected spies inside the KGB; he also worked with defectors in the Soviet Union, including the British defectors Kim Philby and George Blake.

About the same time that the CIA was circulating the Yurchenko biography, the story of his tryst in Canada with Valentina Yereskovsky leaked to the press. "An outrageous, dirty lie," responded Consul General Alexander Yereskovsky in Montreal. "Dirty linen . . . unseemly," said Mrs. Yereskovsky, in a statement released by the consulate.[5]

In Moscow, on November 14, Yurchenko held a press conference in which he said that William Casey's fly was unbuttoned when they dined together at Langley and that, among other tortures, his CIA captors had forced him to play golf, eat with them in expensive restaurants, and pick up the check. Asked about the Yereskovskys, however, he did not add his voice to the chorus of denials. He confirmed that he had known the couple in Washington. And he knew Valentina?

"That is a highly private matter," Yurchenko replied.[6]

---

[5]On November 5, the day after Yurchenko surfaced in Soviet hands in Washington, Svetlana Dedkov, the forty-eight-year-old wife of a Soviet trading company official, plunged to her death from a twenty-seventh-floor window in Toronto. The police ruled her death a suicide. Both Canadian and Soviet officials said it had no connection with Yurchenko or his visit to Canada.

[6]After the press conference Yurchenko dropped from public view until March 14, 1986, when he was shown on West German television in a brief sidewalk interview in Moscow. The interview took place shortly after reports in the West German press that Yurchenko had been executed. Reporter Lutz Lehmann, who claimed he had bumped into Yurchenko by chance, asked him, "Are you really Vitaly Yurchenko?" "Do I have to show you my passport?" Yurchenko replied. On August 9 Yurchenko was quoted in an interview in the newspaper *Moskovskaya Pravda*. "As you can see I am alive and well," the interview reported

There were others who were watching the Yurchenko drama unfold with more than casual interest.

In Santa Fe Mary Howard, reading that Yurchenko had gone back to the Soviet Union, hoped it might be safe for her husband to come home. After all, the government had just lost its original witness, the man who had triggered the investigation of Edward Howard.

But it was five months before she had a chance to suggest this to her husband. When Howard telephoned her from Latin America in March 1986, he said, "She kept saying Yurchenko had gone back. I said it didn't change anything. They are still trying to put me in jail."

---

he said. "In March I started work in my old job." More than a year went by before there was any word of Yurchenko. Then, on September 20, 1987, *Izvestia* carried an interview quoting Yurchenko as mocking Western reports that he had been executed.

29

"We Screwed Up"

On Capitol Hill, when Howard's escape became known in October, there were immediate calls for congressional investigations in the House and Senate.

Senator David Durenberger, the Minnesota Republican who was chairman of the Senate Intelligence Committee, and Patrick J. Leahy of Vermont, the Democratic vice-chairman, announced that the Senate panel would conduct a detailed examination of the case.

Both the Senate and House intelligence committees did make limited inquiries into the Howard affair. The Senate panel held secret hearings at which Casey, Clair George, Hathaway, and Gerber all testified.

"We screwed up," CIA Director William Casey testified in secret session to the House Intelligence Committee.

But the CIA was not about to lay out in depth the alarming record of the Howard case for the congressional panels: his hiring despite a history of drug use and the waiver of the normal standards for CIA employment in such cases; his selection for Moscow despite the knowledge inside Langley of his alcohol problem; his abrupt dismissal; his bizarre embassy calls; the driveway confrontation; his confession of his lingering outside the Soviet consulate; the decision to pay for his psychiatrist after that confession in hopes of containing the damage in-house; the concealment of the case from the FBI for more than two years; the crucial delay by the CIA in identifying Howard, even after Yurchenko's disclosures, that permitted him to slip off to Vienna for a third time, unobserved by the FBI; and the failure to tell the bureau about Bill Bosch.

Heavily sanitized versions of this history were provided to the committees and touched on in brief testimony by agency officials in secret session. The House panel, headed by Democrat Lee H. Hamilton of Indiana, had a particularly difficult time getting a straight story from the agency about Howard's drug use. The CIA submitted conflicting information, first providing an extensive, detailed list of the drugs Howard had used, by year and type, then attempting to pull back and minimize his drug problem.

Neither committee issued a public report on the case, however. Months later, there were only brief references to Howard in separate, broader reports on U.S. counterintelligence issued by each panel.[1]

In a breakfast interview several months after Howard's escape I asked Senator Durenberger about the CIA's handling of the case. "Somebody's covering up," he said. "We'll never know the truth."

Perhaps one reason that the committees did not probe in greater depth was that the executive branch promised to conduct its own inquiries.

Two internal investigations of the Howard case were carried out at the CIA. The directorate of operations conducted its own secret study. Casey also ordered a report by the CIA's inspector general. There was an awkward problem, however. John Stein, the IG, had been the deputy director for operations when Howard was selected for the Moscow station and when he was dismissed; he could not very well conduct the internal investigation and write

---

[1]The intelligence committees also examined the Yurchenko affair. Acting CIA Director Robert M. Gates conceded to the Senate panel that there were "organizational deficiencies" in the handling of defectors. Henceforth, he said, "a single individual and a single organization" would manage defectors, with one case officer in charge, "so that a defector isn't facing a whole new set of people all the time and there is somebody there that he gets to know and that he can depend upon and that understands him and . . . can identify when he is going through a particular psychological crisis."

the report. Stein had to recuse himself and the task fell to his deputy, Carroll Hauver.

The CIA inspector general's report neatly sidestepped the question of why Howard, given his history of drug use, had ever been hired. The agency glossed over the whole question of drug use and why those standards had been waived when Howard was employed. Instead, the report emphasized that Howard had been dismissed when his problems were discovered.[2]

In addition, the President's Foreign Intelligence Advisory Board, a civilian group, investigated the Howard case and issued a report. A Harvard political scientist, James Q. Wilson, coordinated the inquiry with the assistance of the PFIAB staff. The classified report, which was not made public, sharply criticized both the CIA and the FBI for their handling of the case.

The report to the President also criticized what the advisory panel viewed as poor working relations between the CIA and the FBI. William Webster, then FBI director and later CIA director, wrote a letter to the President's intelligence board, assuring it that the FBI would take steps to improve its relations with the CIA.

At the working level in both agencies the critical report and the Webster letter rankled. "Sure, it broke down in this one case," an FBI man said. "But we had good relationships. Of course, when the Howard thing happened, our guys were pissed off. The agency guys were pissed when we lost the surveillance. Institutionally there are always going to be differences."

But the congressional committees, the CIA inspector general, and the President's advisory board did not want to face the unpleasant facts of the Howard case or to draw the obvious conclusion: enormous damage that might have been avoided was done to U.S. intelligence.

---

[2] A House Intelligence Committee report released on February 4, 1987, faulted the CIA inspector general's report and observed that "curiously, CIA management focused more attention and action . . . on the manner by which Howard was fired . . . and gave relatively little attention to how he was hired in the first place. The extent of Howard's drug use was underplayed in this review."

Moreover, the disturbing truth was that the CIA never told the FBI about Howard. "It was Yurchenko who told the FBI," a former CIA officer said. "Perhaps the CIA would, in time, have told the FBI, but there's no way to know that. It was a joint interview with Yurchenko. The FBI guys came back from the interview and said there's a problem. The CIA had no choice at that point. The files on Howard were produced because the FBI asked for them."

The Senate Intelligence Committee report on counterintelligence, drastically watered down in negotiations with the CIA, came closest to pinpointing the trouble. "In the Edward Lee Howard case, CIA security officials failed to alert and involve the FBI in a timely fashion," the report said. The FBI, it added, should be told when employees with access to extremely sensitive information resign or are dismissed under circumstances that might create "motivations for espionage."

Privately William Casey acknowledged the obvious: the CIA's concealment of the case from the FBI even after Howard's confession about lingering outside a Soviet embassy building was clearly a mistake. That was a failure; his people didn't take it seriously enough.

In a free society even former CIA employees with rarefied clearances and sensitive access cannot be placed under surveillance or their telephones tapped on mere suspicion. The objectives of counterintelligence collide with the values of civil liberties in a democracy. No one would suggest that police state methods be employed against former case officers who fall under suspicion.

The argument might be made, therefore, that even if the CIA had informed the FBI when Howard was dismissed and at subsequent key points along the way, there would have been little that the bureau could have done to prevent his spying. FBI officials disagree with that thesis.

Certain steps could have been taken to check on Howard's activities. The standards for investigating a suspected agent of a foreign power are contained in guidelines, issued by the attorney general, that are themselves classified. These place restrictions on such techniques as car beepers, which are placed under bumpers to permit agents to tail someone, and mail covers, which allow the government to record the addresses on mail sent or received by a suspect. However, attorneys familiar with the secret guidelines say that they permit considerable latitude in cases where there is reason to believe espionage has been, or will be, committed.

Phil Parker said of Howard, for example, "Someone with his clearances and the information he had, we could do more with him than the average citizen. The guidelines would allow surveillance. There are two types of investigations: preliminary, which are very restricted in what you can do, and then a full. Or you can go right to a full."

Well before Howard confessed the consulate episode, the FBI, had it been told of his dismissal and subsequent erratic behavior, could have taken countermeasures that would not have involved direct surveillance of Howard. Parker said, "There were other things we could do. We could alert people who might see him, for example. We would let it be known that this person might be making contact with the Soviets at installations in this country. We would have a higher degree of alert for a specific person if he showed up in the vicinity. We could have checked travel records and done record checks of various kinds."

Another former FBI agent said that Howard's confession of loitering around a Soviet embassy building "would have been enough to put surveillance on him." Even if the CIA could defend its silence up to that point, once Howard had confessed, the agency's failure to notify the FBI was unconscionable.

Not only the CIA was at fault in the Howard affair, but the FBI also erred in that Howard was able to escape through a cordon of its agents in place in Santa Fe. The bureau lost Howard not once but twice on the night he escaped: it failed to see him leave his house and then did not reinstitute surveillance when it could have after his intercepted call from the restaurant.

Howard's escape appeared to be chiefly the fault of a single agent who did not see the couple drive away from their house. While conceding a mistake in "our on-the-scene operations," Geer called the escape an "aberration" and said he saw "no institutional weakness."

Nevertheless, both the CIA and the FBI took unannounced disciplinary action in the aftermath of the Howard case. Each agency reprimanded three officers.

The FBI issued reprimands to the young agent who was on duty in the trailer, to one supervisor, and to Rodney K. McHargue, the assistant special agent in charge of the Albuquerque division. Within the FBI it is traditional to discipline the ASAC when something goes wrong.

At the CIA three officers, all in SE division, were reprimanded, beginning with Thomas Mills, the Soviet branch chief. The brunt of the disciplinary action appeared to have fallen on Mills, who was Howard's boss and the one official who seemed to feel some concern about the agency's treatment of Howard.

"Mills was the fall guy," one CIA source said. "A letter of reprimand in the file virtually means you have no chance of an overseas assignment or promotion."

Gus Hathaway, the counterintelligence chief, and Burton Gerber, the chief of the Soviet division, both of whom played key roles in the mishandling of the Howard case, emerged unscathed.

"The three guys were called in by Clair George and given their letters of reprimand," the CIA source said. "Gus was not one of them. The agency felt he had taken appropriate action to get Howard a psychiatrist."

Phil Parker had much better luck in tracking down Yurchenko's other mole, the former employee of the National Security Agency who had come to the Soviet embassy in Washington in January 1980, at a time when Yurchenko was the KGB officer in charge of security for the SK, the Soviet colony.

The FBI had recorded the man's telephone call to the embassy at 2:30 P.M. on January 15:

CALLER: OK, um, how? . . . Do I just ring the bell and someone lets me in? How do I get in?

YURCHENKO: No, no, you'll enter through the gate directly.
CALLER: And, OK, they'll let me in?
YURCHENKO: Of course, no question.

Until Yurchenko revealed that the caller, who walked into the embassy soon after, had worked for the NSA, the FBI had not known where to look for the man. Yurchenko disclosed that the visitor had worked for the NSA and had given away Ivy Bells, the NSA's underwater wiretapping of Soviet communications, and other sensitive secrets. But he remembered him only by his KGB code name, Mr. Long. Yurchenko also provided a physical description of the walk-in and described the run-down house that he thought was near Beltsville.

The FBI pored through its tapes of telephone calls to the Soviet embassy and located the conversations. It began playing the tape for NSA employees, hoping that someone would recognize the voice. In mid-October an NSA employee said, "That's Ron Pelton."

On November 24, 1985, two FBI agents interviewed Ronald W. Pelton in an Annapolis motel. He confessed to extensive spying for the Soviets, including two trips to Vienna to meet with agents of the KGB. Just before midnight the agents arrested Pelton. His own statements were used to convict him at his trial six months later.[3]

* * *

---

[3]Pelton was arrested at the conclusion of the motel interview and tried in May 1986. A federal jury convicted him of espionage, and he was sentenced in December to life imprisonment. In addition to Ivy Bells, Pelton gave the Soviets information from a sixty-page "encyclopedia" on Soviet communications, called the Signal Parameters File, that he had authored while working for the NSA and other sensitive intelligence. He received a total of thirty-five thousand dollars from the Russians. The run-down house that Yurchenko remembered casing turned out to be in Bowie, seven miles from Beltsville, at 12203 Maycheck Lane. Neighbors recalled the driveway's being strewn with broken automobile parts.

A week after Pelton's arrest Victor B. Kenton, a Los Angeles criminal lawyer, got a call at his office in Century City from Bill Bosch. Kenton gave him an appointment.

A few days later Bosch drove up from Mission Viejo in his black 911 Porsche and parked in the underground garage of Kenton's office on Santa Monica Boulevard.

"I'm being followed by the FBI," Bosch told the attorney.

Kenton, then thirty-seven, a dark-haired easterner who had earned his law degree in California, had heard statements like that before and was highly skeptical.

Bosch took him downstairs. "Sure enough," Kenton said, "there were three cars in the alley by the gas station next to the garage: a white Porsche and two sedans. Four guys in down jackets in the cars. I walked up to a car and said, 'I'm Victor Kenton, Mr. Bosch's lawyer.' "

"We're lawyers, too," one of the men replied.

Kenton scribbled down the numbers of the license plates. Uncertain whether the men in the down jackets were really FBI agents and alarmed for the safety of his new client, Kenton hauled Bosch back into the lobby and dialed 911. He read off the numbers of the license plates. "The Los Angeles Police Department said, 'There are no such plates.' So now I was sure they were FBI."

Kenton went back out, got the name of the agents' supervisor, Gary Auer, and called him the next day. The FBI man confirmed that Bosch was under surveillance, and he had a favor to ask. Would Bosch please not drive so fast? They had already had to rent the white Porsche to keep up with Bosch's black Porsche.[4]

The surveillance continued—at one point an FBI agent joined Bosch and Kenton for a hamburger at McDonald's—and in January Kenton wrote to both California senators and the Department of Justice to try to get the FBI agents to stop following Bosch. The surveillance, Kenton pointed out, was now in its fifth month, and Bosch had not been charged with a crime.

Auer had told Kenton that Bosch would not be arrested

---

[4]When Bosch drove to California from South Padre Island that fall, the FBI, in a Plymouth, had a great deal of trouble keeping up with him.

unless he tried to cross an international border. Finally Kenton told Auer that he planned to get a reporter from the Los Angeles *Times,* drive Bosch to the airport, and put him on a plane to Acapulco. He assumed Bosch would then be arrested, at which point Kenton would file a suit against the FBI. "Five days later," Kenton said, "the agents disappeared, like Brigadoon."

The Justice Department had decided by that time that it had no grounds to prosecute Bosch for espionage. He was in the clear.

Edward Howard's spying was still unraveling the CIA's operations in Moscow. Paul Stombaugh, the CIA officer expelled by the Soviets, had been caught in June 1985, along with Howard's asset, Adolf Tokachev.

On March 14, 1986, the Soviets announced the expulsion of another CIA officer, Michael Sellers. He was serving under diplomatic cover as a second secretary in the U.S. embassy in Moscow. Sellers was accused of spying and holding a clandestine meeting with a Soviet citizen.

On May 7 the KGB grabbed another CIA officer, Erik Sites, as he strolled along Malaya Priogovskaya Street to contact a Soviet asset. Sites was listed as a civilian employee of the defense attaché's office.

A lengthy account in *Izvestia* detailed operational procedures that would have sounded familiar to the Howards. The account said that Sites's wife, Ursula, was waiting by a car for her husband to return from the agent meeting.

According to the Soviet account, Sites carried a blue bag containing an electric razor with a secret compartment to conceal a miniature camera, "the size of a tube of toothpaste, designed for photographing secret documents." A vial of the type used for vitamins contained tablets that dissolved in water for secret writing. Sites also carried innocuous letters addressed to persons in Brookfield, Wisconsin, and Texas. Secret messages could be encoded between the lines of the letters in invisible ink. A message concealed inside a notebook asked the agent for information "about the tactical and technical characteristics of aircraft, the location and purpose of defense facilities, and the personnel working there." The message added: "We wish you a pleasant summer and await a meeting with you in the autumn."

The Soviet newspaper added dramatically:

> The passers-by and the inhabitants of the block who are sitting on the benches on this warm May evening hardly pay attention to him. Eric Sites is indistinguishable from a Muscovite: he wears jeans, a checked shirt, a zippered jacket and a cap bought in a Moscow shop. He carries the blue bag. . . . Sites looks nervously from side to side. It seems there is nothing suspicious. At exactly 21:15 a man appears carrying a rolled-up newspaper that is the sign. Sites approaches him, gives the password, he hears the answer, invites him to take a walk. . . . Caught red-handed, Sites stands there, deathly pale, as if thunderstruck.

Sites, too, was expelled. Reports circulated in Washington that two more CIA officers had been quietly ousted from Moscow.

The arrests and expulsions shattered the Moscow station. Other operations in the Soviet capital went bad, and the CIA concluded that all these had been betrayed by Howard.

There was one more blow to come. On October 22 TASS announced the outcome of the trial on charges of espionage of a former researcher, Adolf G. Tolkachev. A military tribunal had convicted him of "high treason in the form of spying."

The Moscow announcement described Tolkachev as "a staff worker of a Moscow research institute." The announcement added: "It was established in the course of the investigation that Tolkachev in pursuit of selfish ends and on account of his hostile attitude toward the Soviet state had maintained espionage contacts with U.S. intelligence agents who had been in Moscow under the guise of U.S. embassy personnel."

Tolkachev, the Soviets said, had been arrested by the KGB and "exposed as an agent of U.S. intelligence."

Tolkachev's appeal had been turned down, the news agency said, and he was executed.

30

From Russia, with Love

When Howard walked into the Soviet embassy in Budapest in June 1986, he was, as he described it, a "nervous wreck" from his eight months on the run.

"They convinced me I would go to jail if I went back to the United States," Howard said. "After a week of discussions, in late June, they put me on a plane to Moscow."

His odyssey was over. Edward Lee Howard, by his account, had finally made it to Moscow. He arrived in the Soviet capital three years late, not as a CIA man but as a spy under the protection of the KGB. He was the first CIA officer ever to defect to the Soviet Union.

"In Moscow I got a hypo and tranquilizers," he said. "I was very nervous. They gave me a thorough physical. About a month later they discovered ulcers and prostate trouble."

Howard said he drank a lot at first. Did he consider himself an alcoholic? "I know that now I'm not. I know I had a drinking problem in Santa Fe. My definition of alcoholic is when alcohol causes problems in my life. Maybe in the past year four or five times I've had too much to drink. Mostly in the first four months.

"They gave me a Russian tutor. I was very scared when I first arrived. 'I can only stay awhile,' I said. 'I've got to go back and get my wife.' They said, 'Your wife is probably under control.' The Soviets worked hard on my wife to come. They sent her a letter saying she and Lee could go back [to the United States] if they came."

The FBI, Howard claimed, had warned Mary it might be risky to try to visit him in Moscow. "The KGB man in Greece defected to the United States with his mistress and son, and his wife wants the son back. The FBI warned Mary they [the Soviets] might try to swap her for the kid from Greece."[1]

After the medical exam, Howard recounted, "they said we have to make your presence official." On August 5, 1986, Howard called his wife, who had moved from Santa Fe to the St. Paul area, and told her to expect an announcement shortly. "I told her where I was and that I wanted to see her and Lee. She said it would take a few days to make the arrangements."

The same day Howard telephoned his parents in Garland, Texas, and told them to expect an announcement from Moscow. He asked his parents to visit him, but Kenneth Howard said he would postpone any trip until he retired in about six years; he explained he did not want to jeopardize his security clearance at Texas Instruments.

On August 7, almost a year after Howard had vanished in New Mexico, he was surfaced by the Russians in Moscow. TASS, the Soviet news agency, announced that Edward Lee Howard, "a former CIA officer," had been granted political asylum in the Soviet Union. The request was approved by the Presidium of the Supreme Soviet, which acted on "humane considerations." Howard had asked to live in the Soviet Union, the announcement went on, because "he has to hide from U.S. secret services which unfoundedly persecute him."

A week later Howard called Mary again and asked when she was coming to Moscow. "She said she didn't think it was advisable just now, with the press, and the Justice Department."

When I first met Mary Howard in September 1986 in

---

[1]In May 1985 Sergei Bokhan, forty-nine, the deputy director in Athens of the GRU (Soviet military intelligence), defected to the West and was brought to Washington to be debriefed by the CIA. News reports at the time said that the Greek government had agreed to Soviet demands that Bokhan's wife and child be returned to Moscow.

St. Paul, I had asked her about her plans for the future. We had been talking for hours, and near the end of the interview we stood by the window looking down at the courtyard of the Sheraton Midway. It was getting dark outside.

"I plan to stay in this country," she said. "I came back to Minnesota because I like it here. I have good friends, since kindergarten."

"You've got to make some decisions," I said.

She nodded. "You can't have a marriage with one person in Moscow and one here."

On September 14, a little more than a month after the announcement in Moscow, Howard appeared on Soviet television, interviewed by journalist Genrikh Borovik. He had grown a mustache. In the interview Howard spoke in English for the most part, with Russian voice-over.[2] He described his background and CIA training and claimed: "I love my country and my people. I have never done anything which inflicted damage on Americans or jeopardized the security of my country." Howard said he had sought refuge in the Soviet Union because he was getting tired of life on the run. "One cannot hide from the CIA for the rest of one's life," he said.

It was Howard's only public appearance since he escaped from the FBI in New Mexico. He gave no other interviews until he met me in Budapest, and we talked intensively during six days in late June 1987.

The KGB treated Howard well in Moscow. He was, after all, the first CIA defector. He had provided important intelligence information to the KGB before fleeing the United States, and he was a continuing source of information about CIA operations, personnel, and procedures.

In Moscow Howard lives in an apartment a couple of blocks from the Arbat, a main avenue in the Soviet capital,

---

[2]Howard ended the TV appearance by speaking a few words in halting Russian to the Soviet people. *"Bolshoe spasibo* [thank you very much]," he said, continuing in Russian, "for the help which you have given me at a difficult moment. Many thanks to the Soviet people and to the Soviet state. You are very kind."

and he has been given a dacha in the countryside. The apartment, spacious by Soviet standards, is 88 square meters, or almost 950 square feet.[3] Howard lives on the second floor of the building, and there are three-star generals among the other tenants.

The dacha, Howard said, is "on the outskirts of Moscow. It's a brick dacha. It has two bedrooms, a living room, dining room, kitchen, and a small upstairs study. It's not very big. I don't need much. It is a little bigger than my house in New Mexico."

Howard gave me a color photograph of the interior of his dacha. It shows a living room furnished with two wide chairs and a couch. A stereo and two small speakers can be seen on a shelf above the couch, flanking framed color photographs of Mary and Lee. A wooden stairway leads up to the balcony that forms the study, which has a picture window.

On the back of the photograph Howard wrote: "My house outside of Moscow—the living room. Ed Howard 6/27/87."

At the dacha, Howard said, he grills shashlik.

Howard, who is dark-haired, compact, and a shade under five feet eleven inches, had lost twenty-five pounds from his weight in Santa Fe, partly because he had taken up smoking in the spring. He weighed 170 pounds when I interviewed him in Budapest, down from 195. He said several times that he planned to stop smoking.

In Moscow Howard keeps in shape by playing volleyball and tennis on KGB intramural teams at the Dinamo sports complex. "Dinamo is a sports club," Howard said. "The MVD [Soviet internal police] and the KGB have soccer and tennis teams. All the teams are KGB and MVD. I'm on the volleyball team."

He shops at special stores in Moscow. "They let me shop at the diplomatic store," he said.

"Don't you worry you might run into some Americans?"

"So what? I have a right to be there. I saw some ma-

---

[3]If the apartment were square, it would be approximately 31 feet by 31.

rines at the store and almost joked, 'You guys ought to be careful who you take home to bed.' '' But Howard said he did not say anything to the marines, nor did he reveal his identity to them.[4]

Howard goes to a Roman Catholic church behind the KGB headquarters in Dzerzhinsky Square every three or four weeks, he said. ''I don't like it as well as the church in Budapest because in Moscow the mass is said in Russian. In Budapest it's in Latin, which I understand.[5]

In keeping with his importance to the Soviets, in Moscow Howard's welfare is personally supervised by the powerful number two official of the KGB and the head of its foreign operations, Vladimir Aleksandrovich Kryuchkov. A stolid-looking man of sixty-three, Kryuchkov, although little known in the West, is the deputy chairman of the KGB and chief of its First Chief Directorate, in charge of all foreign operations. As the official in charge of Soviet espionage all over the world he is one of the most powerful men in the Soviet Union.*

Kryuchkov, who is an ethnic Russian born in Sverdlovsk, rose through the apparatus of the Communist party's Central Committee. He was in a construction unit during World War II, then worked his way up through the party machinery. By the 1950's he was managing Hungarian affairs for the Central Committee. In 1956 he was third secretary in Budapest when Yuri Andropov, the ambassador, helped crush the revolt in Hungary. When Andropov

---

[4]Marine Sergeant Clayton J. Lonetree, the only U.S. marine in the Moscow embassy to be tried for espionage, claimed in his defense that he had been dealing with the Soviets in the hope of capturing Edward Lee Howard and spiriting him out of Moscow to the United States. Lonetree was convicted on August 24, 1987, and sentenced to thirty years.

[5]I wrote to Howard after our meetings in Hungary, enclosing a map of Moscow and asking him to pinpoint the church he attended. He wrote back, enclosing the map and circling the spot. On the map he wrote: ''Area of the Catholic church I attend. I don't know the name. It's the only one in Moscow that is active.'' He signed the map ''EH.'' The Roman Catholic Church of St. Louis is located on Lubianka Malaya Street, behind KGB headquarters, close to the circle Howard drew for me on the map.

*Kryuchkov was promoted to head of the KGB on October 1, 1988.

took over as chief of the KGB in 1967, Kryuchkov went into the KGB with him. He traveled a lot to Hungary for the KGB in the 1960's. By 1978 Kryuchkov was head of the KGB's First Chief Directorate, and in March 1986 he was elected a full member of the Central Committee.[6]

Howard, who clearly considers himself a protégé of the KGB's deputy chairman, was enthusiastic in praise for his mentor. "I can't say enough about the man," he said. The KGB official "has been kind to me; he has taken me personally under his wing. He is very human."

Howard also seemed to admire Kryuchkov's political skills, the way he had maneuvered to become Andropov's protégé and risen through the party and KGB bureaucracy.

Kryuchkov, in turn, had good reason to treat Howard well and assure his comforts and perquisites. As the price of asylum in the Soviet Union, Howard was thoroughly debriefed, just as any defector would be in the United States. Whatever he had not previously revealed about the agency's operations in Moscow or about the CIA in general, he certainly told once he had arrived in the Soviet Union.

I asked Howard about the line in the letter to Mary that he left with Phil Baca: ". . . maybe I'll give them what they think I already gave them."

"Yes, that's what I said to Mary in the letter," he replied. Howard did not deny what it meant: he had been exhaustively debriefed by the KGB on everything he knew about the CIA, including the agency's Moscow operation, the assets, the communications plans.

"It's obvious," Howard conceded. "I can't say that. No comment."

How then, I asked, could he say on Soviet television that he had never done anything to harm his country?

"My dispute is with the CIA and, as a result, with the FBI. America is a very big country with all kinds of people and philosophies. I know now the mentality of CIA is

---

[6]Howard was reluctant to identify Kryuchkov by name but said that his patron was chief of the KGB's First Chief Directorate. Kryuchkov held that position from 1978 until his appointment as head of the KGB in 1988.

just a minor portion of America. I still love my country, but with those institutions frankly I'm at war.''

Howard was relieved to discover, during his interrogations in Moscow, that the KGB does not believe in polygraphs. At least, he realized, he would not have to go through that again.

Defectors, especially someone like Howard who served for only two and a half years in the CIA, are wrung dry and of little use to the host intelligence agency after a time. One way that Howard could be of continuing use to the KGB, however, would be to help identify CIA officers in Moscow and perhaps other stations. He certainly knew a great many of the people working in SE division and virtually all those in the Soviet branch.

Howard went over photographs of suspected CIA officers, identifying them to the KGB. He may even have gone out with KGB surveillance teams and identified American case officers on the street. Some evidence that he may have done so came up in the trial of Sergeant Lonetree.

Lonetree approached a CIA officer at a Christmas party in the U.S. embassy in Vienna in December 1986 and blurted out a tale of dealing with the Soviets in his previous eighteen-month tour in Moscow. In a subsequent interrogation by the CIA, Lonetree told how his love affair with Violette Seina, a young Soviet woman employed by the Moscow embassy, led to his meetings with ''Uncle Sasha,'' a KGB agent named Alexi Yefimov.

''Uncle Sasha,'' Lonetree told the CIA man, brought up Howard's name and said that Howard was identifying agents on the streets in Moscow, had even walked up to them on the street. Lonetree told his CIA interviewer that he would be willing to go back to Moscow to try to lure Howard out of the Soviet Union.

''He offered to go back to Moscow and do whatever was necessary to bring Howard out in any kind of a game they wanted to play,'' Michael V. Stuhff, one of Lonetree's attorneys, told me. How would this have been accomplished? ''Kidnap him or do something,'' Stuhff replied. The CIA politely declined the marine sergeant's offer.

In secret testimony at Lonetree's court-martial the CIA

agent who had debriefed him confirmed the marine sergeant's account of what "Sasha" had said about Howard as well as Lonetree's offer to return to Moscow to lure Howard out.[7]

I asked Howard how he spent his days in Moscow, aside from answering questions put to him by the KGB. He spoke vaguely of economic work but said he had no office other than the study in his dacha. "The Soviets ask my opinion on gold bonds," he said. "They are big gold producers. Other countries float gold bond issues; they are interested in perhaps issuing gold bonds. I might be asked to do research on what other countries do."[8] He added: "They have gone to great lengths to see that I have something to do.

"I don't work for the KGB," he said. "The Soviet government takes care of me. I don't know whose budget it comes out of. You can draw your own conclusion. Yes, the KGB provides security. I've been granted political asylum, and they want to protect me."

Although Howard obviously spends a lot of time with the KGB, he said he had not met any other defectors, including Kim Philby, who was a Soviet mole while serving as chief of the Soviet branch of MI6, the British secret intelligence service.

Howard claimed that he does not do everything that "they" ask. "I was invited to the GDR [German Democratic Republic, or East Germany] on the fortieth anniversary of the CIA, to go on TV, and I said no."

Howard said he had traveled to Tbilisi, in Georgia, Estonia, Leningrad, and Kiev, "getting to know the coun-

---

[7]If Howard was identifying CIA officers in Moscow in person, however, it would seem more logical for him to do so with a surveillance team in a car than to walk up to anyone on the street; a personal encounter would only give away the fact that the CIA officer had been spotted by the KGB.

[8]If so, the research would not have kept Howard very busy. Ernest E. Keith, chief trader in gold-based investments for the Bank of Nova Scotia, in Toronto, said, "I do not know of any countries that deal in gold bonds, although France issued a gold-related bond in 1973 that comes due in 1988."

try. The Soviets encouraged me to do this, to see and become familiar with the country."

In January 1987 Howard telephoned Mary in Minnesota, again asking her to visit him with Lee. "She made airplane reservations. Then, about two days before the flight, Mary called to tell me that an FBI counterintelligence man from Washington visited her and made her 'voluntarily' surrender hers and Lee's passports, citing 'national security.' The man told her, 'Give them to me now or we'll take them from you at your connection in Chicago.' "

That night, Howard said, he got drunk.

Mary Howard confirmed the story about the passports, although she told it with different nuances that made the episode sound a shade less coercive. The FBI, she said, "was so concerned about national security, and for Lee's and my safety, that they wanted to be sure we would not leave the USA. So they asked me to give them our passports, and we could get them back at a later date. It was voluntary; however, they said something about it being better to let the FBI have them then rather than at the airport in Chicago."

Mary Howard said she assumed the FBI "must have had a pretty good reason" to be so adamant, so "I gave them our passports."⁹

The following month I met with Mary Howard in St. Paul again. She said she had no plans to settle in Moscow

---

⁹Under State Department regulations, the secretary of state can revoke or refuse to issue a passport on the ground that the travel would be likely to cause "serious damage to the national security or the foreign policy of the United States." The principle was upheld by the Supreme Court in 1981 in *Haig* v. *Agee*. The Court ruled that the government could revoke the passport of Philip Agee, the former CIA case officer whose writings, including a best-selling book, *Inside the Company: CIA Diary*, had exposed the names of CIA agents and operations overseas.

A spokesperson for the State Department's passport services office, citing privacy laws, would not say whether Mary Howard's passport had ever been revoked but added that such action would be "extremely rare." The FBI declined to comment when asked whether Mary Howard had surrendered her passport to the bureau, voluntarily or otherwise.

with her husband, although "I still love him." She added: "I would be crazy to go over there. I don't think I would like it in Russia. I don't want to live in Russia. I like Minnesota." She paused and said, "I might go to visit."

She did. Early in March Mary Howard asked the FBI to return the passports, she said, "and they did so with no problems." At the end of April Mary and Lee flew to the Soviet capital.

Howard had not seen his wife and son for nineteen months. Lee was two when Howard jumped from the car in Santa Fe; now he was four.

The trip was unpublicized, and the KGB made special security arrangements for the visit. Mary Howard did not get to see her husband's apartment or dacha. Instead, she said, "we were all together in a big guesthouse somewhere near Moscow."

They went to the Bolshoi, to the churches in the Kremlin. "We went to Lenin's tomb, and the Armory, and St. Basil's Cathedral. Also the Pushkin Museum. I was there on two holidays; there were banners out; it was nice and colorful."

Did they go out at night? I asked. "We went out once to a show in a hotel, where they had dancers, and to a restaurant and to the circus with Lee."

Mary sounded buoyant, no longer subdued as she had seemed in St. Paul when she spoke of the future. "You sound happy," I said.

"It was nice to be a family again," she replied. It was clear that Mary Howard was still in love with her husband.

"Did the trip give you any different thoughts about the future of your marriage?" I asked.

"We have to think about it a little more," she said. "I plan to go see him periodically."

Howard said he hoped his wife and son would visit "every few months." Would Mary come to Moscow to live? "No, because of Lee," he said. "She wants him to grow up in the States. And I do, too."

Howard said that he and Mary had traveled together to Leningrad and Budapest in May. "In Hungary we went to Lake Balaton and drove along the Danube."

Early in August Mary Howard and Lee returned to Budapest for another, much longer visit. Again the trip was unpublicized. The Howards traveled within Hungary and to Prague, but not to the Soviet Union.

Late in October the Howards wrote to me, two letters in the same envelope, mailed from Budapest. Mary would be leaving for the United States in a few days, Howard said. "Her home is in Minnesota with her family and friends. For us, these past two-and-a-half months have been a time of reflection and preparation for our futures. Although it is sad . . . we will go our separate paths."

Mary Howard struck much the same tone in her letter. "Lee, Ed and I have greatly enjoyed being together again as a close, loving family and I feel very sad to leave for Minnesota so soon, but it is returning 'home.' And even though we will be going our separate ways, the decision to do so will have been made under more normal circumstances."

One morning in mid-January 1988 Howard telephoned me at my office in Washington. Although the letters I had received seemed to suggest that their relationship had changed, he disclosed that Mary had been to see him again in Moscow, her third secret trip. "We're going to visit," he said. "She came over for Christmas."

And their marriage? "We're still married," he said. "We don't feel like getting a divorce. I hope I'll see her in the summer."

Why did Howard agree to see me, and why did the Soviets let him? Any answers are, of necessity, speculative. Mikhail Gorbachev's policy of *glasnost,* or openness, has been accompanied by a much more sophisticated understanding of public relations, and of public opinion in the West, by the Soviet leadership. The interview took place against this background.

Howard himself replied, "Yes, *glasnost* was a factor," when I asked why he and the Soviets had agreed to the interview. "My decision to see you was my decision," he insisted. Perhaps so, but obviously it had to be approved at a higher level.

Howard and, by extension, the KGB may have hoped to convince me that he was innocent of any espionage before he fled the United States. In this he failed. The evidence does not support him. As a fallback Howard must have hoped that by talking with me he would at least get his side of the story on the record. He would have a chance to describe the CIA's mishandling of his case and the abrupt manner in which he was dismissed.

There were two good reasons for Howard to insist during our interviews in Budapest that he never gave secrets to the Soviets until after he fled the United States, despite substantial evidence to the contrary. If he ever returned, however remote that possibility, any public confession of guilt might constitute evidence that could be used against him.

Furthermore, it would be to the advantage of the KGB, Howard's protectors, to keep the CIA and the FBI uncertain about how much Howard had revealed to the Soviets while he was still living in the United States. That is basic counterintelligence strategy: to make the damage assessment by the opposition more difficult by revealing as little as possible.

Howard had obviously cooperated fully with the KGB since arriving in the Soviet Union, but he would not acknowledge it in so many words:

A. I'm not going to say that.

Q. OK, you deny any espionage before arriving in Moscow, but not since. Isn't it a little like a hit man getting convicted for the wrong hit?

A. I'm not going to say that and convict myself of espionage.

It was clear that anything Howard told me about CIA operations in Moscow he had already told the Soviets, and in greater detail. Yet at several points during the interviews Howard declined to discuss certain CIA procedures; he would not reveal the digraphs for Moscow cable traffic, for example. "I don't want to give away agency secrets," he said with a straight face; "it may come up on another charge against me."

I pressed Howard again about Tolkachev:

Q. Was Tolkachev going to be one of your agents?

A. I would go to a park, meet a guy, give the password; he would give his password. I don't know his name. I know his code name. The first time I read Tolkachev's name was in the American press.

Q. But he [Tolkachev] could have been one of the agents you would have handled?

A. Yes, he very well could be one of the assets I would have handled . . . There was one person working on military electronics. Tolkachev could fit the description of a couple of people in the agents' reports I saw. A couple of people were giving us defense information.

Q. You have been accused of betraying Tolkachev and causing his execution.

A. [in a very soft voice, eyes clouding over] I don't want to kill anybody. I wouldn't do that.

Q. You seem to be a very religious man. Doesn't the accusation that you betrayed an agent who was executed trouble you?

A. Yes, *because I don't believe I did that* [emphasis added].

Q. What do you mean, you "don't believe" you did that? If you didn't contact the Soviets until June of 1986, why is it a matter of belief?

A. [shrugs] OK, it's not possible.

That slip of the tongue was perhaps the closest Howard came in six days of interviews to admitting that he had spied before fleeing the United States. But there were other ways in which he edged close to the truth. "Tolkachev was arrested two years after I left the CIA," he said. "Why didn't they change the commo [communications] plan? Assume I met with the Soviets in September of 1984, why hadn't they changed the plan? If I did know all the assets, the commo plans would have changed."

Howard almost seemed to be saying that it wasn't his

fault if the CIA had not changed its procedures for contacting agents.

"They [the KGB] did destroy the Moscow station," Howard said. "The Second Directorate knows what's going on.[10] It appears in the last couple of years they have rolled up four to five CIA case officers. Which means they did a fairly devastating job on Moscow station."

I asked Howard about Yurchenko. Why had he provided the information to the CIA that led to Howard?

"Yurchenko is full of shit," he replied.

What would Yurchenko's motive be in pointing to you? I asked.

"I don't believe he had all the facts," Howard answered. "Yurchenko is troubled. He splits from Moscow. He has to talk to the agency about something. So he gives them a spent asset [Pelton] and peripheral knowledge of 'Robert.' "

Q. You must have asked why he fingered you.

A. Yes, I asked about Yurchenko, but they won't say; but it's obvious they are not happy with what happened.

Q. Have you ever met Yurchenko?

A. No. They showed me videotapes of his press conference. Since then through casual contacts, not official, I've been told he's alive, well, and working. I suspect he'll lead a quiet life. The FBI told Mary he was executed, but I have a friend who sees him in the [KGB] parking lot. I assume Yurchenko is OK as a demonstration that defectors can go home.

Q. Will Yurchenko ever get high-level work?

A. If we [the CIA] had an officer in a similar mess, he'd be given an administrative job.

Howard was very nervous at our first meeting on the Margit-sziget. The first time we went to dinner he had obviously had a few too many beers before meeting me

---

[10]The KGB's Second Chief Directorate is in charge of the surveillance of diplomats, journalists, tourists, and other foreigners inside the Soviet Union.

and had another with his meal. But he drank nothing but soft drinks or citrons on every other occasion and seemed entirely sober. "In Budapest," he noted, "one drink and you lose your driver's license and its a ten-thousand-forint fine."

Our working day usually began early in the morning, on a park bench on the island. We broke for lunch or a cool drink at an outdoor café and met for dinner several times.

As we walked through the park on the first day, we passed the ruins of a thirteenth-century Dominican convent. It reminded Howard that there are Roman ruins as well in Budapest. The city, he observed, was "the northern-most point of the Roman empire," the last barrier between the civilized world and the barbarians.

Howard, although permitted to talk to me, was on a tight leash. He said the first morning that he had been instructed to meet me only in public places, in case he had to yell for help.

Clearly the KGB was worried that my presence in Budapest might be part of a trap set by the CIA, Howard implied. "I trust you," Howard said, "but they don't know who you are." It seemed clear from later oblique remarks, that "they" were mid-level KGB officers who had accompanied him from Moscow to Budapest.

Once, when Howard was on the sun deck of the Thermal Hotel, I saw what appeared to be a security man on the roof, watching. Other than that I saw no overt signs of surveillance, no KGB men lurking in the bushes near our park bench. But it was obvious that Howard was reporting back each night on what he had discussed with me.

"They know I'm talking to you," he said. "They told me, 'Tell the truth, but don't hurt yourself.' "

As the week wore on, Howard gradually became more relaxed about our meetings. He said it was nice to talk English again to someone. On Saturday, and again on Monday, we met in my hotel room. Gone was the stricture on meeting only in public; his fears, or those of his control, that I had come to Budapest to kidnap him appeared to have dissipated.

I did notice, however, that when we met in the hotel room, every hour he would go out on the balcony of the room. "To have a smoke," he said, lighting up another Marlboro. But I had the clear impression it was to show himself to his security, to demonstrate that he was in no danger.

I found Howard highly intelligent and easy to be with. I could see why his friends in the United States, almost without exception, found it difficult to believe he was a Soviet spy. He came across like the pleasant neighbor next door, the well-spoken young professional who would be glad to lend you charcoal for the barbecue grill if you ran out.

While Howard is very angry at the CIA, his feelings about the FBI are not as strong, although he seemed annoyed that the bureau had taken away his fuzz buster. "They still have my radar detector," he said bitterly.

He seemed to regard his escape from the FBI as the normal result of his training as an intelligence agent. Only once, very briefly, when he talked about the tape-recording ruse, did he gloat about having outwitted the federal agents. "To let the FBI know I was still around or make them think I was, I had Mary call the doctor in Santa Fe and have his recording talk to mine. I would have loved to see the look on their faces when they realized it was a tape."

Since Howard would not admit he had spied, that effectively blocked any questioning about his motives. But it seemed clear that the driving force was not ideology but revenge. No doubt the money was, or became, an important factor, but it is not likely that it impelled him to take the first step.

In six days of interviews only once did he sound blatantly like a party-line propagandist. "I was looking at the Bible this morning," he said. "John eight: thirty-two. I came across the quote that is in the CIA lobby. 'And ye shall know the truth and the truth shall make you free.' But they don't quote the first part. It says, 'Follow my word and ye shall know the truth. . . .' The agency doesn't follow in Jesus' word. Any agency that plots assassinations isn't following Jesus' word.''

''But that didn't bother you when you were there,'' I observed.

''Some things started troubling me, even in training class,'' he said. ''Tom Mills is a devout Catholic. I wonder how he can work on the Soviet desk and give agents L-pills [to commit suicide to avoid torture] to take if they are caught.''

Subtly Howard is adapting to his new world. On Sunday, my fourth day in Budapest, we had planned to take a break; but he showed up unexpectedly at my hotel, and I invited him to dinner. At the Margitkert restaurant I asked casually, ''What's going on in the world? I haven't seen a paper.'' He leaned over the table, intense.

''Well, the big thing in this part of the world is the plenum. They're getting ready for a Central Committee meeting in Moscow.'' He said it in the same manner that an American back home might discuss an upcoming Democratic National Convention in an election year.

The next night Howard insisted on paying for dinner, our last. We went to the Kisbuda and sat in the garden. There were wandering violins and an accordian. I ordered black caviar. He talked about Tom Mills and the L-pills, how he had grown a beard on the run from the FBI, the virtues of the special stores in Moscow. The musicians were playing a schmaltzy song, and I realized it was ''Somewhere My Love,'' from *Doctor Zhivago*.

The whole setting was surreal: sitting in a garden in Budapest with a KGB spy, listening to gypsy music, and discussing the fine points of whether the CIA's Soviet branch chief should provide his agents with suicide pills.

We parted after dinner and had a final meeting at the terrace café of the Thermal Hotel the next day. I told him that I had listened to him carefully for six days and took note of his denials, but I believed that he had passed secrets to the Soviets before fleeing from Santa Fe. There was too much evidence against him.

''If I were you,'' Howard said, ''and listened to me and

looked at all the evidence, I might come to the same conclusion, perhaps that is where I would come out, too, but it didn't happen.''

"You're beyond the reach of U.S. law now," I reminded him. "You can tell me the truth."

"I could say it, but I don't want to, because I'm not responsible for those things," Howard replied. "It's a political battle. I crossed the line. I'm the first one from the agency to do it."

We talked some more, and then, in the late afternoon, we parted. We shook hands, and he slipped away, walking along the edge of the park. In a moment he was gone.

That night I went out on the balcony of my hotel room, wondering if the KGB was still watching. As darkness fell over the Danube, the lights were winking on across the river in the Buda hills. There was a soft haze in the summer air. I thought, *Tomorrow I'm going home, to the West. Howard will still be here in Budapest.*

I remembered something he had told me in the garden of the Kisbuda restaurant the night before. "When Mary came to Moscow in April," he said, "she was met. I sent roses since I couldn't go to the airport." For security reasons the KGB did not want him there. "They asked me if I would like to write something to go with the roses.

"So I wrote, 'From Russia, with Love.' "

Epilogue

The CIA always conducts a damage assessment in the aftermath of an important espionage disaster. Naturally the damage assessment in the Edward Lee Howard case is highly classified, not a publicly available document.

But Stansfield Turner, the director of the CIA during the Carter administration, has said that United States intelligence was "very badly hurt" by Howard, who had "very critical information about operations inside the Soviet Union."

Another intelligence official put it more bluntly:

"He wiped out Moscow station."

The House Intelligence Committee report concluded that the information Howard provided to the Soviets had "severely damaged U.S. intelligence collection capabilities."

Methods as well as sources were revealed. "There was not only compromise of ongoing operations but also compromise of techniques," one intelligence official said. "The MO in Moscow had been built up over many years and is very hard to duplicate.

"It wasn't just the human assets. It was far deeper than that. All the technical assets were rolled up. The damage was tremendous. He closed us down over there."

There is little reason to doubt these assessments. In the spring of 1987 the CIA was quietly suggesting that the marines in the U.S. embassy in Moscow, not Howard, had been responsible for compromising the agency's operations. It was to the agency's advantage to blame its troubles on the military rather than on a CIA officer.

But the most serious charges in the marine scandal were dropped. The marines did not have access to the highly sensitive, guarded details of the CIA's Moscow operations. Howard did.

He should never have been hired. He was, despite drug use and alcohol abuse, and then, incredibly, selected for SE and Moscow. His dismissal was handled abominably, and his firing and subsequent bizarre behavior went unreported to the FBI even after his confession. The massive cover-up inside the CIA lasted for more than two years and continued even after the FBI had entered the case. He got away, to the bureau's everlasting chagrin.

Edward Lee Howard, in the end, was a man caught between the superpowers. He changed sides, but did he escape? For Howard, there is no exit. He is a man who abandoned his homeland, who belongs nowhere, living in an alien culture, the future of his marriage uncertain.

He betrayed his country and must live with that knowledge for the rest of his days. But the agency, accountable only to itself, abused its power and the trust of the American people. The CIA was more interested in protecting its image than in catching a spy.

The FBI, its pride injured, wants him badly. Although the bureau would not say so publicly, Division 5 hoped that Mary Howard would not decide to join her husband permanently in Moscow. After her extended visit to Budapest in the summer and early autumn of 1987, and the decision the Howards appear to have made, that seemed, for the moment, less likely. But the FBI still feared that with each trip, the couple might be drawing closer. There was less of a chance that Howard would ever return to the United States if his family was with him. And the FBI still hoped that, however unlikely it seemed, Howard might one day be brought to trial for espionage.

"The case," James Geer said grimly, "is still open."

Edward Lee Howard lives in Moscow, occasionally enjoying the relatively greater freedom of Budapest. His wife and son, as these words are written, are still in Minnesota. Bill Bosch lives in Southern California and drives a Corvette. Phillip Parker retired from the FBI in May 1986 to his home in Norfolk, Virginia. He sold the *Alexandra*.

"Joseph Addison," Howard told me in Budapest, "says that a man needs something to do, something to love, and something to hope for. They [the KGB] try to do that for me."

He worries a lot about being abducted by the CIA. "I have to worry that the agency might try to kidnap me. Every time I come to Budapest the agency salivates. It wouldn't take much—a hypodermic needle, throw me in the trunk of a car, it's only two hours to the border."

He longs for chunky peanut butter and pizza. "I miss Skippy peanut butter, chunky style." Why not ask his wife to mail a jar? "When she was here, a friend in Moscow warned her the peanut butter might be poisoned by the CIA. My parents heard that, and now they won't mail me any food. I suppose there's only a one in five hundred chance [of being poisoned], but why risk it?

"I can't go back. If I did go back and I beat the espionage charges, I'd still go to jail for probation violation. I can build a good life here. I'm not going to give them the satisfaction of going back."

And then: "I guess the roulette wheel didn't turn so well for me.

"I think the biggest mistake of my life was leaving AID. I'd be overseas doing development projects.

"I have no intention of renouncing my U.S. citizenship. I love my country. I guess I'm just a lost American, maybe.

"Even though people here treat me well, I'd rather live a middle-class life and go to the PTA with my wife and son. I'd rather be with my people. But I've crossed the line. I'm trying to build a life."

He had called Minnesota the weekend I was in Budapest. "I talked to Lee and said, 'Lee, come over here and come fishing with me.' He said, 'Daddy, we have a dock here. You should come here.' I said, 'Maybe, some-day.' ''

Howard told me he had built model airplanes since he was ten. ''In Santa Fe I flew gas-powered planes near the house. Lee would get excited. I was building one when I left. I had just started.''

Maybe Lee would finish that plane when he was older, I said.

Howard said he hoped so. Suddenly he had a thought. ''Maybe I'll buy him one. I think they have good ones in Czechoslovakia.''

Author's Note

I was intrigued by the story of Edward Lee Howard, the CIA's first defector to Moscow, from the moment I learned he had vanished into the New Mexico desert on September 21, 1985. When, in the summer of 1986, *The New York Times Magazine* asked me to investigate the case, my interest grew to fascination as I acquired new details of the story. Gradually a portrait of Edward Lee Howard began to emerge, like a print in the developing tray of a darkroom. My article on the Howard case was published as the cover piece in *The New York Times Magazine* on November 2, 1986. This book followed.

There were still missing pieces in the emerging portrait. I needed to know what had happened behind the scenes, inside the CIA, during the Howard case. And how had the FBI managed to let its quarry slip from its hands? Vitaly Yurchenko, the enigmatic KGB officer, was obviously an important key to the story as well.

Researching any book about intelligence presents a substantial challenge. Most of the information sought is secret. Moreover, in this instance, the central figure, Edward Lee Howard, had disappeared, although he had surfaced in Moscow in August 1986, seemingly beyond reach. His wife, Mary Cedarleaf Howard, was living in seclusion somewhere in Minnesota, her phone number unlisted. She had not talked to the press or to any writer.

I began by trying to make contact with Mary Howard. At first I was able to obtain only a post office box number, and we exchanged letters. Then came a phone call, next a meeting in St. Paul. For more than a year I corresponded with Mary Howard and interviewed her seventeen times, including two lengthy, face-to-face meetings.

Often, in our talks, Mary Howard emphasized that it was really her husband's story; I should talk to him. That seemed impossible. In the history of the cold war the Soviets had never permitted a defector from an intelligence agency to be interviewed. Nor was it clear whether Howard himself would agree to talk.

It had to be tried. Early in January 1987 I wrote to the Soviet embassy in Washington, asking to interview Howard. I never received a reply to my letter. I later learned that it had been forwarded to Moscow and that Howard had been told of it. In April Mary Howard was preparing to fly to the Soviet Union with her young son to visit her husband. I asked her to put my request for an interview directly to Howard. Late in May, after Mary Howard had returned from Moscow, she said that Howard would contact me.

The telephone call came one morning in mid-June, from Budapest. Howard agreed to meet with me there and asked when I wanted to come. As soon as I can get a visa, I replied. Within a week I was secretly on my way to Budapest, accompanied by my nineteen-year-old son, Jonathan, a college student and an accomplished photographer. Howard telephoned me at the Thermal Hotel as agreed, and we met for thirty hours over six days in late June. Most of our meetings took place in the park on the Margitsziget, the island in the middle of the Danube, but we also talked at restaurants, at outdoor cafés, and in my hotel room.

Jonathan was present at many of these interviews, and he took the pictures of Howard in Budapest that appear in the book. Jon's contribution to the book was invaluable, and I will always be grateful for his help. For that, and so many other reasons, this book is dedicated to Jon.

Many others deserve my thanks, first among them Robin G. Colucci, my enormously talented and resourceful research assistant, whose judgments at every step of the way were unfailingly accurate and deeply appreciated by me. Her enthusiasm and support were unflagging, and her advice exceptional.

More than two hundred people were interviewed for this book, some dozens of times, and I gratefully acknowledge their assistance. First, the principals in this story, beginning with Mary Howard. I appreciate the confidence she placed in me over many months, her patience with my questions, which must have seemed endless, and her role in arranging the meeting with her expatriate husband. Second, Edward Howard, the subject of this book. Whatever his motives for seeing me, he did. He answered every question I asked, no matter how personal or probing, and continued to do so with great patience even after I had made it plain to him that I did not believe all his answers.

I am grateful as well to Kenneth and Mary J. Howard, Howard's parents, who allowed me into their home and responded to my questions on numerous occasions. They struck me as decent Americans caught up in a nightmare not of their own making. Also to William G. Bosch, Howard's friend and confidant, who played a pivotal role in the story, and to his attorney, Victor B. Kenton, who arranged my meeting with Bosch.

This book could not have been written unless I'd had access to dozens of former and some present officials of the intelligence community, including the CIA and the FBI. Most of these men and women cannot be thanked by name, and many took risks in seeing me at all. I believe that the great majority of these individuals talked because they were persuaded of my seriousness of purpose and my desire to tell as balanced and complete a story as possible. I am grateful to all of them. They know who they are.

The CIA declined, more than once, to give any official help, although I was able to discuss the Howard case in two telephone conversations with William J. Casey, the

director of the CIA, in September and early October 1986.
I also talked with Admiral Stansfield Turner, who was the
director of the CIA under President Carter. A former CIA
officer, Donald F. B. Jameson, provided valuable insights
into the psychology of defectors.

The FBI did give me some assistance, limited for the
most part to three interviews with James H. Geer, head of
the intelligence division. I greatly appreciate his willingness to discuss a case that the FBI still regards as open,
and I am also grateful for the help of Lane M. Bonner,
the special agent in charge of the FBI press office in Washington, his assistant, I. Ray McElhaney, and Norman A.
Zigrossi, formerly head of the FBI's Washington field office.

My special thanks go to Phillip A. Parker, former deputy assistant director of the FBI's intelligence division, the
man whose job it was to track down Edward Lee Howard
and who came so close to succeeding.

Many of Howard's former friends, neighbors, and co-
workers freely shared their time and recollections, as did
several officials in Santa Fe. Their numbers are too great
to mention all of them, but they include Philip M. Baca,
staff director of the New Mexico Legislative Finance Committee, whose assistance was vital and much appreciated;
his predecessor, Curtis R. Porter; Judge Bruce E. Kaufman; Nilda Pabon Balderston; Robert and Kate Gallegos;
Rosa and Gary Carlson; Dennis Hazlett; Peter Hughes;
Gina Jackson; James C. Lockwood; John J. Matejko; and
Dr. Marco Ferroni.

Charles F. Ruff, Mark H. Lynch, and Eric L. Richard;
and Laura W. S. Macklin, James Doyle, and Wallace J.
Mlyniec of the Georgetown University Law Center helped
me understand some of the legal complexities of the Howard case; all were generous with their assistance. So, too,
was Michael V. Stuhff.

Many colleagues in the press took time to help, especially Andrew J. Glass, Washington bureau chief of the
Cox Newspapers, and Thomas J. Moore, of the Knight-
Ridder organization, both of whom initiated me into a
higher level of computer literacy and counseled me in other

valuable ways; Stuart H. Loory of the Cable News Network; Marino de Medici, the Washington correspondent of *Il Tempo* of Rome; Michael Evans, defense correspondent of the *Times* of London; Allan W. Cromley, senior correspondent of the *Daily Oklahoman;* and Kent Walz of the Albuquerque *Journal*. The editing skills of Alex Ward, Randall Rothenberg, and Edward J. Klein contributed greatly to the original piece in *The New York Times Magazine*. Daniel Wiedenkeller of Zurich provided generous and valuable research assistance in Switzerland.

It is always a privilege to work with Robert D. Loomis, vice-president and executive editor of Random House and my editor on this and five previous books. His support for this project, from the outset, was steadfast. So, too, was that of my friend and literary agent of thirty-seven years, Sterling Lord, whose wisdom and integrity are unmatched.

In writing this book, I benefited as well from the counsel of my son Christopher, who is working for a peaceful world in which spies, and nuclear weapons, would be unnecessary. Most of all, I acknowledge, with gratitude, the love, encouragement and understanding of my wife, Joan, during the long journey and considerable adventure that became the story of *The Spy Who Got Away*.

DAVID WISE

Washington, D.C.
October 21, 1987

Index

DAVID WISE is a writer based in Washington. He is the coauthor of *The Invisible Government*, a landmark number-one best-seller that has been widely credited with bringing about a reappraisal of the role of the Central Intelligence Agency in a democratic society. He is the author of *The American Police State* (1976) and *The Politics of Lying* (1973), and coauthor with Thomas B. Ross of *The Espionage Establishment* (1967), *The Invisible Government* (1964), and *The U-2 Affair* (1962). He is also the author of three espionage novels, *Spectrum* (1981), *The Children's Game* (1983), and *The Samarkand Dimension* (1987), which is available in paperback from Avon Books. He is a television commentator on intelligence issues for the Cable News Network (CNN). A native New Yorker and graduate of Columbia College, he is the former chief of the Washington bureau of the *New York Herald Tribune* and has contributed articles on government and politics to many national magazines. He is married and has two sons.

FROM PERSONAL JOURNALS TO BLACKLY HUMOROUS ACCOUNTS

VIETNAM

DISPATCHES, Michael Herr

01976-0/$4.50 US/$5.95 Can

"I believe it may be the best personal journal about war, any war, that any writer has ever accomplished."
—Robert Stone, *Chicago Tribune*

A WORLD OF HURT, Bo Hathaway

69567-7/$3.50 US/$4.50 Can

"War through the eyes of two young soldiers...a painful experience, and an ultimately exhilarating one."
—*Philadelphia Inquirer*

NO BUGLES, NO DRUMS, Charles Durden

69260-0/$3.50 US/$4.50 Can

"The funniest, ghastliest military scenes put to paper since Joseph Heller wrote *Catch-22*"
—*Newsweek*

AMERICAN BOYS, Steven Phillip Smith

67934-5/$4.50 US/$5.95 Can

"The best novel I've come across on the war in Vietnam"
—Norman Mailer

COOKS AND BAKERS, Robert A. Anderson

79590-6/$2.95

"A tough-minded unblinking report from hell"
—*Penthouse*

AVON Paperbacks